IMAGES
of America

KALAMAZOO RIVER

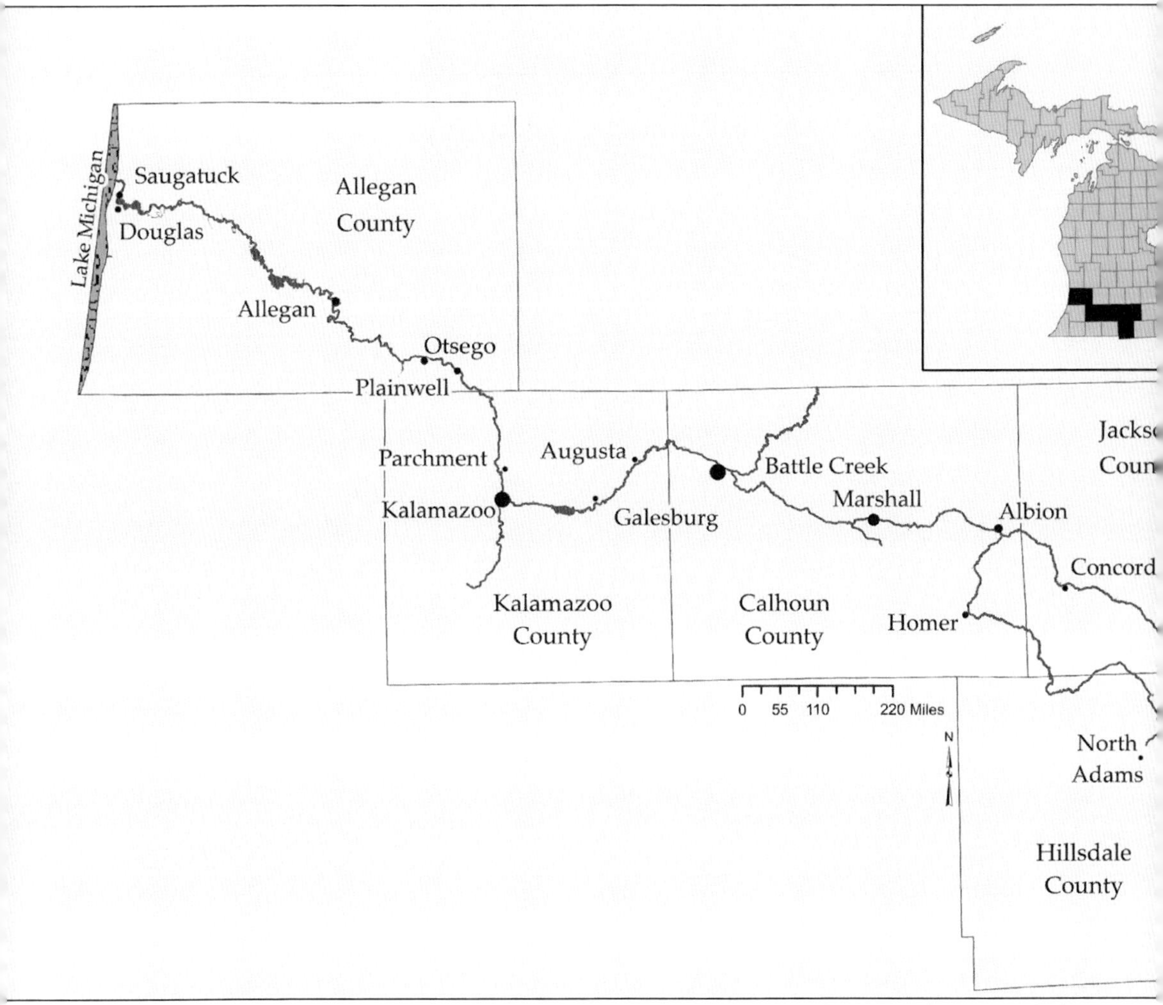

The Kalamazoo River flows through all or part of five counties in southwest Michigan, including Hillsdale, Jackson, Calhoun, Kalamazoo, and Allegan Counties. It also flows through many cities and towns (the larger the dot, the larger the town/city) on its way west to Lake Michigan. Many of these places are highlighted in the book. (Cartography by Trenton Benedict, authors' personal collections.)

On the Cover: These women are enjoying a sunny day above Saugatuck on Mount Baldhead around 1920. The hike to the top is not an easy one and today boasts a staircase of 302 steps to reach the summit. In the background are the Kalamazoo River and the Big Pavilion, which served as an entertainment destination for locals and tourists who came from distant cities by passenger ship. (Saugatuck-Douglas History Center.)

IMAGES
of America

KALAMAZOO RIVER

Lisa M. DeChano-Cook
and Mary L. Brooks

ARCADIA
PUBLISHING

ISBN 978-1-4671-2902-2

Published by Arcadia Publishing
Charleston, South Carolina

Printed in the United States of America

Library of Congress Control Number: 2017961148

For all general information, please contact Arcadia Publishing:
Telephone 843-853-2070
Fax 843-853-0044
E-mail sales@arcadiapublishing.com
For customer service and orders:
Toll-Free 1-888-313-2665

Visit us on the Internet at www.arcadiapublishing.com

To our families for their love and support and to Lauryn Cook, our field assistant, as we explored the many places along the Kalamazoo River.

Contents

Acknowledgments

We would like to thank all the individuals and organizations that provided images included in our book. We would specifically like to thank Keith Martin, Jennifer Wood, Sandy Stamm, Nathaniel Nietering, Jeff Shook, Paul Petosky, Cheryl Vosburg, Luanne Castle, Mark Jenness, Alan Marr, Craig Phillips, Jeff Weisman, John Winchell, and Kendall Christopher for their time and effort in securing digital photographs. Many other people provided us with names and contact information for leads. We thank all of these people collectively as there are too many to name individually. We would also like to thank our title manager at Arcadia Publishing, Angel Hisnanick, for her expertise and guidance throughout this process.

A special thank-you goes to our husbands, Gordon Cook and Bob Brooks, and boss, Benjamin Ofori-Amoah, for their support while we finished our book. Much needed support also came from other family members, including Dave, Cindy, Lee, Marian, Rob, Laurie, Haley, Jake Alexandra, William, Scott, Jessica, Emma, Rachael, and Samantha. Thanks to everyone!

Many images in this volume appear courtesy of the following organizations: Homer Public Library (HPL); Albion Public Library (APL); the Battle Creek Historical Society (BCHS); the Western Michigan University Archives and Regional History Collections (WMU); Kalamazoo Public Library (KPL); Kalamazoo Valley Museum (KVM); Willard Library, Battle Creek (WL); Galesburg Historical Society (GHS); Otsego Historical Society (OHS); Otsego District Public Library (OPL); the Dorothy Dalrymple Collection, Otsego District Public Library (DDC); Ransom Library, Plainwell (RL); Saugatuck-Douglas History Center (SDHC); and the W.E. Upjohn Center for the Study of Geographical Change (Upjohn).

INTRODUCTION

The Kalamazoo River is the result of two glacial lobes, the Saginaw and the Michigan, advancing southwest and retreating northeast across the Michigan landscape over 14,000 years ago. The Kalamazoo River, the seventh-longest river in Michigan, is approximately 178 miles long, flowing west to Lake Michigan from its beginnings in Hillsdale and Jackson Counties. The Kalamazoo River Watershed drains nearly 2,200 square miles and contains 188 miles of tributaries and 287 inland lakes greater than 10 acres in size. The largest of these inland lakes is Gun Lake, which covers 2,661 acres. Three other lakes are actually part of the Kalamazoo River: Morrow Lake (Galesburg), Lake Allegan (Allegan), and Lake Kalamazoo (Saugatuck). Because of the action of glaciers, the gradient of the Kalamazoo River does not change significantly from its headwaters to its mouth, only about three feet per mile on average. The soils along the river are mostly loamy in nature and land uses range from agriculture to forest to urban. Ninety-six percent of the land in the watershed is privately owned. Lands in the Allegan State Game Area, Fort Custer Recreational Area, and the Yankee Springs Recreation Area comprise the four percent that is publicly owned.

The river winds its way through many cities, towns, and villages on its trek to Lake Michigan. The two largest cities along its banks are Battle Creek, home to the Kellogg Company, and Kalamazoo, home of Stryker, Pfizer, Gibson Brands, and Western Michigan University. Smaller locales include Albion, Marshall, Galesburg, Augusta, Plainwell, Otsego, Allegan, and Saugatuck. Some places never grew from their original small settlements, like Marengo, while others have been lost to history, such as Singapore.

Although evidence suggests that the river may have been used continuously for more than 10,000 years, perhaps the first documented group of people to use it was the Potawatomi Nation. They used the river for transportation and established at least one small village, which was near what is now the city of Kalamazoo. It is from these people that the name most likely derived, although there is still confusion about its origins. Kekalamazoo, which is the Potawatomi word for "boiling or sparkling water," is the most likely original spelling.

The Kalamazoo River was an important natural resource for Native Americans and European settlers. Hunting and fishing became primary activities along the river. In the late 1600s, Native Americans and fur traders navigated the river in their bark canoes. While these canoes were good for some stretches of the river, they often ran aground in the shallower portions. By the late 1830s, flat-bottom boats could be seen on the river. These boats could travel more of the river than canoes, and they ushered in the era of river shipping on the Kalamazoo River. The river was the chief means of shipping raw goods from the Great Lakes' ports to inland locations. It also provided a way for settlers' produce to get downstream. A typical flat-bottom boat (16 feet by 32 feet) could carry 300 barrels of flour. As one can imagine, this type of transportation was slow and oftentimes difficult and inconvenient, especially when traveling upstream against the current. It was nearly impossible to ship goods as far inland as Kalamazoo because the shoals near Otsego impeded farther travels even for flat-bottom boats. Goods were typically shipped as far as Otsego and then hauled in wagons for the last few miles to Kalamazoo. The establishment of the Michigan Central Railroad in 1946 and the creation of dams along the river essentially eliminated river transport on the Kalamazoo River except from New Richmond, east of Allegan, to the mouth of the river, which saw an uptick in the use of riverboats for tourist excursions.

Recreation was and still is a primary use of the Kalamazoo River. Through fishing, one could catch enough salmon, catfish, and bass to supply several meals. Canoeing was a favorite activity of young couples because there were miles of solitude and beautiful scenery. Children could be seen cooling off in swimming holes all along the river during the hot summer months. City parks in nearly every community along the Kalamazoo River provided riverfront access as well as picnic and play areas for families.

The erection of dams along the Kalamazoo River and its tributaries brought a new use to the river—power. The first dams were on tributaries and used for powering gristmills and sawmills. Many more milldams were constructed between the 1830s and 1900. Cereal factories, pharmaceutical companies, flour mills, gristmills, and paper mills sprang up along the river's banks, especially between Battle Creek and Otsego, until the early 1940s. Dams built after this time until 1980 were primarily for recreation and waterfront development, changing the use of the river once again. At the peak of dams on the river, there were 13 in the main stream of the Kalamazoo River and more than 100 throughout the entire watershed.

Dams drastically changed the river's morphology as tributaries and the main stream widened and deepened. The once swift-moving water of the Kalamazoo River slowed down, making some portions of the river like a pond habitat. Fish species were severely impacted as fish movement and reproduction was impeded because their habitat changed so significantly. Aquatics species were injured or killed trying to get over a dam. Other animals living along the river also saw harsh changes in their habitats and food supplies, causing them to move away from the Kalamazoo River for survival.

During the heyday of the municipal industry, the Kalamazoo River became the primary disposal site for much of the municipal and industrial waste by-products at the time. Polychlorinated biphenyls (PCB) contamination of the river came at the hands of de-inking practices at many paper mills. Other pollutants dumped into the river included trash, sewage effluents, and various industrial discharge. From the 1940s through the 1960s, pollution in the river was so bad that native species became extinct. Fish died at alarming rates due to a lack of oxygen, swimming in the river ceased because of high levels of toxicity, and it emanated a foul smell. People avoided the Kalamazoo River as much as possible. The Clean Air Act, established in 1970, provided the needed legislation to begin serious river cleanup efforts. Pollution reductions have allowed for the reestablishment of some fish species, although there are limits on the quantity of fish that should be consumed from the river. The offensive smell is gone, and people are returning to the river for picnicking, water sports, and to simply enjoy nature; however, from the city of Kalamazoo to the mouth, the Kalamazoo River is still designated as a federal Superfund site due to this contamination. Remediation efforts have begun but more extensive activities are still needed.

Many of the dams along the river are being taken out because they have outlived their usefulness and have fallen into disrepair. Before this can happen, however, the PCB contamination must be considered. Some of the oldest and most crumbling dams on the river have the highest volumes of PCB-contaminated sediments trapped behind them. Polluted sediments are being removed from behind these dams before they are professionally demolished. The area of the Ceresco Dam, near Marshall, suffered the largest oil spill in the area's history. A pipeline, owned by the Enbridge Oil Company, burst, spilling over a million gallons of oil into Talmadge Creek, a tributary of the Kalamazoo River, and the river proper, from Marshall to Galesburg. As part of its cleanup contract, Enbridge remediated the area of as much oil as possible and removed the Ceresco Dam earlier than originally scheduled by the Department of Natural Resources, costing the company more than $12 billion. The removal of the Ceresco Dam and others along the river is restoring the river to its natural flow state.

Flooding is the most prevalent natural hazard along the Kalamazoo River. While it is not a frequent occurrence, there is a documented history of river flooding. Perhaps the most disastrous event was the March 1904 flood. Heavy rainfall, runoff, snowpack, and frozen soil combined to create this disaster. No lives were lost, but factories were temporarily closed and transportation services were hindered all along the river. In April 1908, Albion suffered significant devastation during that flood event. Nearly 60 inches of snow fell in the area prior to a heat wave, and heavy rains melted the snow and filled the Kalamazoo River. The Homer Dam failed due to the pressure of the swollen river and sent a wall of water downstream to Albion. Buildings in downtown Albion were destroyed, resulting in thousands of dollars in damage. The 1947 flood of the Kalamazoo River sparked a diversion project in Battle Creek. This 50-year flood occurred because two frontal systems swept through the area in April, leaving behind nearly five inches of rain along with melting snow. The convergence of the Battle Creek with the Kalamazoo River compounded the problem in the city of Battle Creek. The flood brought commerce to a dead stop for over a week. In order to avoid future flooding, the city embarked on a flood-control program in which the Army Corps of Engineers encased the Kalamazoo River channel in cement. While flooding ceased, environmental and cultural aspects of this area were destroyed, including wildlife and fish habitats and the heart of the city's African American community. Currently, there is a movement in Battle Creek to restore the Kalamazoo River to a more natural state while employing other methods of flood control.

Indeed, the Kalamazoo River has had many uses over the course of its history, from transportation and navigation to shipping, recreation, and waste disposal. Fortunately, the environmentally unfriendly uses have ceased, and recreation (fishing, kayaking/canoeing, and picnicking) has become a primary use once again. Since cleanup efforts on the Kalamazoo River began, more and more people are returning to the river to enjoy its natural beauty and landscape. The future of the river will likely see more restoration efforts, and its uses may change with the times. The Kalamazoo River lies in the hands of all who live, work, and play on or near it. Come with us as we take you through the history of the Kalamazoo River and its uses through photographs.

One

Headwaters to Albion

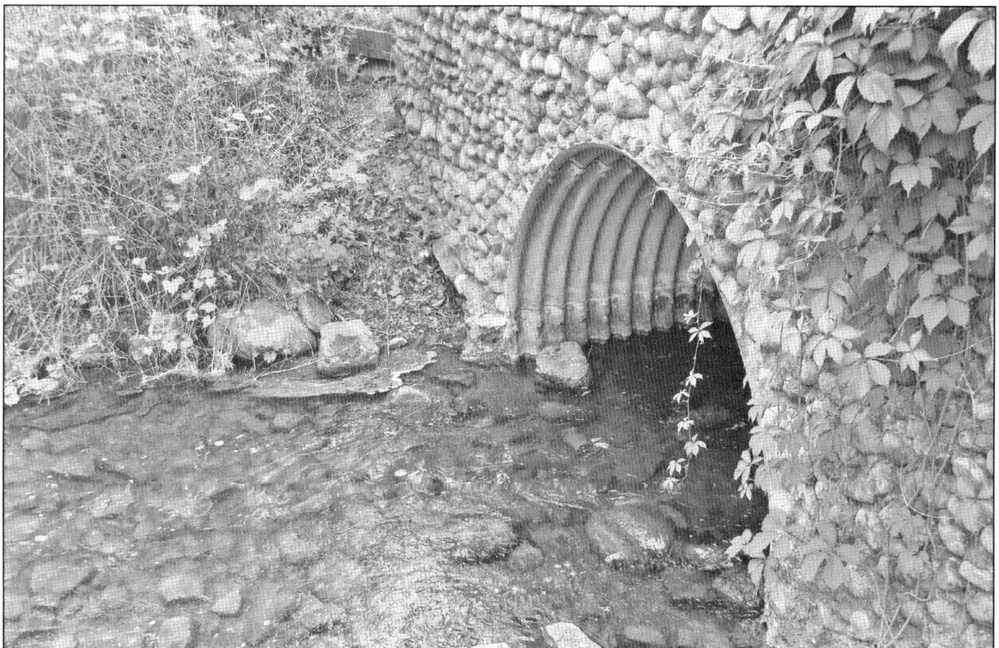

The North Branch of the Kalamazoo River is spring fed by Farewell (or Farwell) Lake in Hanover Township in Jackson County. The water flows out of the culvert under Hanover Road, shown here, on its way 26.5 miles to Albion where it joins the South Branch. (Authors' personal collections.)

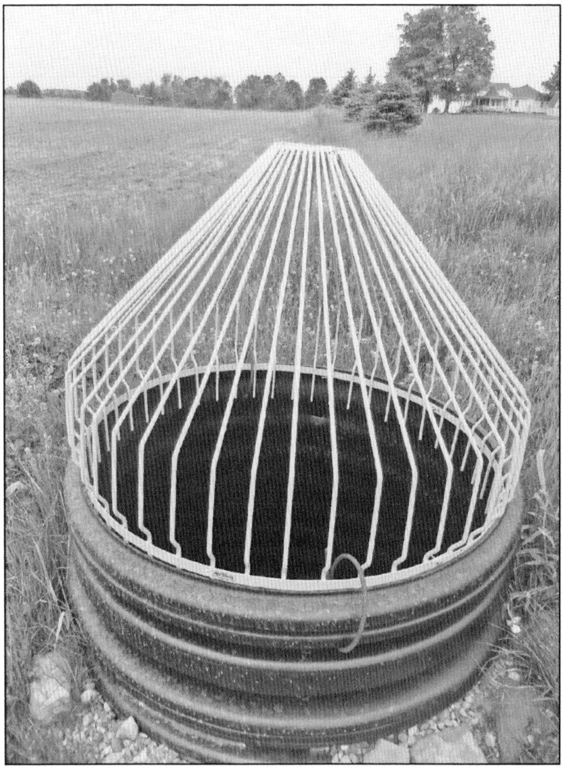

The South Branch of the Kalamazoo River begins in a farm field near North Adams in Moscow Township, Hillsdale County (left). This branch flows approximately 43 miles before it joins the North Branch in Albion. Much of the area that this branch of the river flows through is rolling agricultural land (below) and small wooded lots. The cities of Homer and Albion lie along the South Branch. They are the only two truly developed areas along the South Branch, and the land along the entire length is privately owned. People have fished along the South Branch since the 1950s, when it was stocked with trout. (Both, authors' personal collections.)

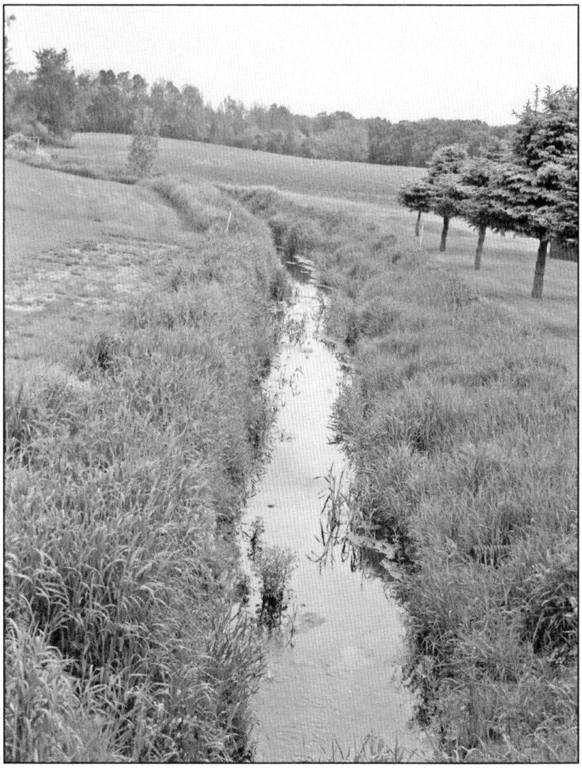

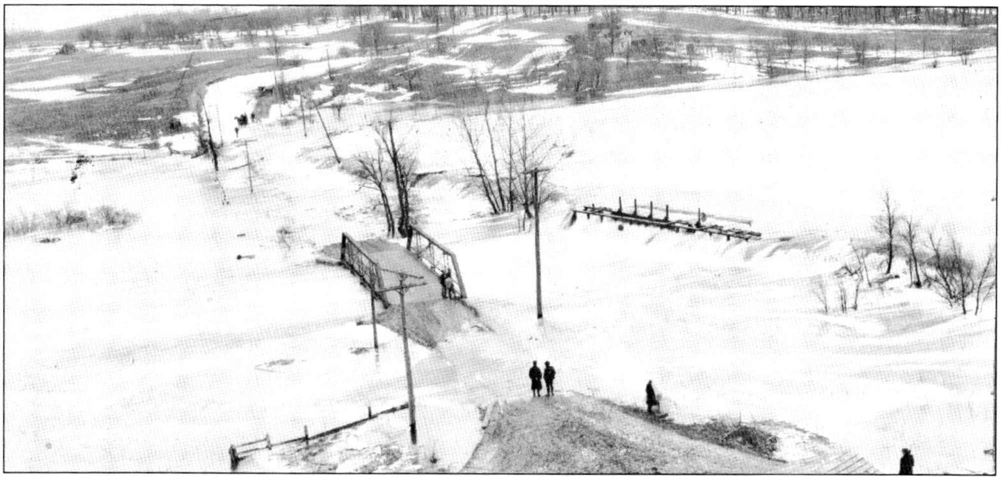

On Saturday, March 7, 1908, a flooding disaster occurred on the Kalamazoo River. In what was dubbed the "Great Flood," the Kalamazoo River swelled rapidly due to heavy rainfall in a short period of time. The excessive amount of water caused the Homer Dam, several miles south of Albion, to fail. A torrent of water swept through Albion, wiping out most of its bridges. (BCHS.)

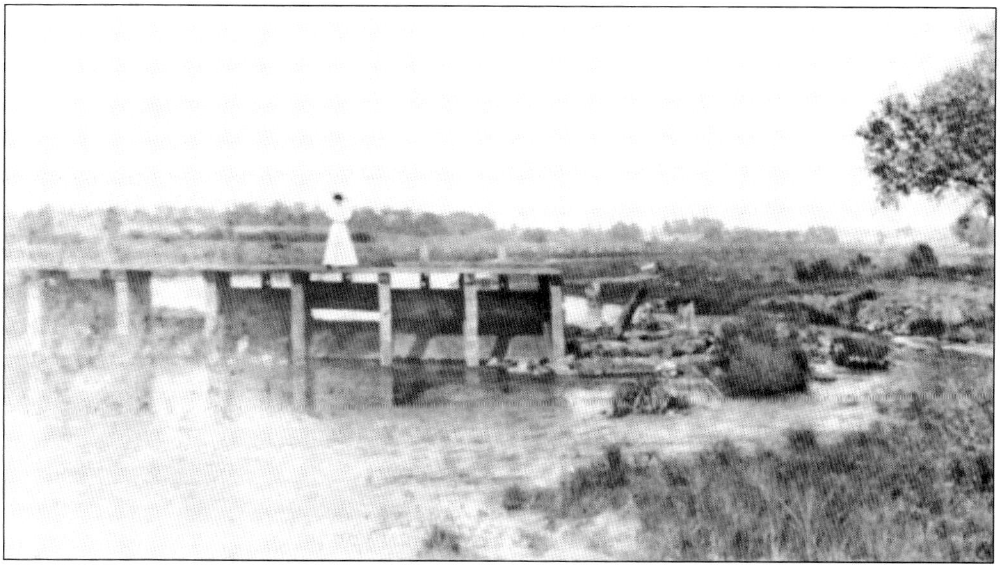

Newburg Mills, constructed in 1844, consisted of a dam and a very large building containing a gristmill, flour mill, and sawmill. During much of the 19th century, local farmers brought their products to Newburg Mills for processing. In 1903, a fire destroyed all but the dam and gates, which were eventually removed. (WMU.)

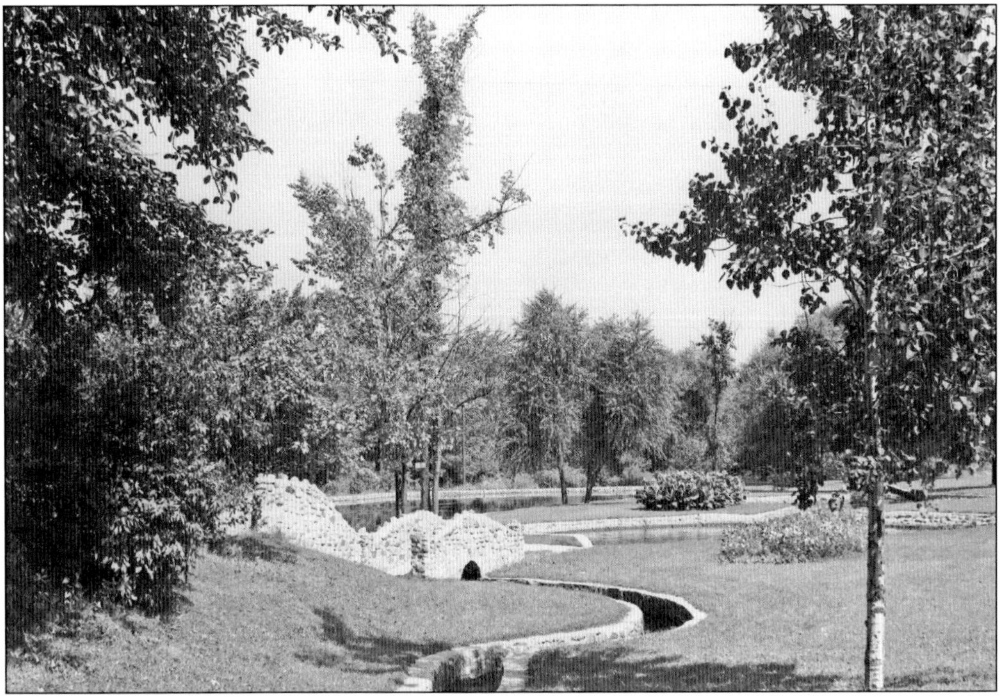

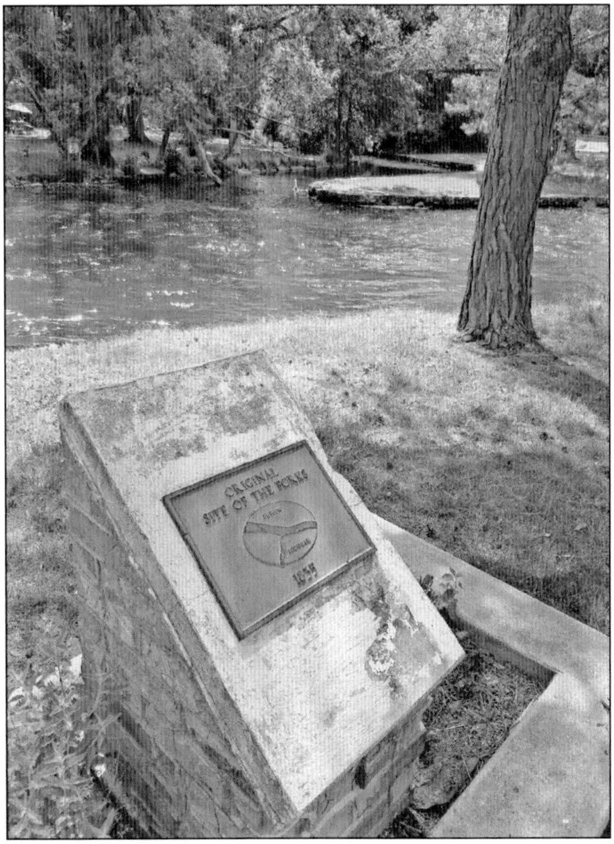

Victory Park is Albion's largest park and opened in 1919. The park honors those who served in World War I. This park also boasts where the North and South Branches of the Kalamazoo River join. The plaque at the forks indicates that Albion was established in 1835 at this site. Many people enjoy the annual Festival of the Forks in Albion, a celebration of the city's beginnings. The stonework seen in the photograph above was installed in the 1930s as part of a Works Progress Administration project. Visitor can cross the meandering river using the stone bridges while they stroll through the park. (Both, APL.)

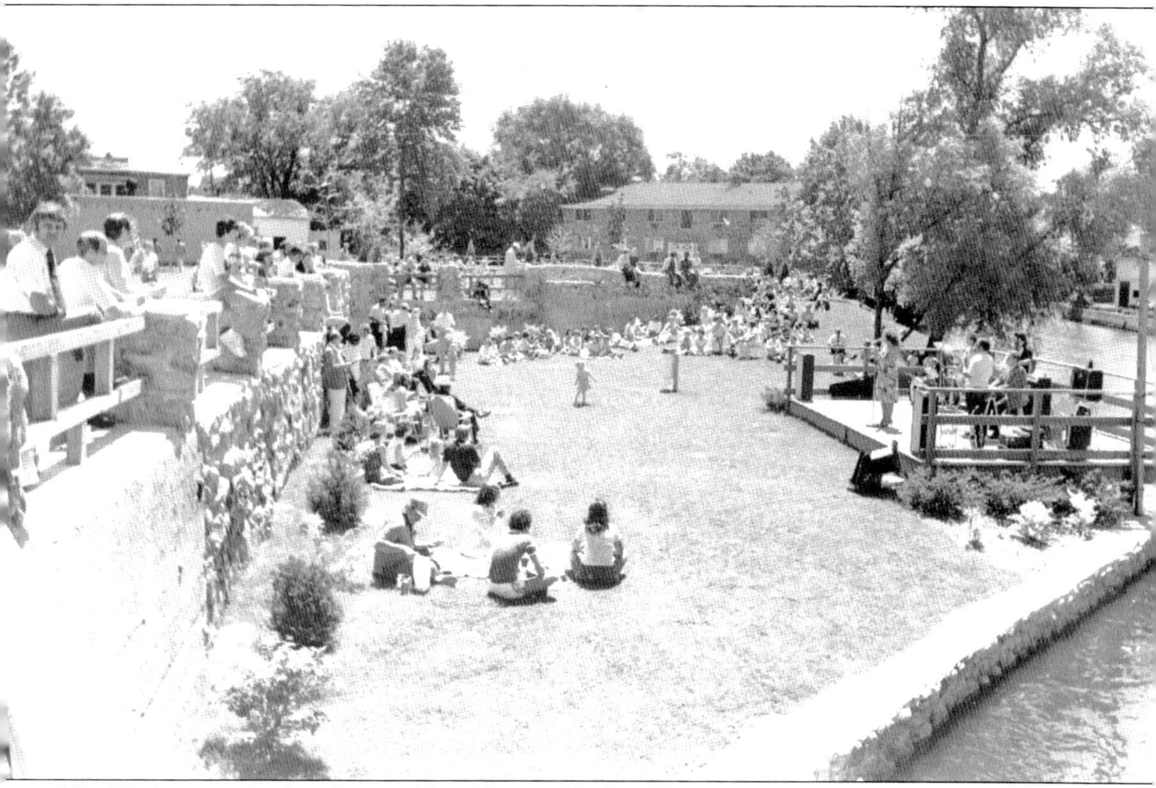

Lloyd Park sits on the foundation of the White Mill. The Albion Civic Foundation wanted to keep the Kalamazoo River as a central focus of the park so it built a sun deck overhead and a canoe landing. This photograph, taken in June 1981, shows the first Lunch at Lloyd, which provided patrons with outdoor concerts once a week during the lunch hour. (APL.)

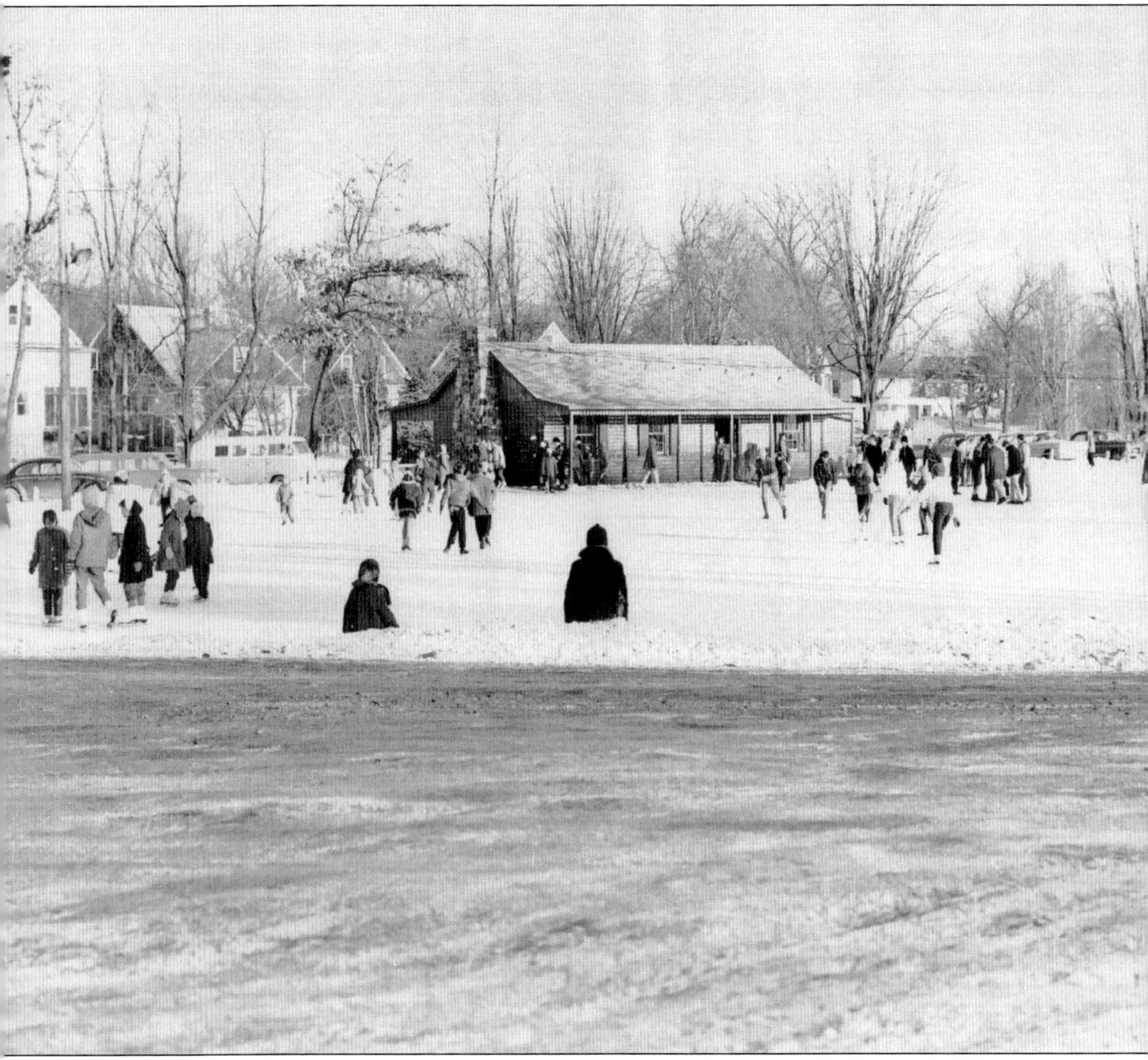

Albion's parks were enjoyed all year long. Millponds and millraces along the Kalamazoo River froze in the winter, providing a smooth ice surface for activities such as ice-skating, hockey, and socializing. People could retreat to a warming building if the weather felt too cold. (APL.)

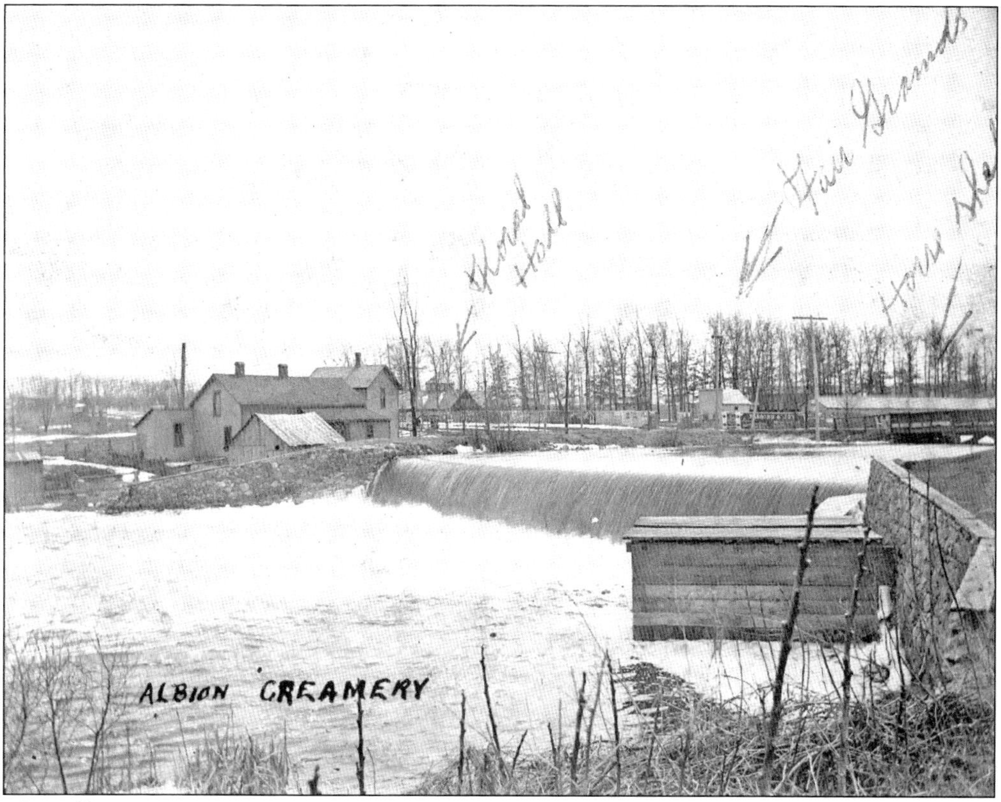

The Albion Creamery and the Albion Fairgrounds, including Floral Hall, were located just south of what is now the Victory Park waterfall. The creamery became the site of the Maple City Dairy Company from 1913 to 1916, when its building burned. Floral Hall, noted on the photograph, has been moved to the current Noble County Fairgrounds and is recognized as the oldest building there. (APL.)

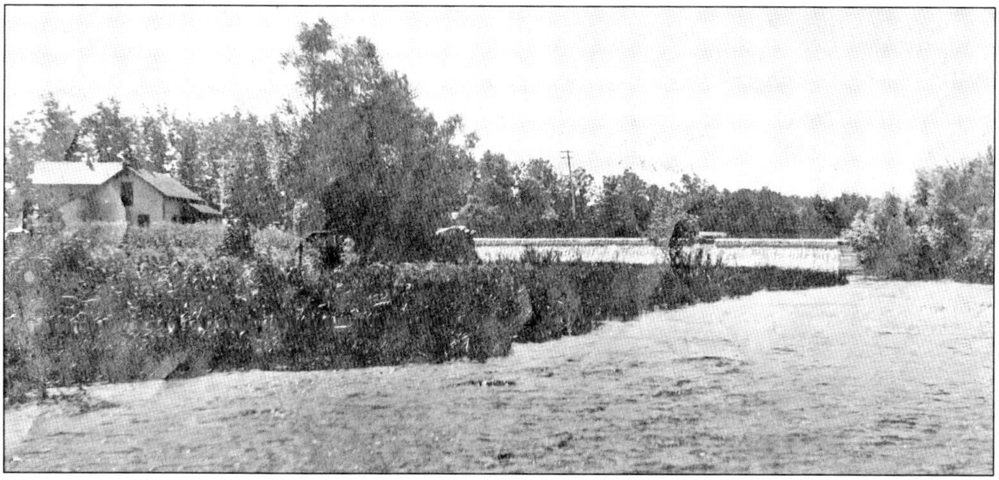

This cement dam was built in 1905 over the old stone dam that had existed since Albion's pioneer days. This dam regulated water from the Kalamazoo River to the Commonwealth Power Plant on East Erie Street. This area has since been developed into Victory Park as a tribute to Albion's World War I veterans. (APL.)

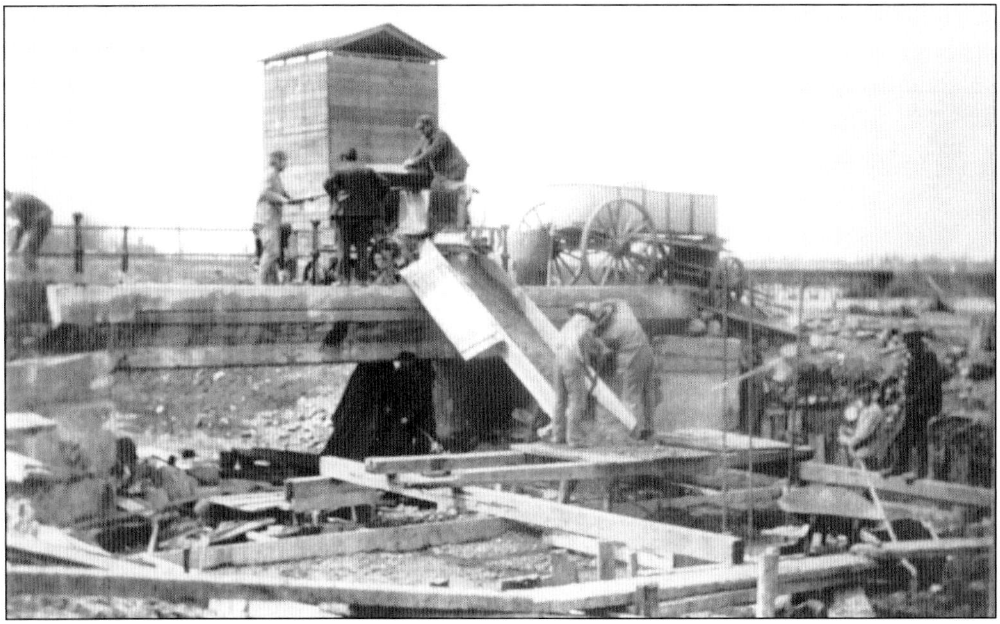

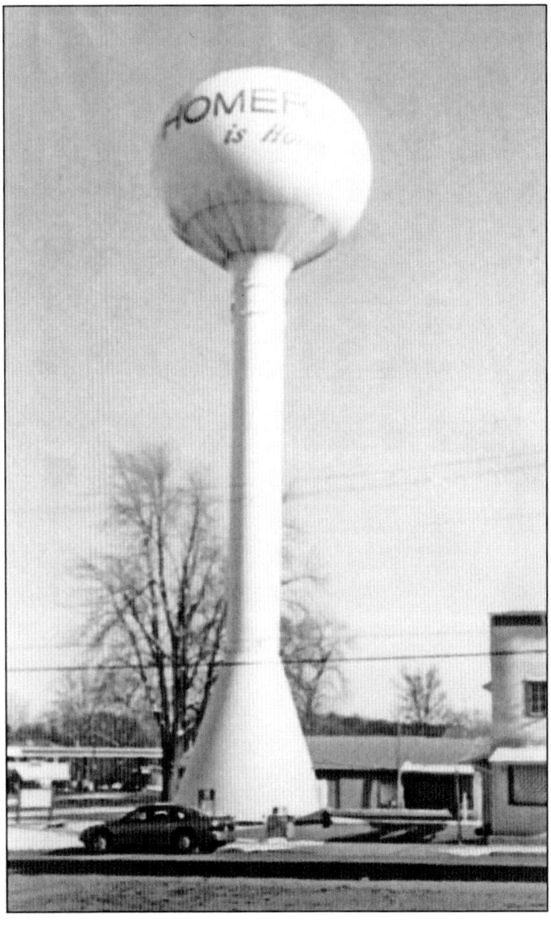

These men are rebuilding the Homer Dam after it was destroyed in the 1908 flood. Two men are leveling the rough gravel cement as it comes down the wooden chute. The roughly laid pour forms help with the overall structure of the dam. The wagon seen on the right would have been used to bring in the raw materials. (HPL.)

Milton Barney, one of the original settlers, built a log cabin, a store, a small mill using waterpower from the Kalamazoo River, and the first hotel in the area. Originally known as Barneyville, the area was renamed Homer in 1834—after Homer, New York, a place many other villagers had previously called home. The spirit and commitment of the residents is reflected on the water tower declaring "Homer is Home." (HPL.)

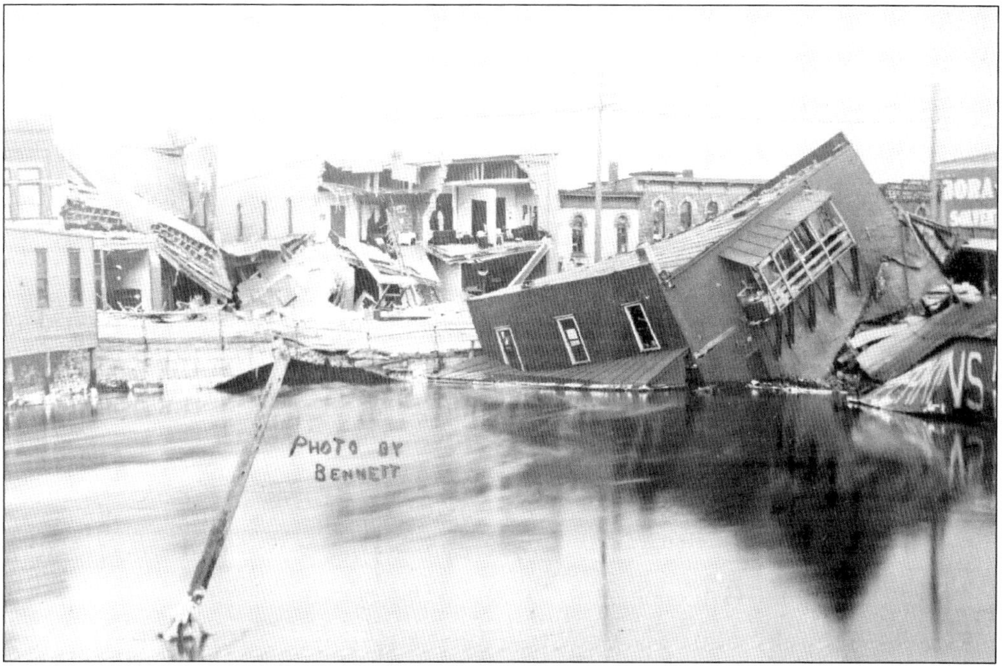

The 1908 flood disaster that occurred in Albion was due to the Homer Dam being destroyed by floodwaters. In Albion, these floodwaters were so strong that they washed out foundations of buildings, toppling them into the Kalamazoo River. Nearly all of the downtown buildings that sat along the river were damaged. (HPL.)

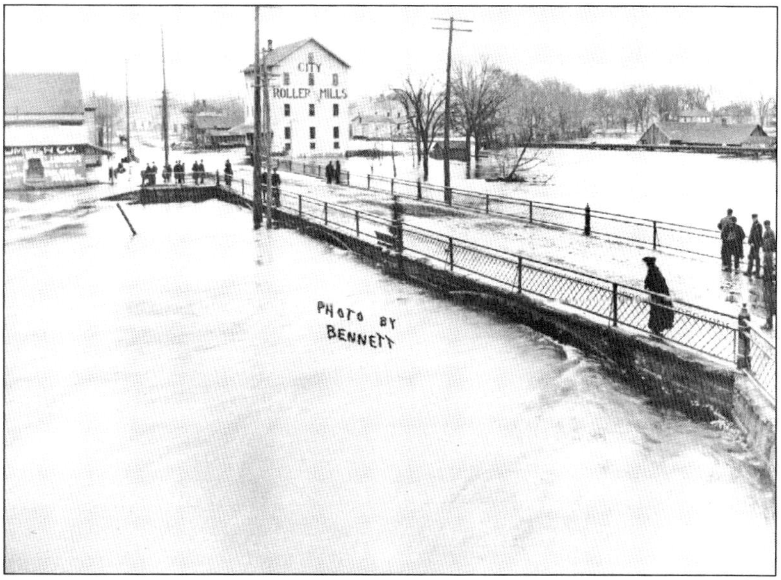

This photograph depicts the flood of 1908 in Albion. Residents were curious to see how high the water level was and what had been flooded in the city. This flooding was exacerbated due to the breach in the Homer Dam, upstream from Albion. (BCHS.)

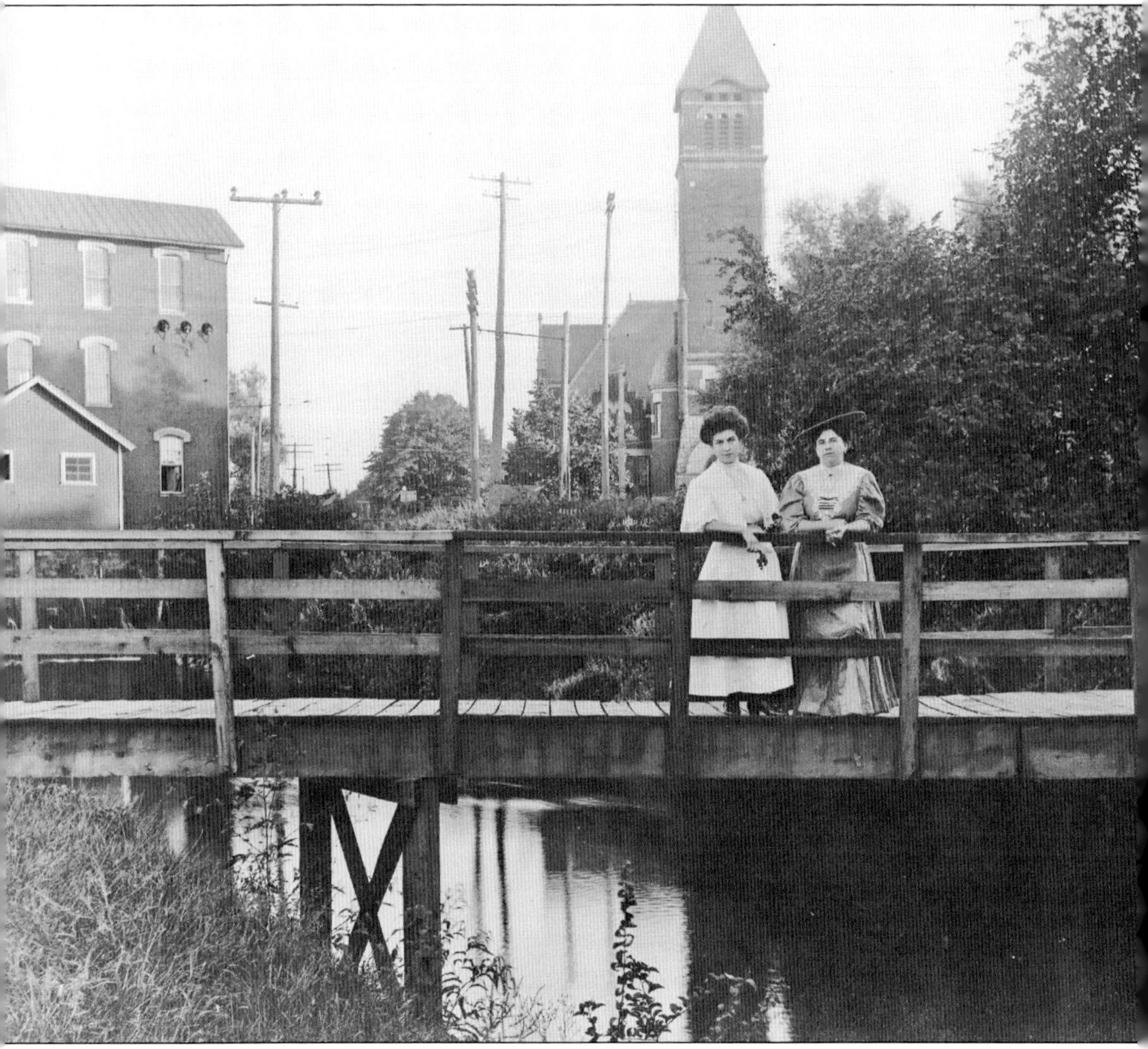

Based on the attire of the women on the bridge, they are probably out for a stroll over the Kalamazoo River on a sunny afternoon. This was a common activity before air-conditioning was invented in order for people to stay cool. These women may have been coming from a social activity at the Methodist church, seen behind them. (APL.)

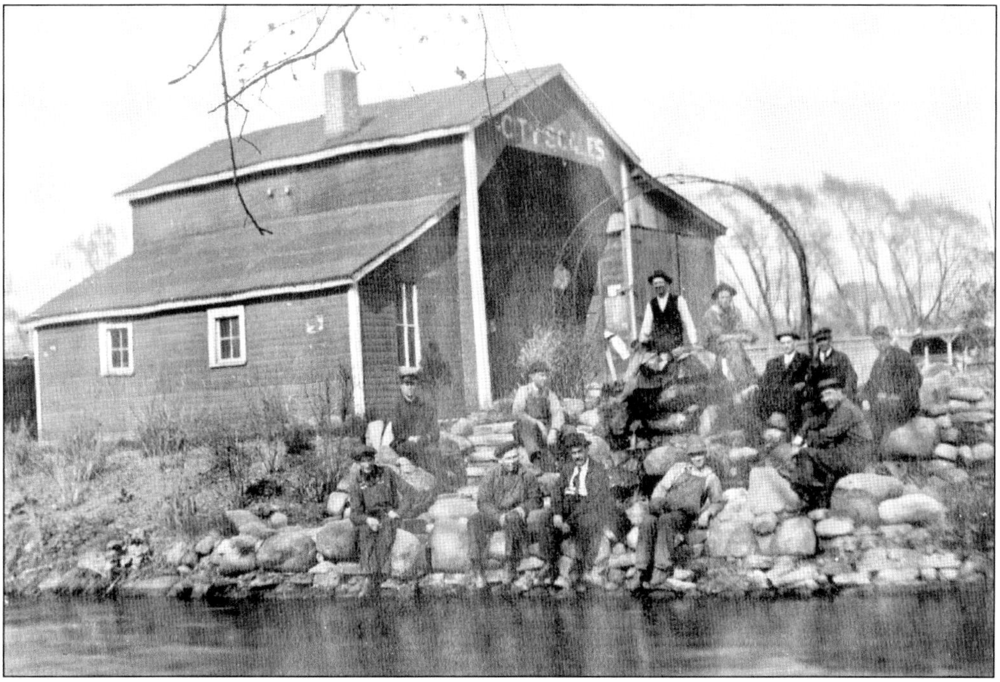

Albion City Scales, located on the banks of the Kalamazoo River, represented a mixture of businessmen and farmers working together to grow the city. On this day, everyone went outside for a break and this photograph was taken. Note the stone stairs (at center) leading to the river. This indicates that products were shipped from Albion City Scales. (Homer Historical Society.)

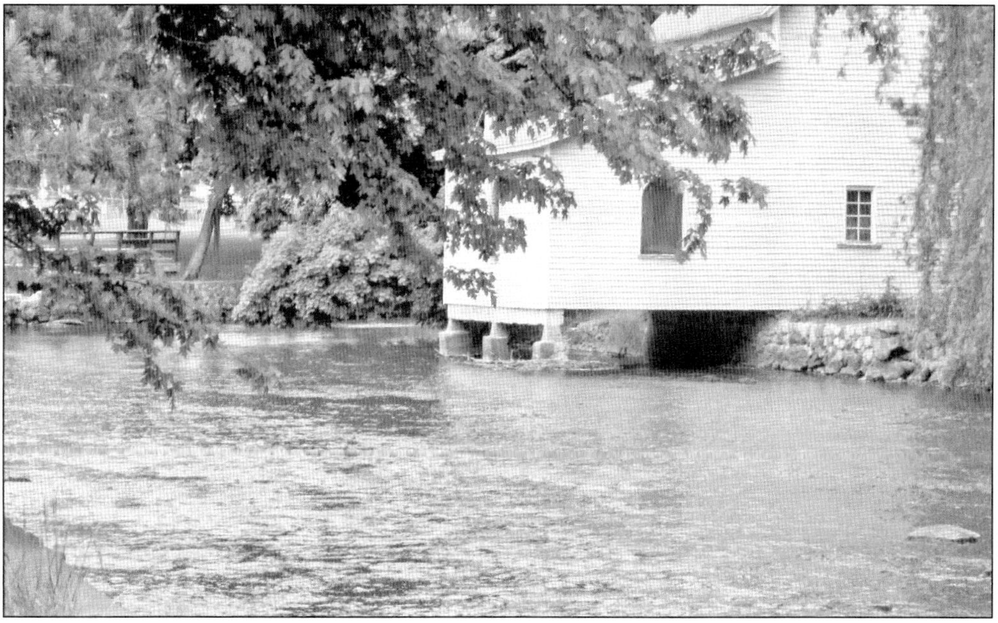

This house partially sits in the Kalamazoo River. The back portion of the building was constructed on pylons so that the river could flow underneath it. Prior to the invention of air-conditioning, this was one method used to keep a building cool. The stonework along the banks of the river was necessary to keep them intact. The building is still occupied today. (Authors' personal collections.)

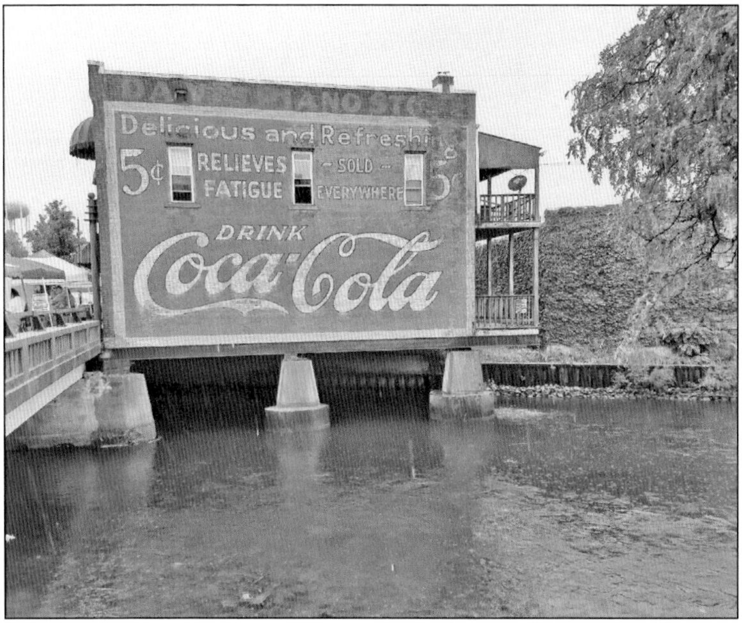

A lot of buildings sit along the Kalamazoo River, making the sides of the buildings perfect for advertising different items. This two-story building with the Kalamazoo River flowing under it, near the intersection of Cass Street and Superior Street in Albion, still advertises for Coca-Cola, although the price is not what it used to be. (Authors' personal collections.)

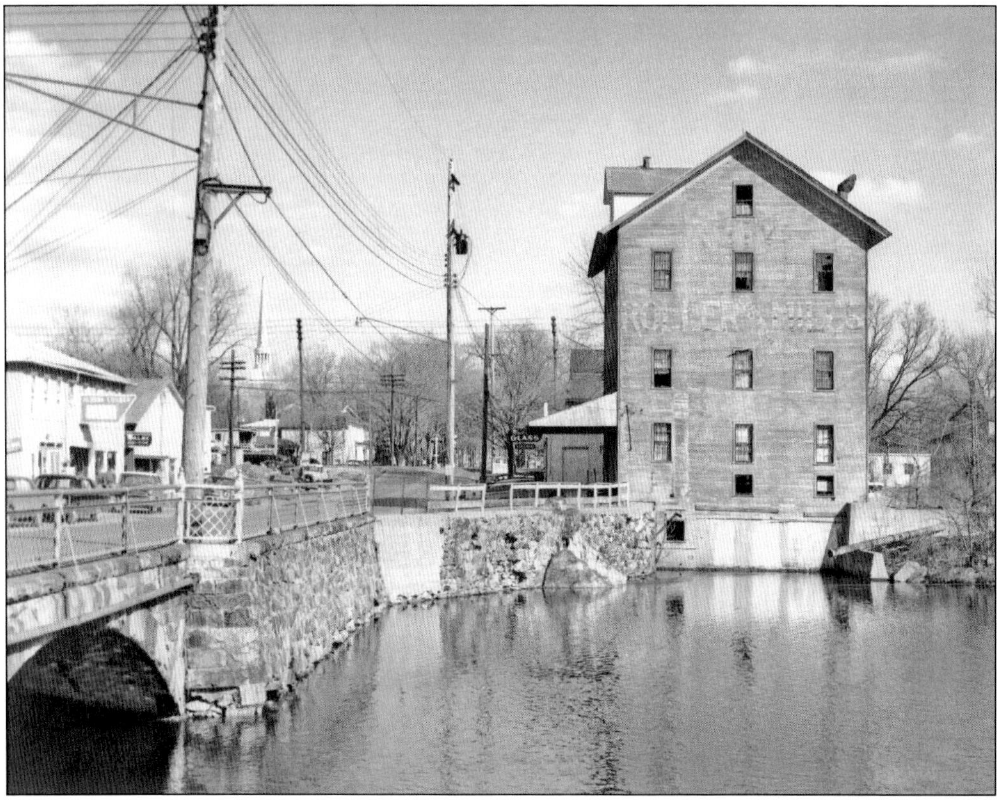

This photograph is a perfect example of how quarried stones were used to channelize the banks of the Kalamazoo River. The stone structure had to be strong enough to support the road and railroad crossing as well as withstand the magnitude of the river's flow and high enough to hold back the frequent floodwaters. (APL.)

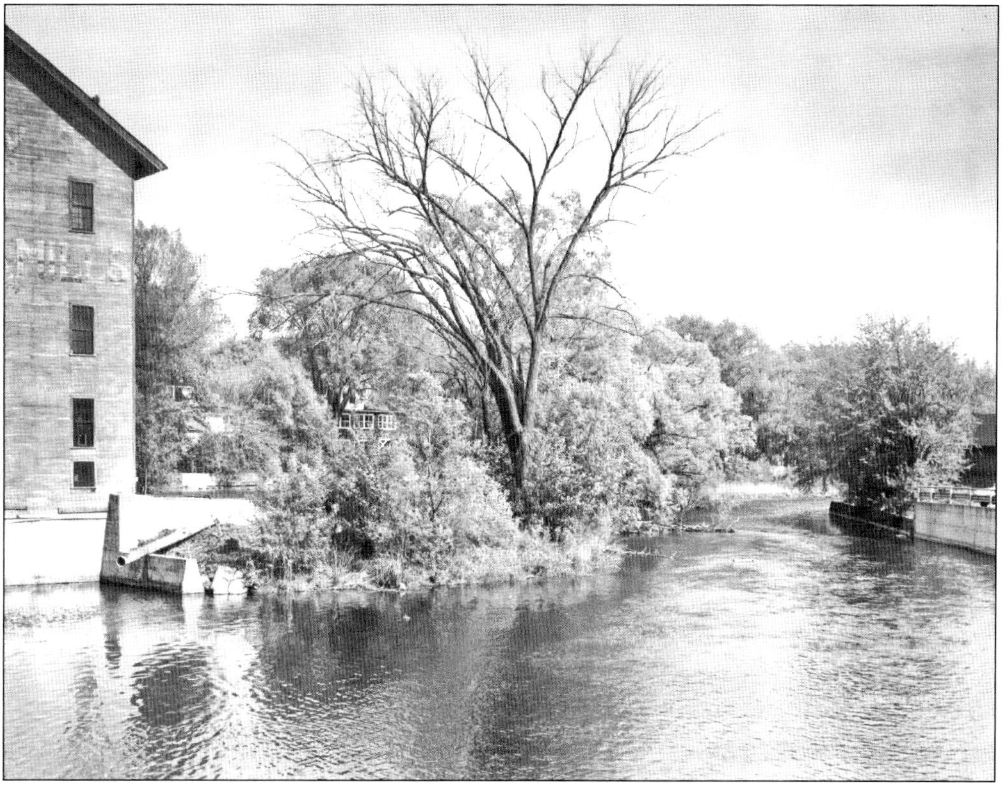

As the Kalamazoo River flows past the White Mill, note the concrete foundation for the mill and the parking lot at right. This was done to help channel the water to the mill for power. Farther downstream, the water is left to flow naturally. (APL.)

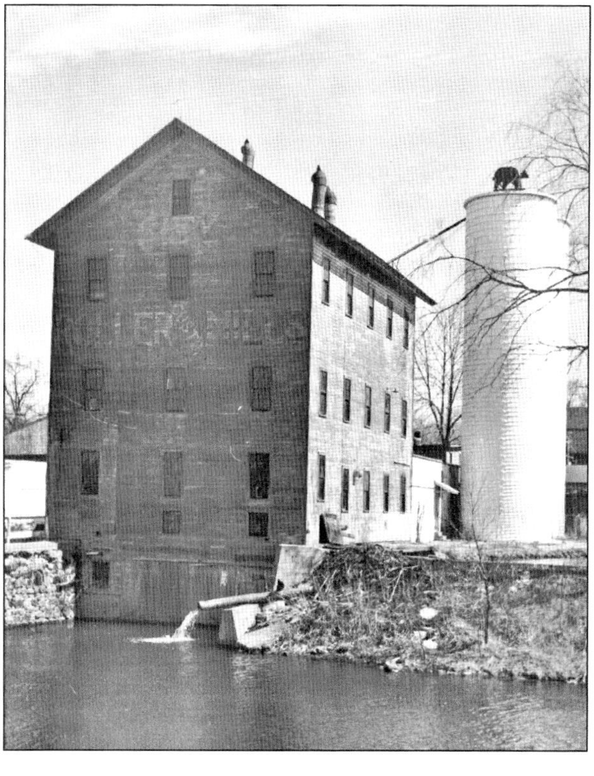

To replace an upstream mill that had burned earlier that year, the White Mill was built in 1876. It operated until 1957. The mill produced a popular brand of flour. The mill's specialties were whole wheat pancakes and muffin mixes. This is what the mill looked like around 1960. In 1974, the upper portion of the building burned, and the rest was subsequently removed. (APL.)

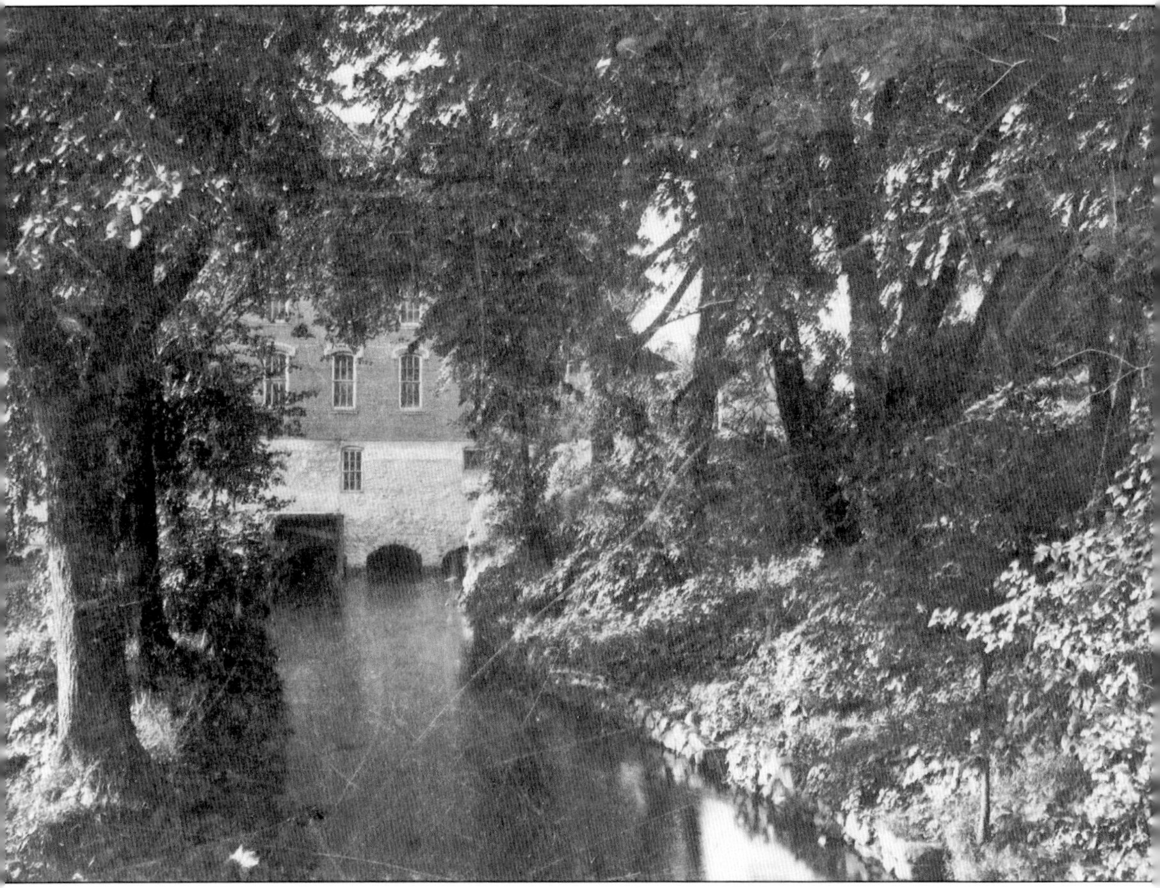

The Old Red Mill, built in 1845, was used as a feed mill because electricity could be generated from the Kalamazoo River, which ran under the structure. In 1909, the mill was converted into a hydroelectric powerhouse. Consumer's Power replaced this powerhouse when it burned in 1913. (APL.)

Two

West to Battle Creek

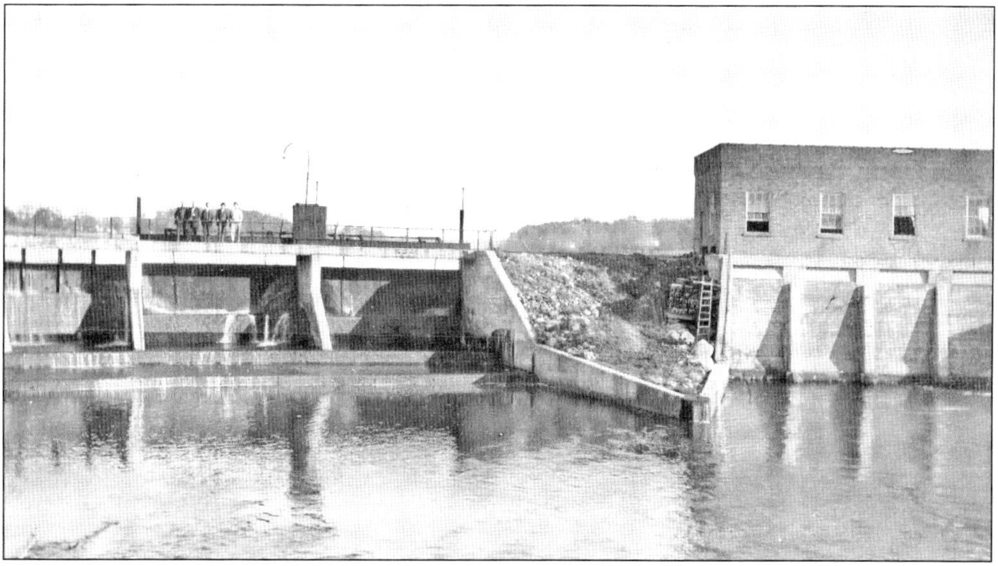

The Ceresco Dam was built in 1839 about five miles west of Marshall. It provided power to flour mills and sawmills in Ceresco. The dam created a 75-acre lake and became the centerpiece of the town. The most recent owner, Enbridge Oil Company, demolished the dam in 2013 as payback to the state for some damage incurred during the 2010 Enbridge oil spill. (BCHS.)

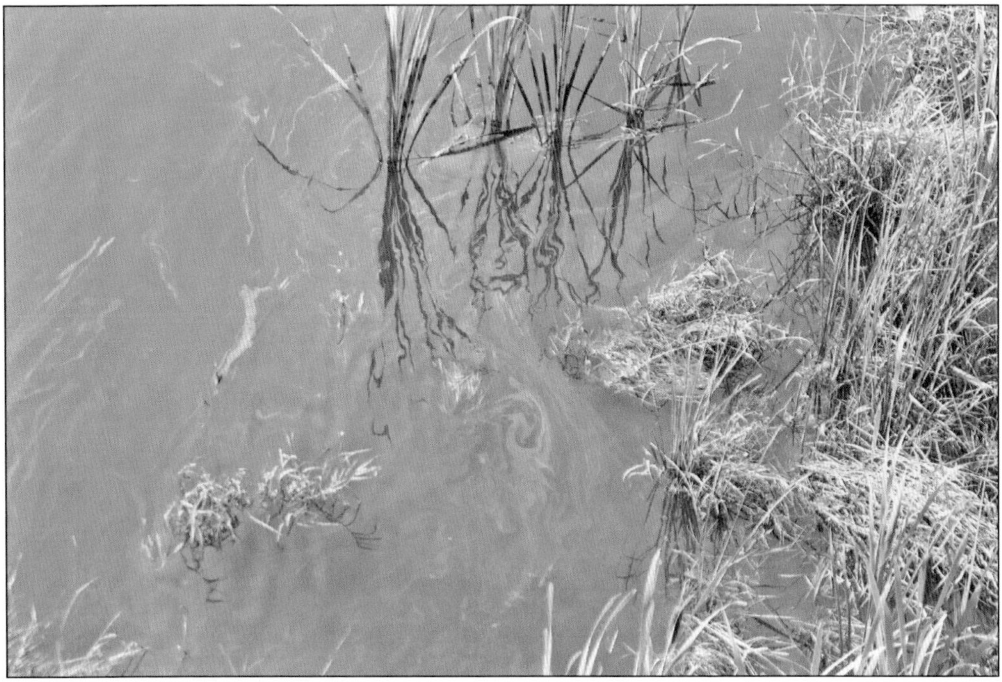

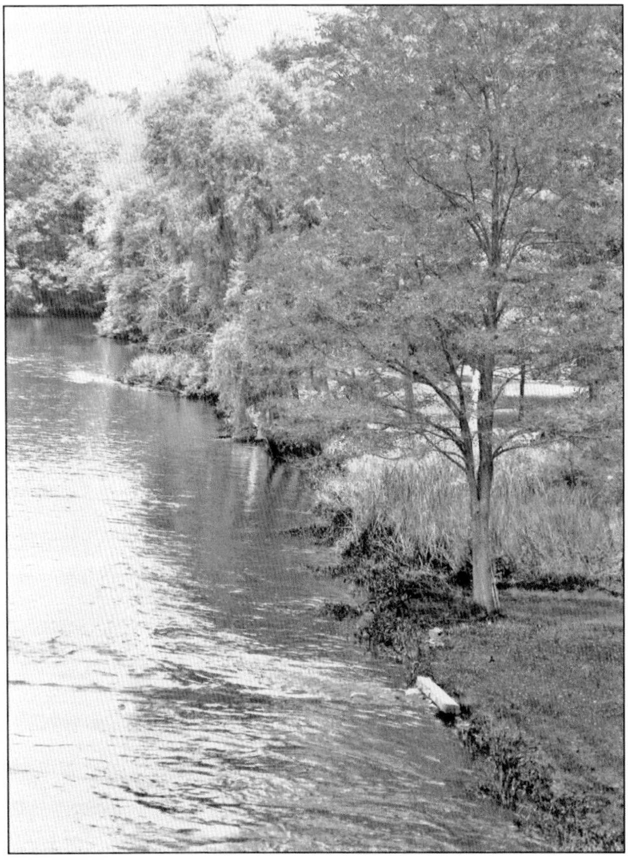

Twenty-five miles of the Kalamazoo River were contaminated when oil was spilled into the Talmadge Creek and Kalamazoo River. All of the lighter streaks in the photograph are oil. Due to the turbulent nature of the water near the banks, the oil formed a swirling eddy, which can be seen at center. (Mark Jenness.)

Dilbit, a form of crude oil that floats in water but sinks over time, spilled into Talmadge Creek, a tributary of the Kalamazoo River, affecting vegetation along its banks. This expanse of bank has oil damage in the grass and reeds, hindering their ability to grow and perform their natural processes, such as photosynthesis, which means putting clean oxygen back into the atmosphere. (Cheryl Vosburg.)

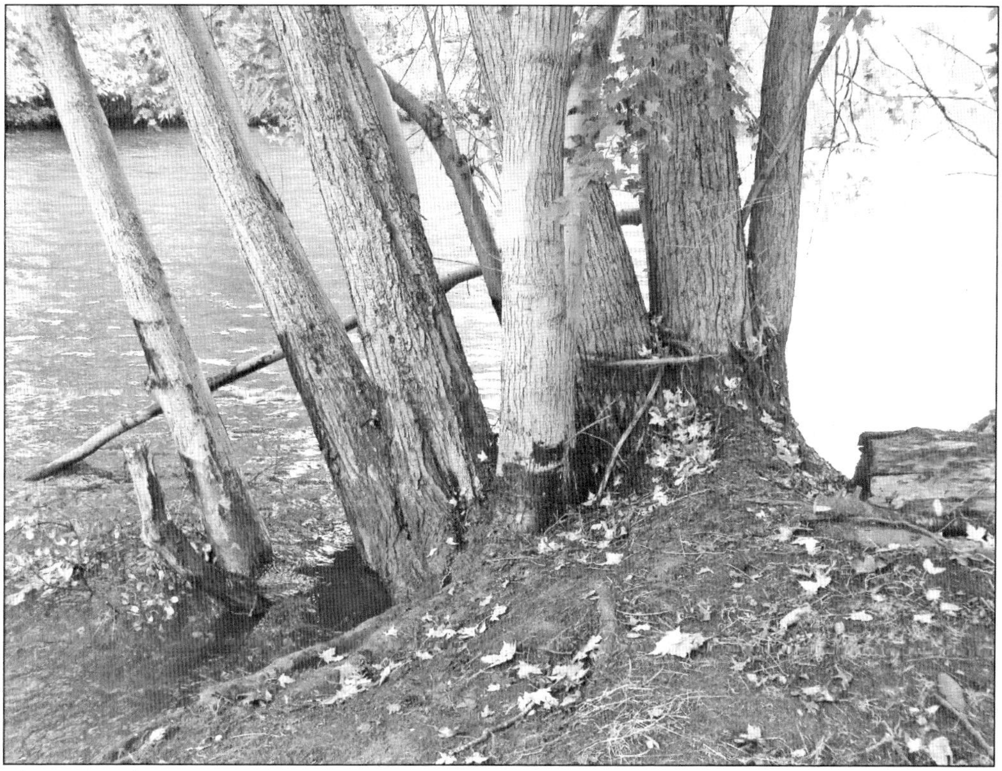

The leak only lasted a few days until Enbridge fixed the rupture. However, the cleanup efforts lasted for many years afterwards. Tree trunks covered in heavy crude oil could be seen all along the 25 miles of river that experienced the oil leak. Vegetation, like these trees, was not a priority for cleanup at the time this photograph was taken. (Cheryl Vosburg.)

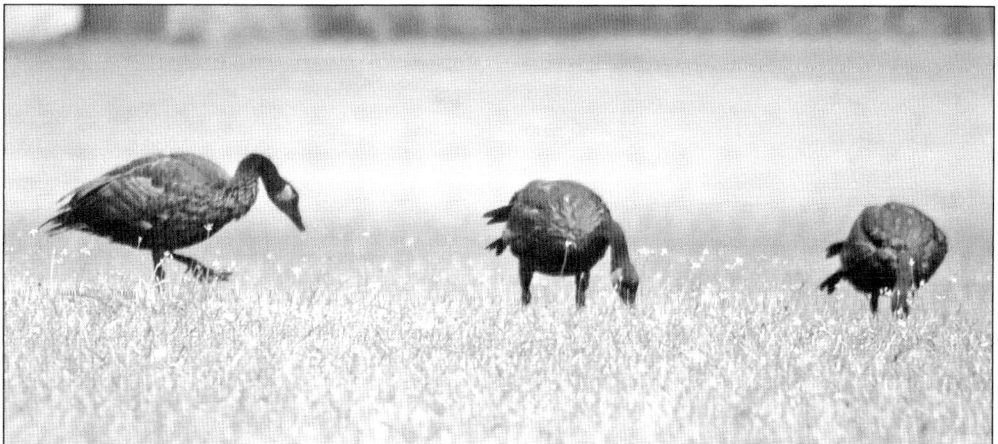

When the Enbridge oil spill occurred on Talmadge Creek, a tributary of the Kalamazoo River, everything that went into the water was covered in oil, like these geese. The geese then took that oil with them when they wandered onto dry land, spreading oil even farther inland than just the banks of the river. (Mark Jenness.)

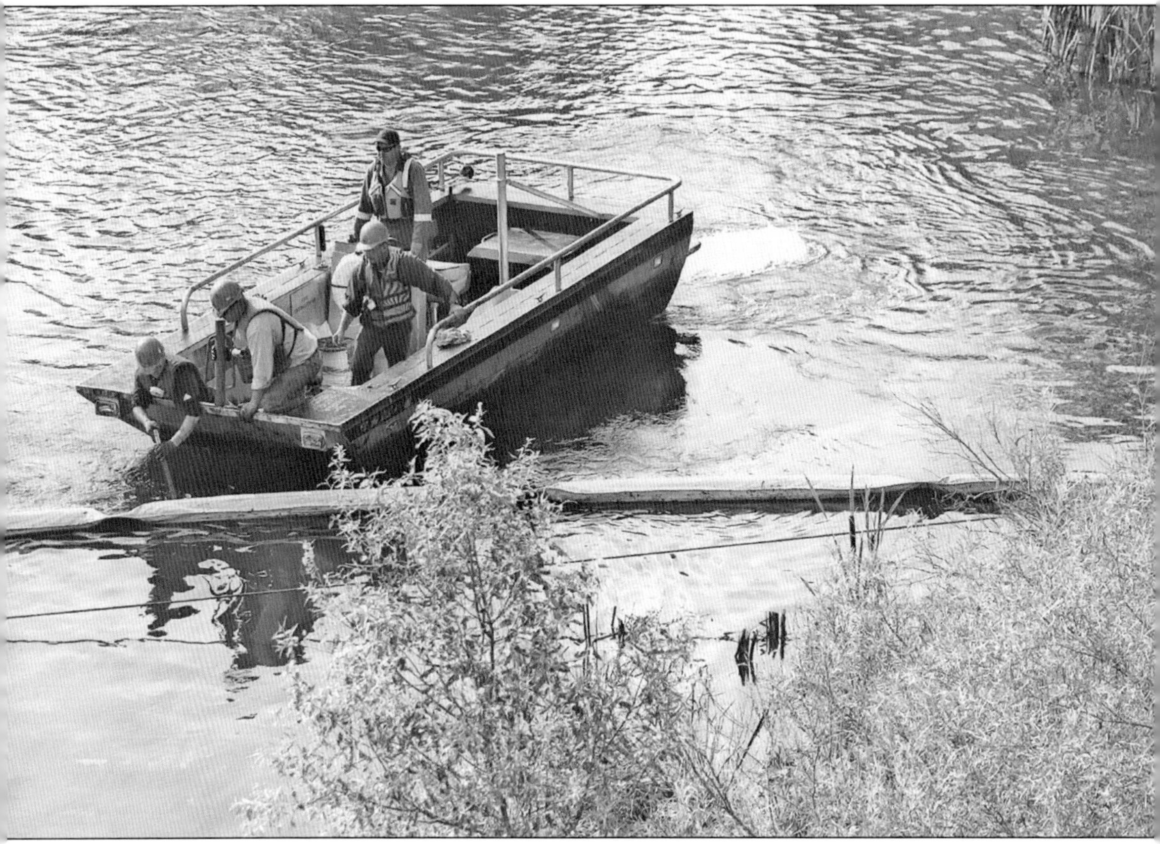

Cleanup of the Enbridge oil spill was an arduous task because oil was floating downstream in the Talmadge Creek, eventually making its way to the Kalamazoo River. This photograph shows a few of the several hundred people working on cleaning up the spill. The Kalamazoo River was closed for recreation during the months it took for cleanup efforts. (Mark Jenness.)

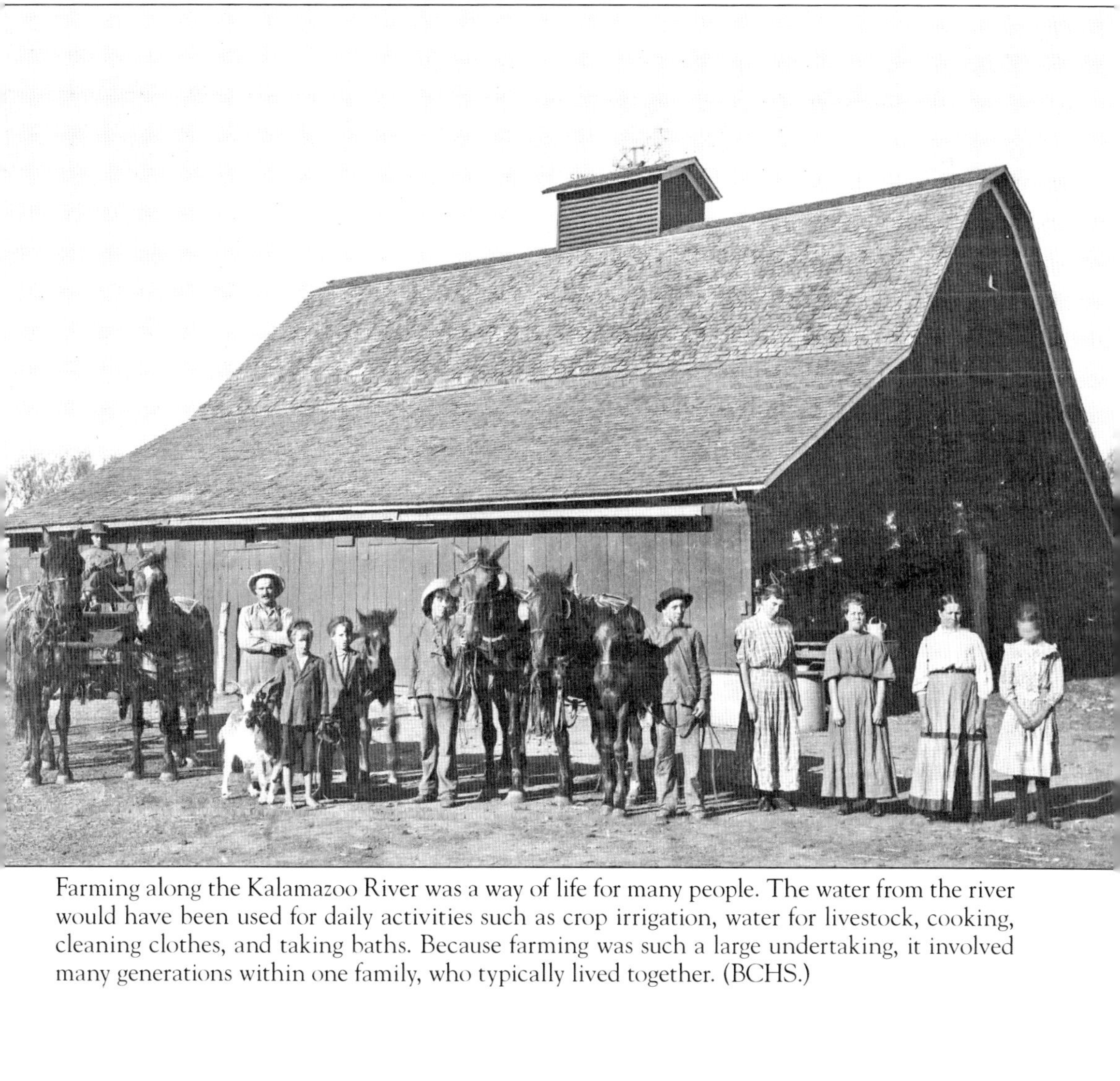

Farming along the Kalamazoo River was a way of life for many people. The water from the river would have been used for daily activities such as crop irrigation, water for livestock, cooking, cleaning clothes, and taking baths. Because farming was such a large undertaking, it involved many generations within one family, who typically lived together. (BCHS.)

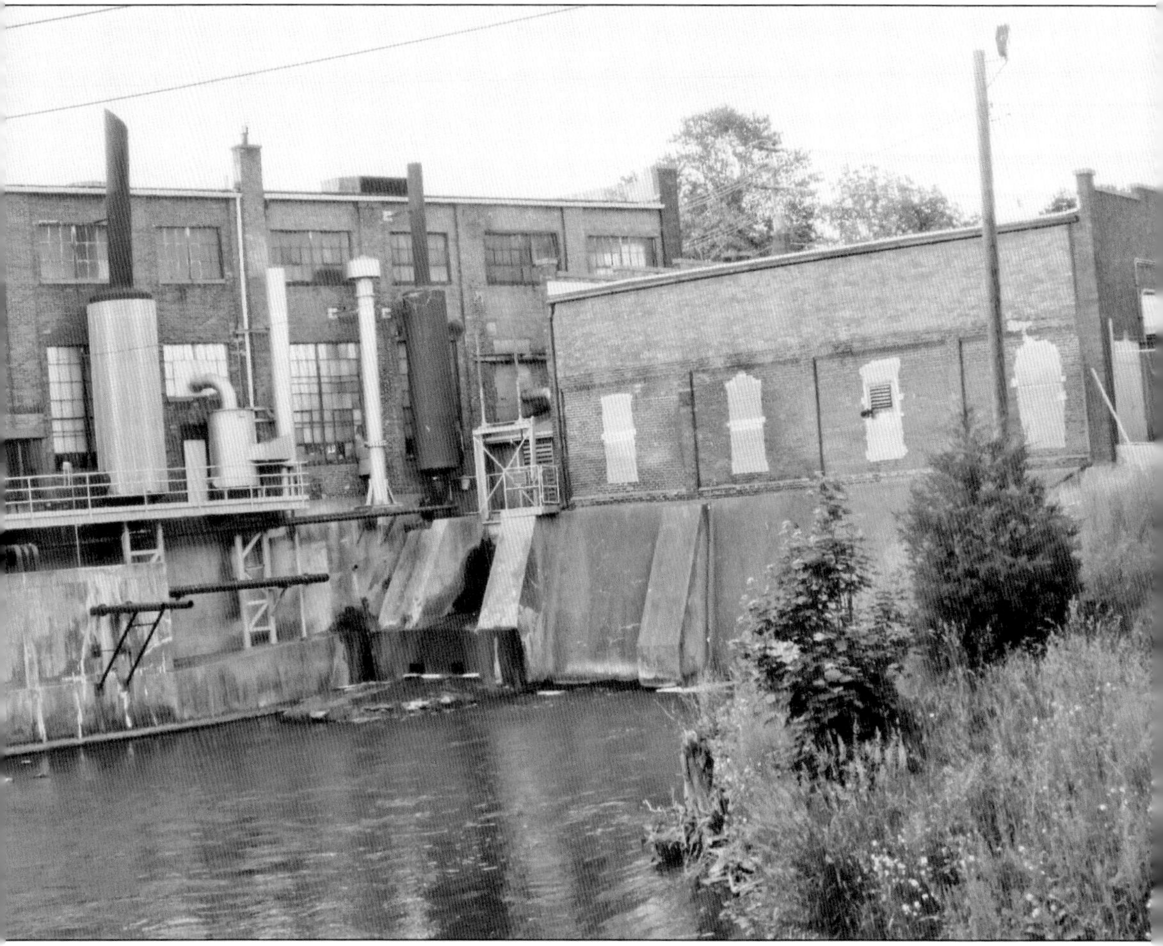

The Marshall Power Plant is located in what was once known as Perrinville, now part of the city of Marshall. The water from the spillway flows south and then heads west to rejoin the Kalamazoo River right behind the plant. The plant that uses the water energy here is one of the oldest hydroelectric operations in the United States. (Mark Jenness.)

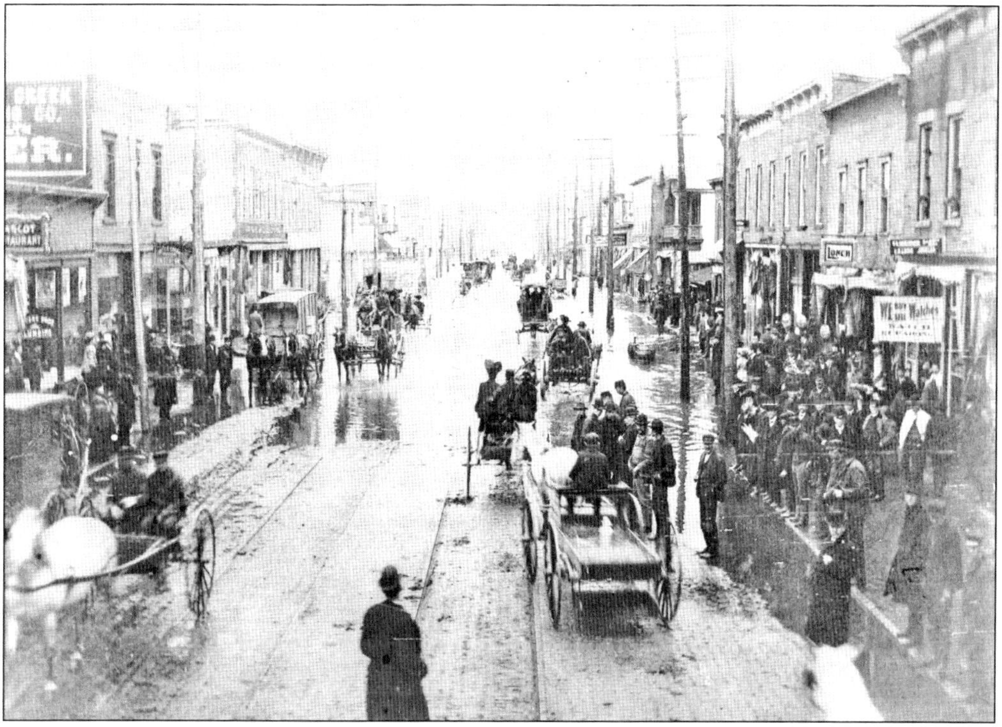

The city of Battle Creek lies along the Kalamazoo River and the Battle Creek River so it experiences flooding frequently. This 1904 view of Michigan Avenue shows that even though businesses may not be very close to the river, they were not exempt from rising floodwaters. (BCHS.)

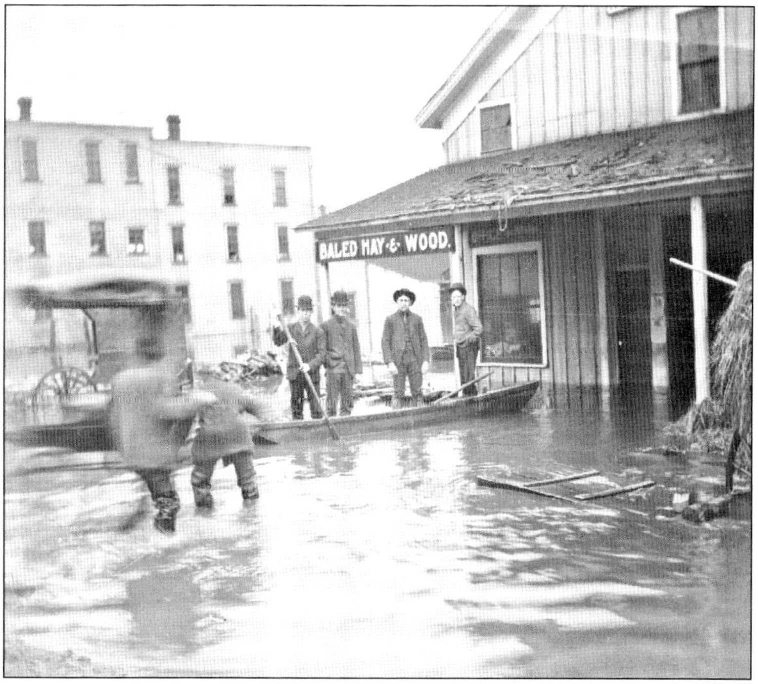

During the flood of 1904, getting around was quite difficult. This photograph shows that the water in the street was knee-deep and walking through it was very dangerous. One of the modes of transportation then was using shallow boats. The men standing in the flat-bottom boat would push off the street under the floodwaters to get around. (BCHS.)

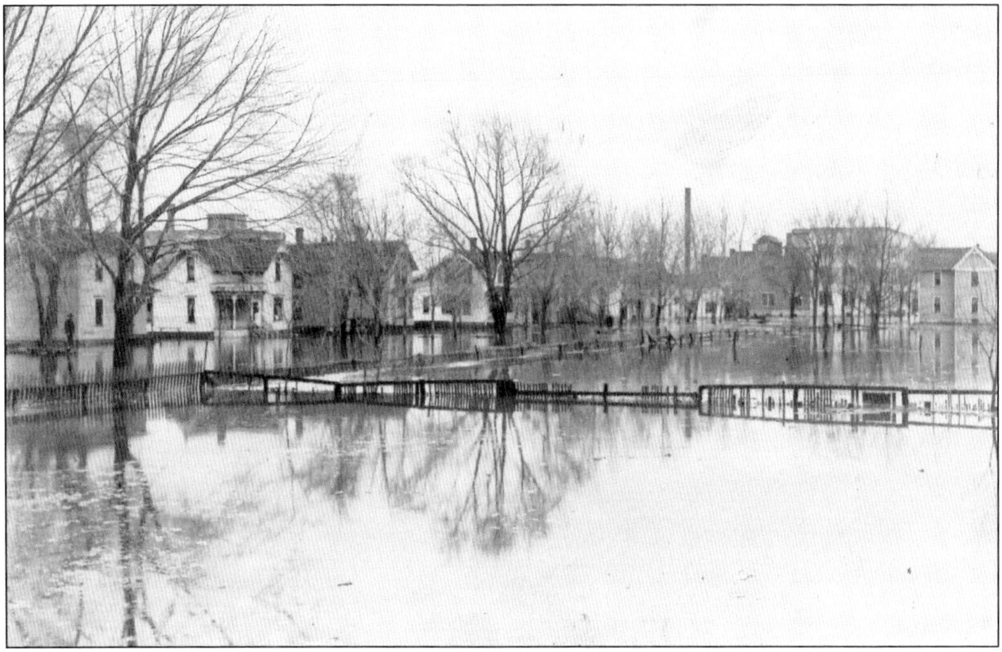

This 1904 photograph has a view looking out over flooded lawns facing Peninsular Street, which ran in front of the homes pictured. The man leaning against the white house is out surveying the damage. It appears the water was vast but shallow as it did not go over the foundations of the homes. (Authors' personal collections.)

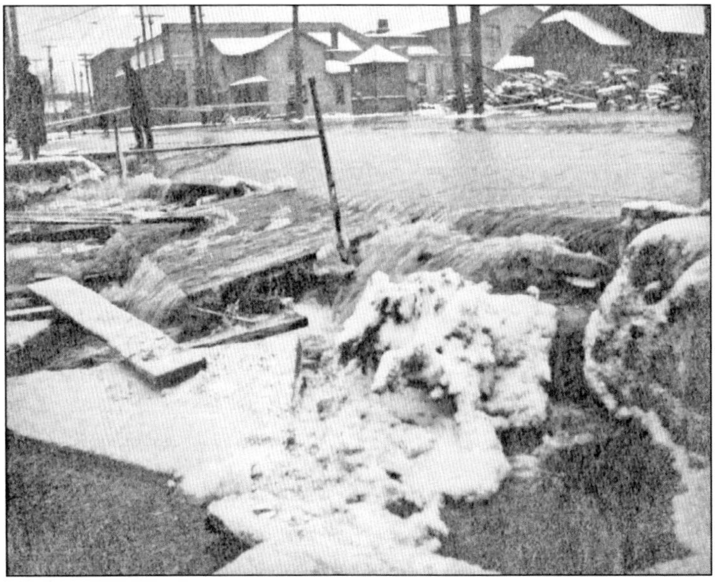

In 1904, South Jefferson Street sustained immense damage, including the washing out of this man-made barrier trying to contain the water. The structure was no match for the floodwater, though. Here, men survey the damage. At the time of this photograph, the water level had significantly dropped, and it was able to flow freely over the damaged containment. (Authors' personal collections.)

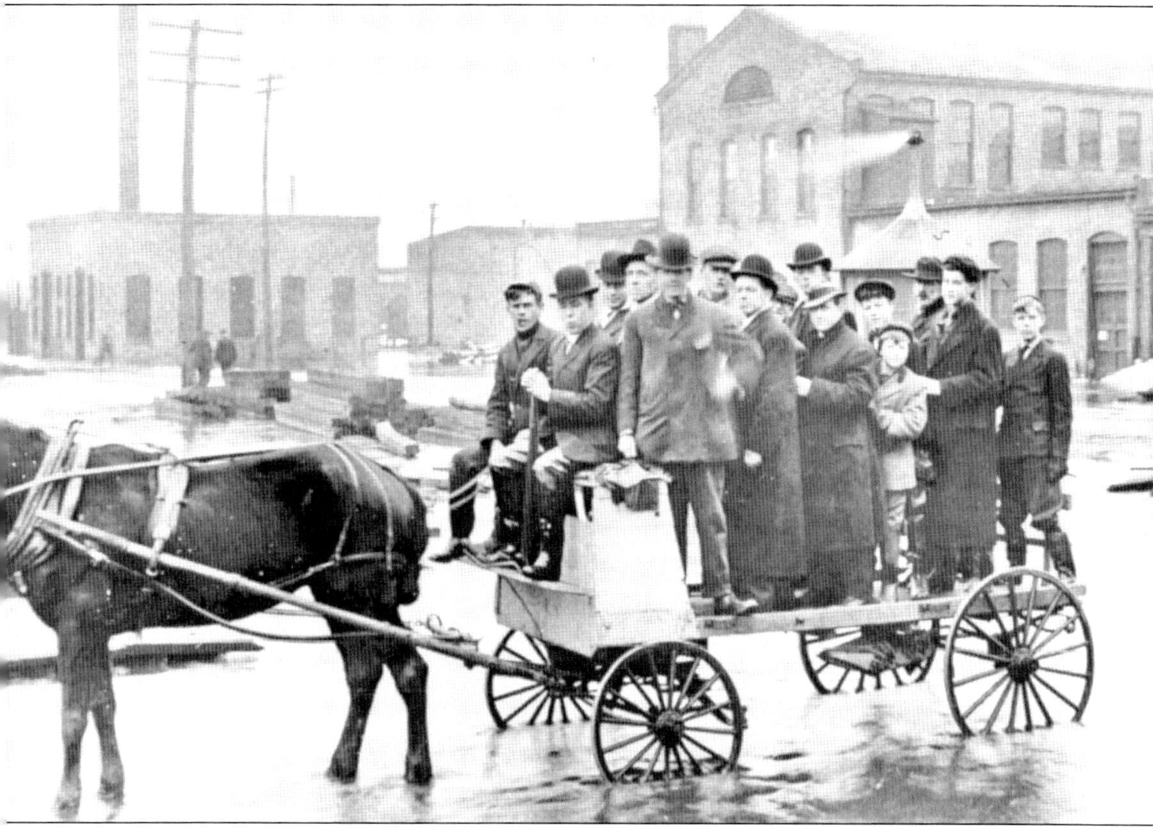

During times of flooding, residents had to be creative in how they got around town and did everyday things. The man who owned this horse and cart helped his neighbors by taking them where they needed to go because he knew he would be able to traverse the floodwaters, essentially creating a flood taxi. (BCHS.)

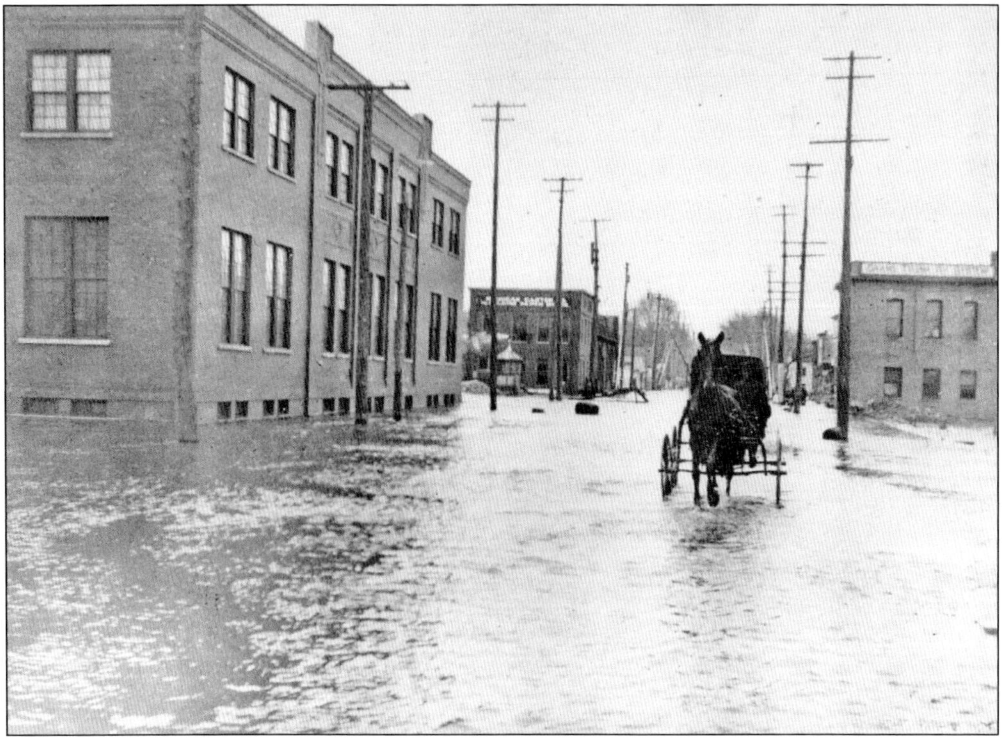

Businesses on Jefferson Street in Battle Creek had to endure many floods. This view from 1908 shows Jefferson Street, in a view looking south. Floodwaters were not very deep based on the wagon wheels; however, it did move swiftly, so people had to be careful when traveling. (BCHS.)

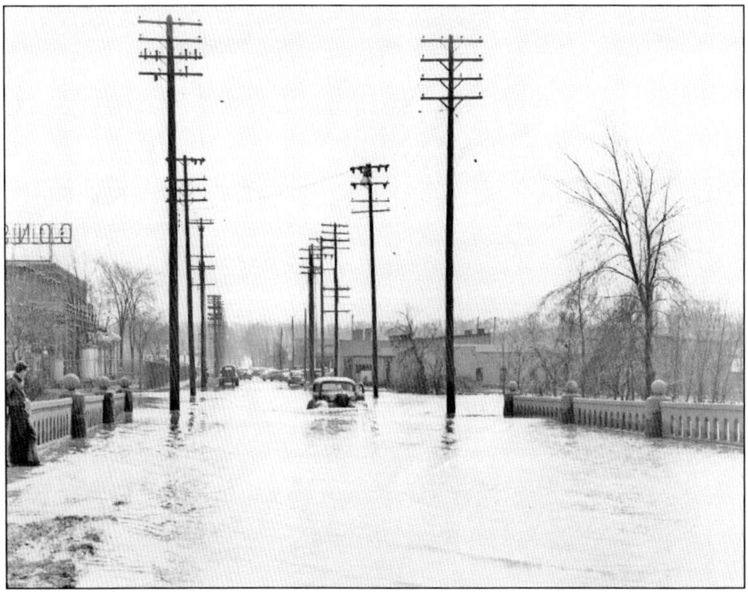

Battle Creek suffered another major flood in the 1930s. Automobiles were now the main mode of transportation. In places, floodwaters were deep enough to submerge the bottom half of cars that tried to get through. The raised sidewalks experienced flooding as well but were high enough that people could stand and watch motorists try to ford the water. (BCHS.)

The 1930s flooding affected the railways through Battle Creek. In the center of the photograph, smoke from a train can be seen at the Shredded Ralston Cereal Company, later known as Chex. The company relied on trains to transport their products to other market cities. When flooding occurred, shipping products slowed. (BCHS.)

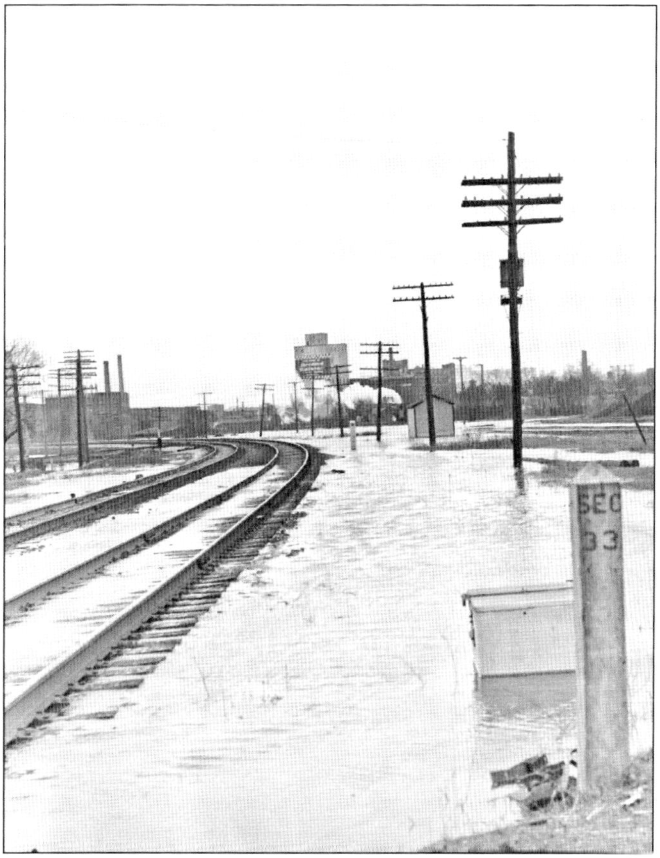

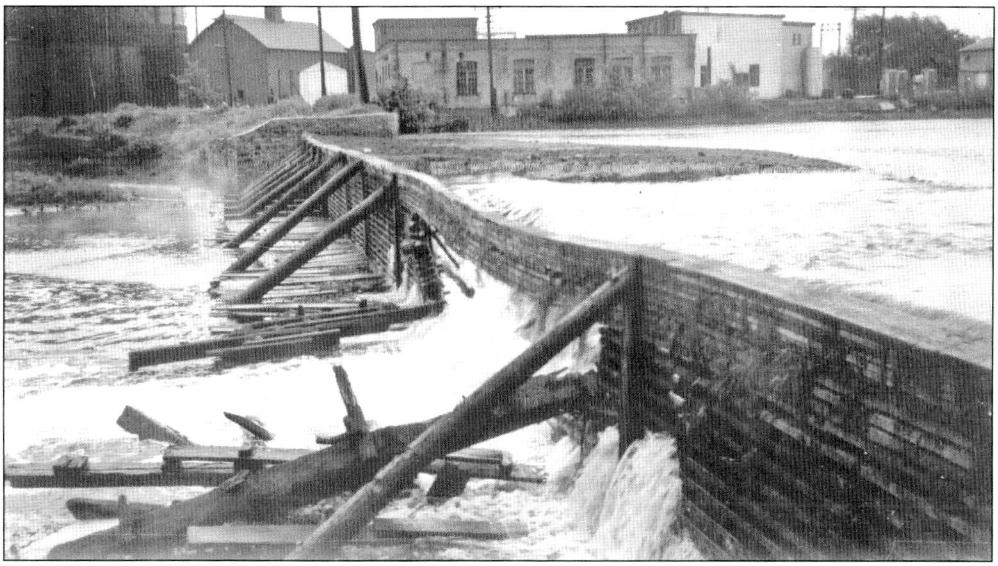

There are many dams in and around Battle Creek that help keep river water out of the town. In the spring of 1938, local rivers experienced a higher than normal amount of water flowing into them, causing flooding throughout the city. This dam had hit its capacity and threshold for holding back water as evidenced by the gaping hole and rushing water. (BCHS.)

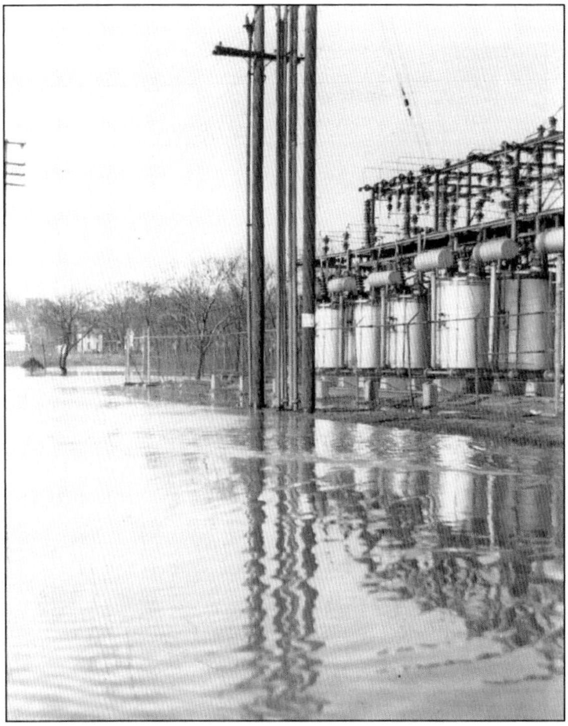

Not only was floodwater bad for crops, animals, and transportation, it was also dangerous for people because water could spark fires when close to electricity. This photograph from the 1947 floods shows water is encroaching on the transformers. If the water had gotten any closer to this substation, parts of Battle Creek would have been in jeopardy of losing power. (BCHS.)

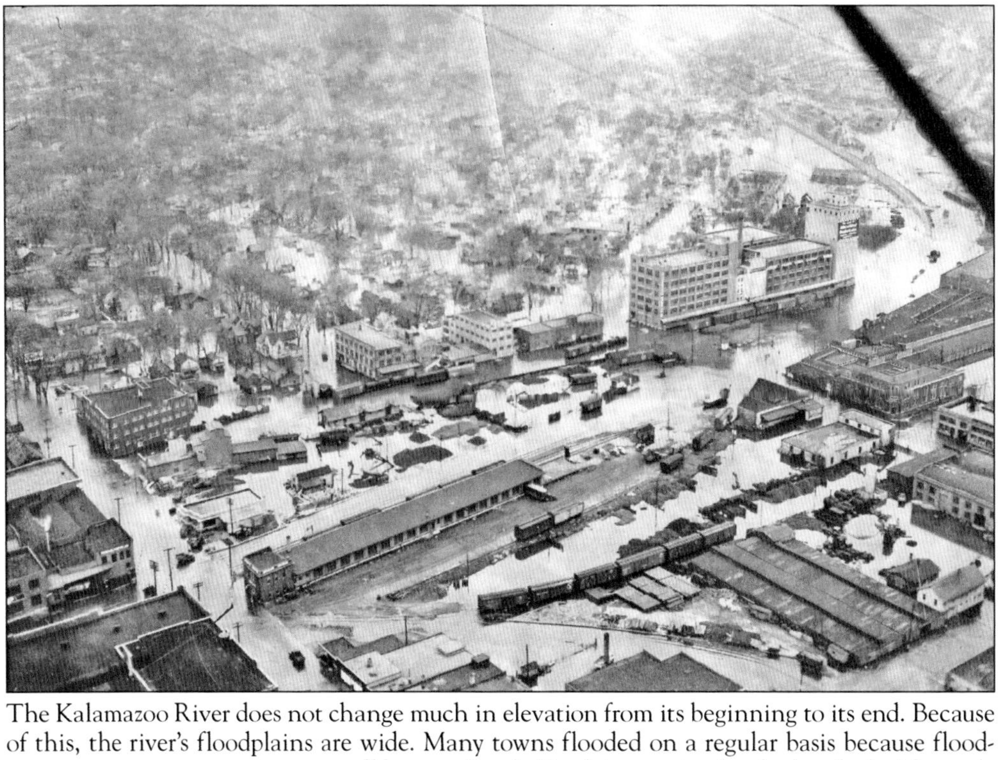

The Kalamazoo River does not change much in elevation from its beginning to its end. Because of this, the river's floodplains are wide. Many towns flooded on a regular basis because flood-management processes were not well known. Battle Creek is one city that had to deal with nearly annual flooding until the water diversion project was completed. (BCHS.)

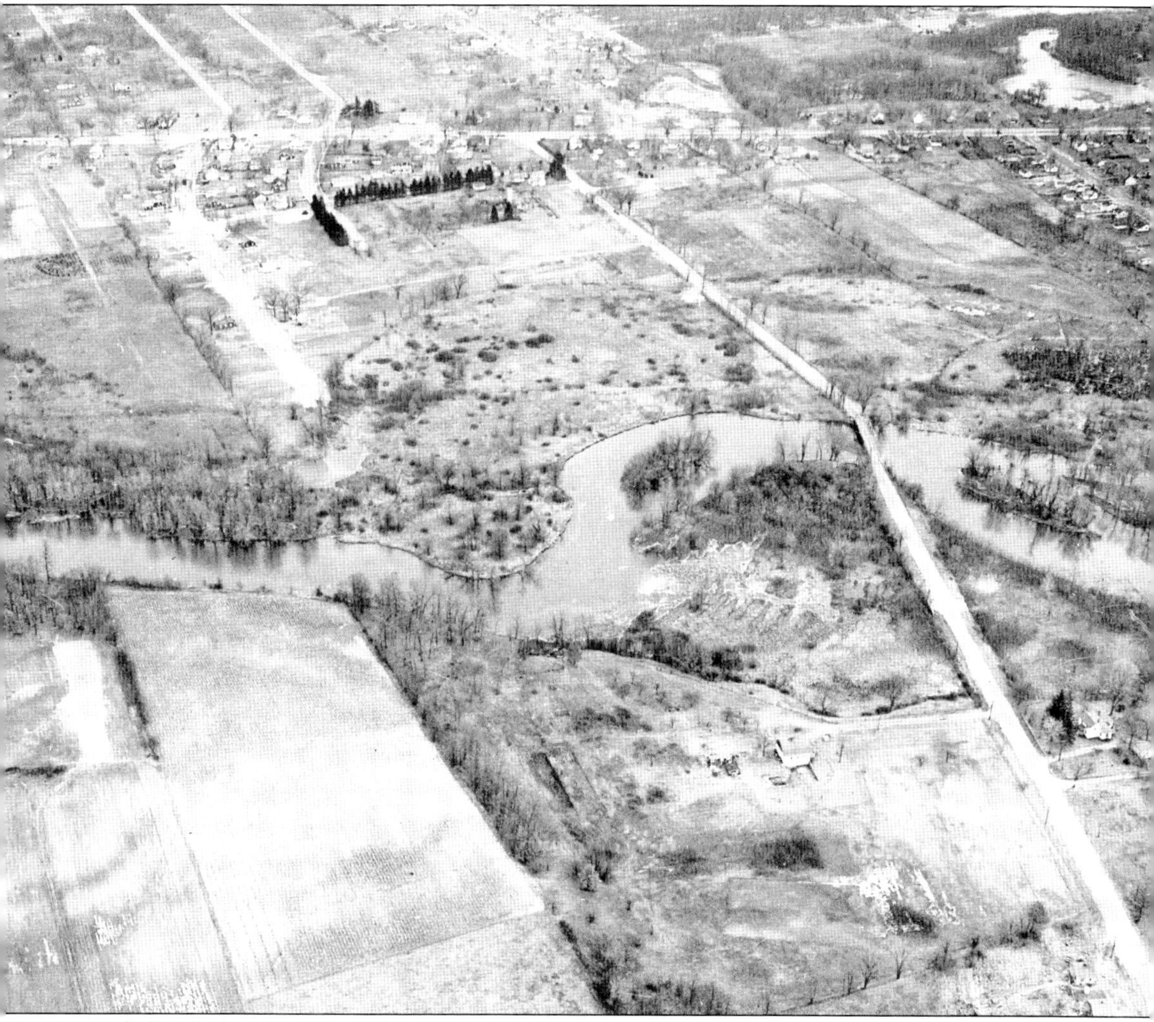

In 1947, Battle Creek experienced a flood that was more widely documented than in the past because airplanes were now being use to survey damage. This image shows a rural area outside of Battle Creek that was flooding, as evidenced by the much wider-than-normal channel of the Kalamazoo River. (BCHS.)

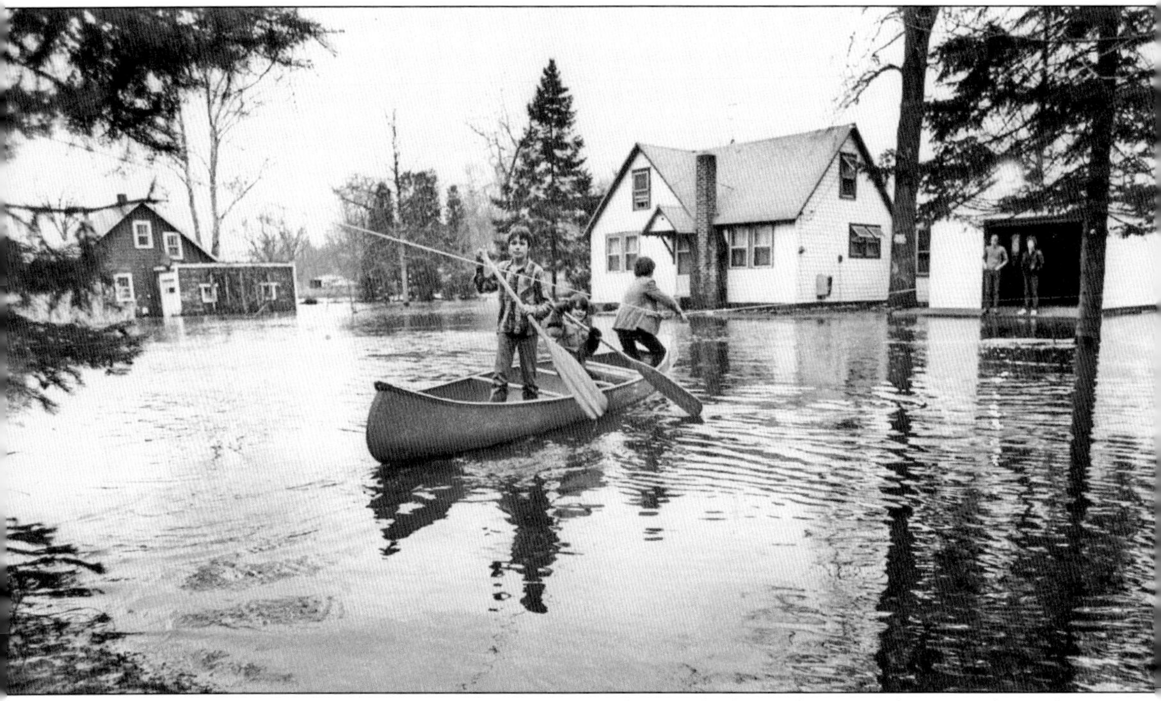

These creative children on Climax Drive in Battle Creek devised a way of getting from their home to the neighbors using a canoe and a clothesline. When the water gets too swift for them to use only the oars, they grab on to the clothesline to help get them across. Their parents watch from the garage door opening. (BCHS.)

Ice jamming in the spring is a hazard along the Kalamazoo River. As ice breaks up from the warming temperatures, it can jam in narrow locations along the river causing flooding. These men try to keep the ice chunks flowing downstream to prevent a flood in Battle Creek. (BCHS.)

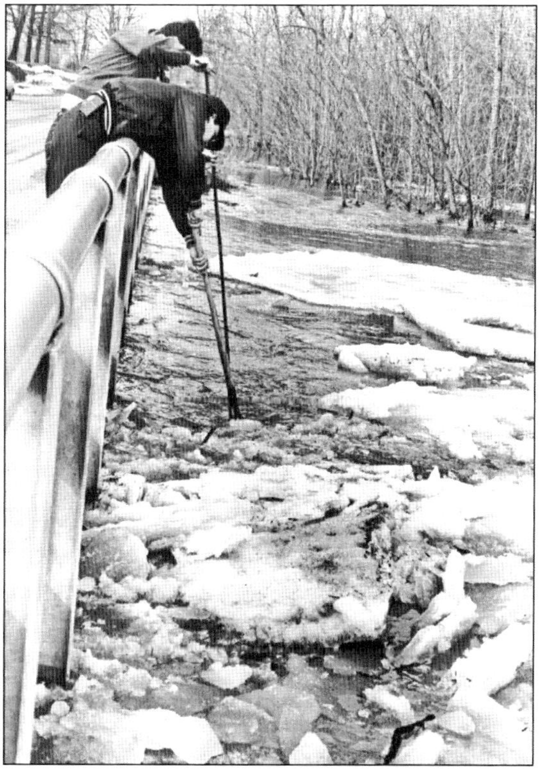

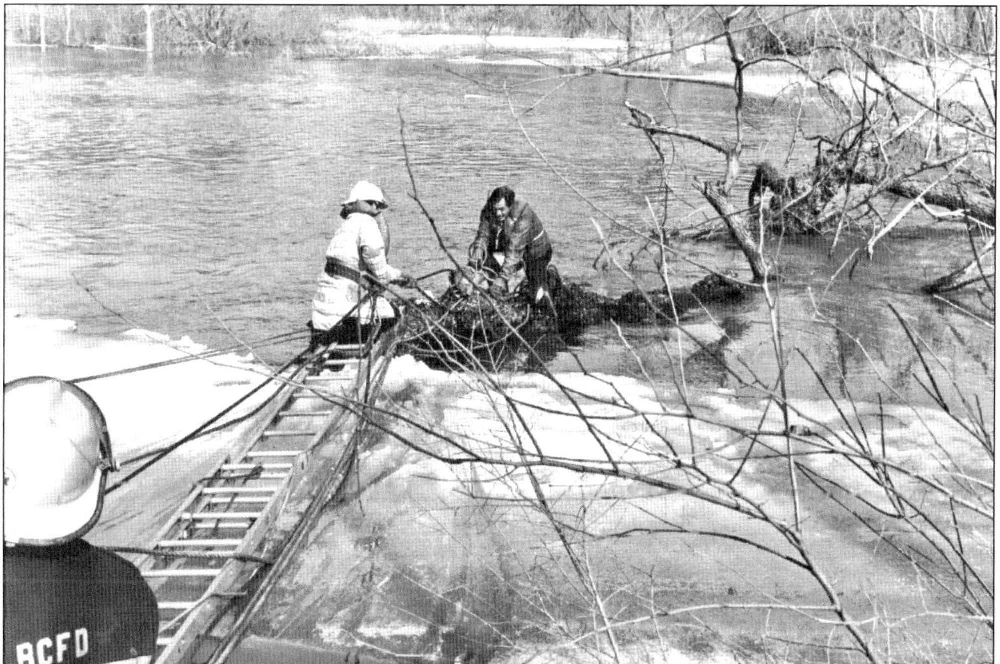

The ice's thickness along the banks of the Kalamazoo River in spring can be deceiving. Many people believe that the ice will hold their weight when it really cannot. In these instances, the local fire departments are called out to help rescue those that have fallen into the river. (BCHS.)

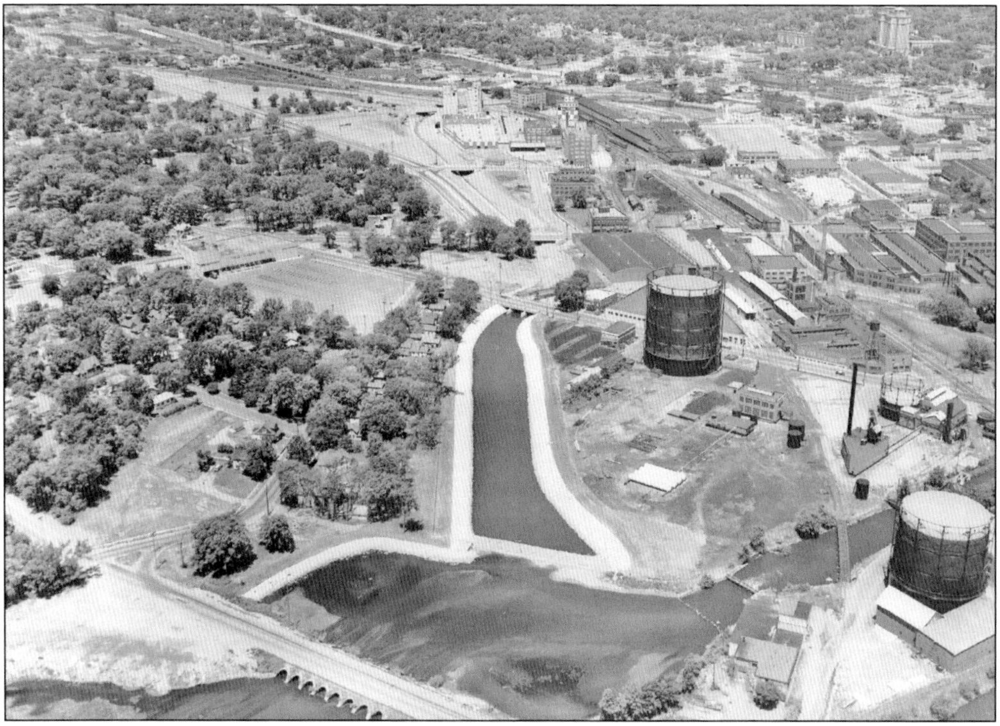

The diversion project in the city of Battle Creek began in 1954 with a price tag of $7 million. In 1961, the Kalamazoo River flowed through the newly cut channel for the first time. Both of these photographs shows the Kalamazoo River as it enters the city from the south. The above photograph shows the new channel (at center) while it was still blocked from completely flowing through. The old channel (at right) allows water to flow naturally. The photograph below displays the Kalamazoo River running through the new channel while the old channel is almost nonexistent. The bright white along the banks of the channel is new concrete that was poured to keep the river from meandering across the landscape. (Both, BCHS.)

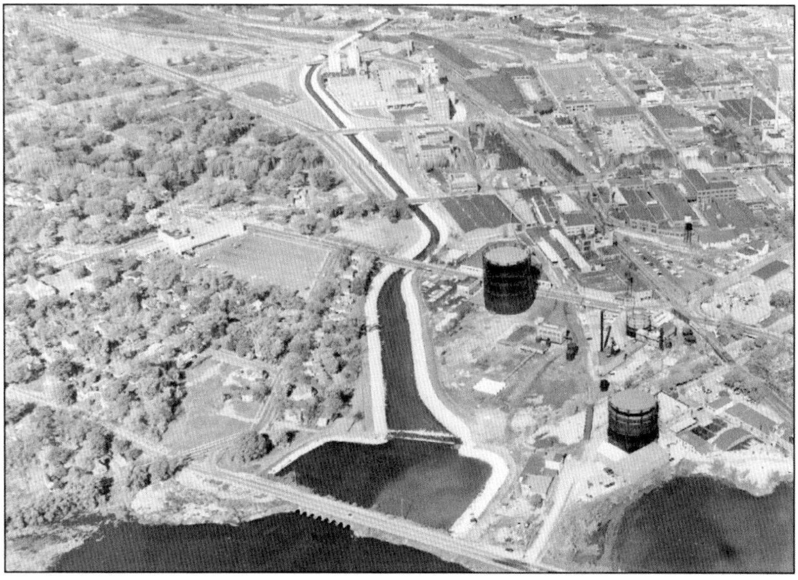

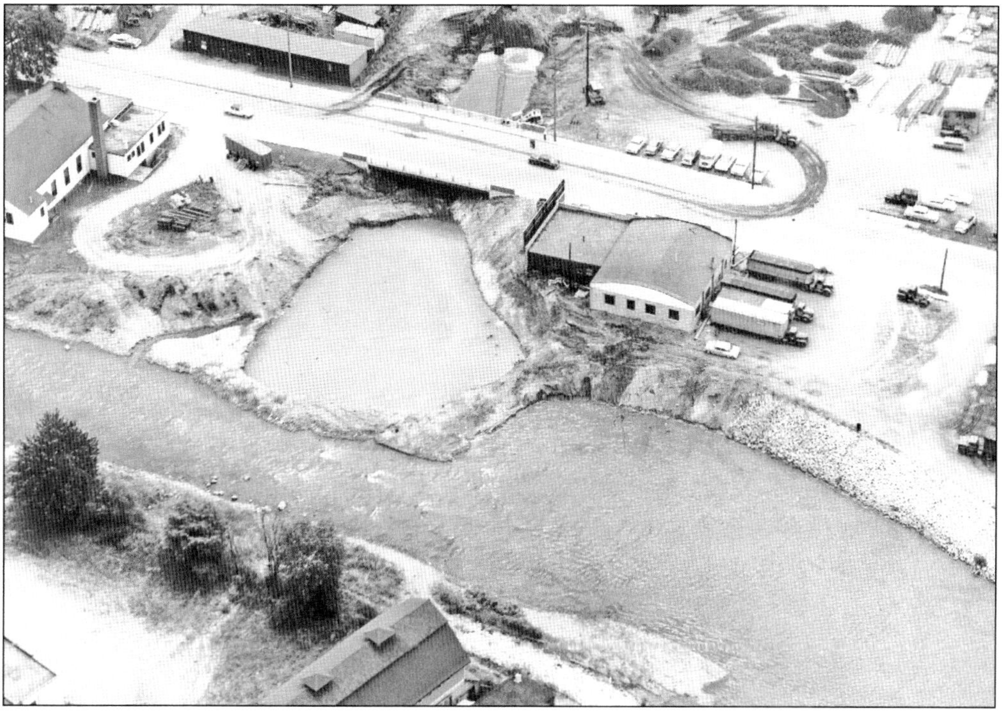

The Bottoms, located in Battle Creek along the Kalamazoo River, was known for experiencing devastating floods in 1904, 1908, 1912, and 1916. By 1927, the first flood control plan for the city was developed. Another plan was proposed in 1937. The flood of 1947 sparked the urgency to implement a flood control plan. In the photograph above, the beginning of stone-lined banks is taking shape and the diversion of the Kalamazoo River and the channelization of the Battle Creek River (in the foreground) can be seen. The image below shows the same area later, with more progress apparent. The crane at bottom right is digging out sediment to widen and deepen the Battle Creek River to match the velocity of the Kalamazoo River. (Both, BCHS.)

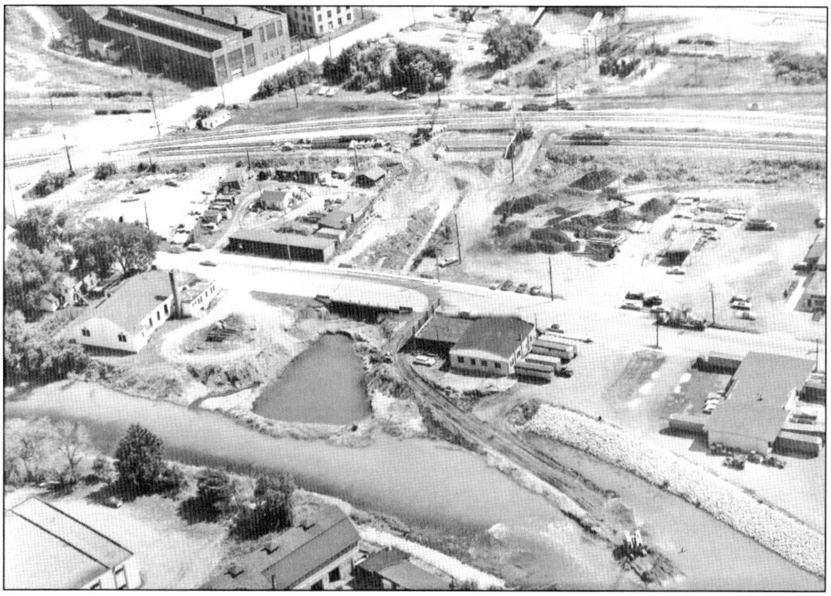

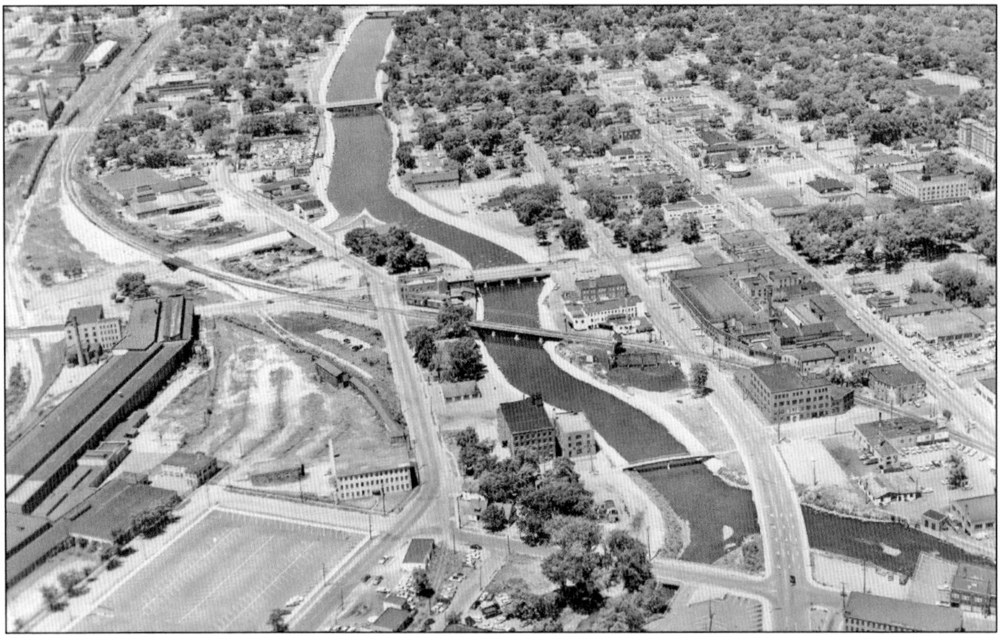

This view of the city of Battle Creek area shows how Rice Creek merges with the Battle Creek River (right corner) and then how the Battle Creek River merges with the Kalamazoo River (center). The water was channelized through the city by concreting the banks. (BCHS.)

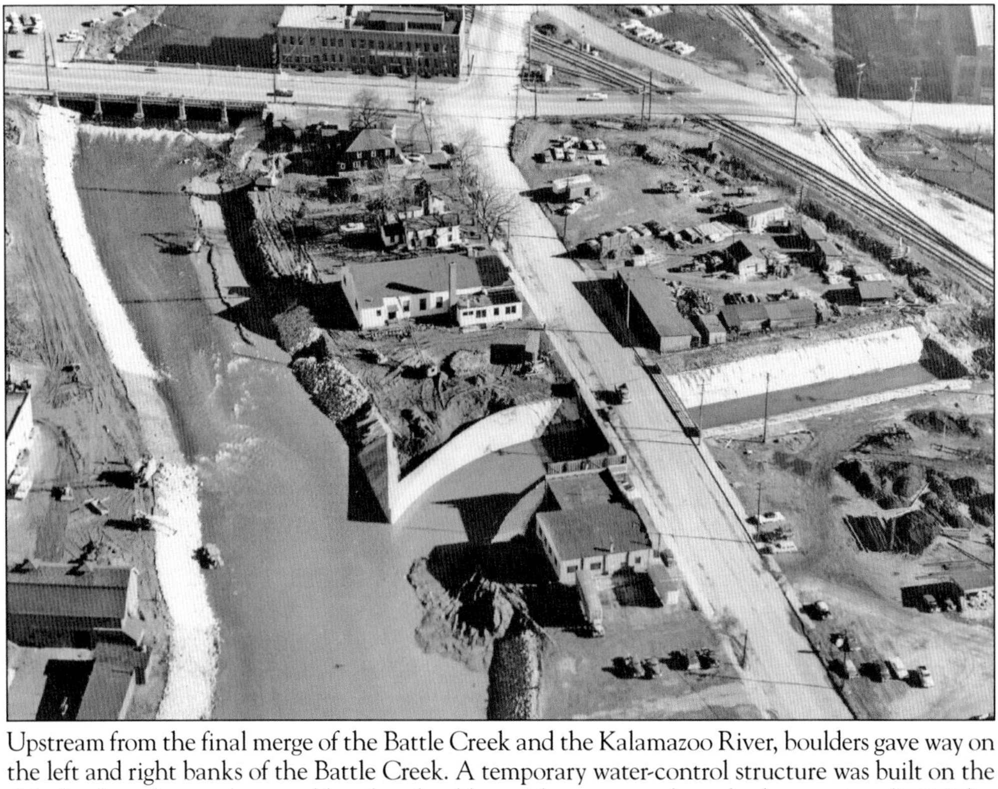

Upstream from the final merge of the Battle Creek and the Kalamazoo River, boulders gave way on the left and right banks of the Battle Creek. A temporary water-control structure was built on the right bank so that workers could replace boulders without worry about further erosion. (BCHS.)

Three

West to Galesburg/Augusta

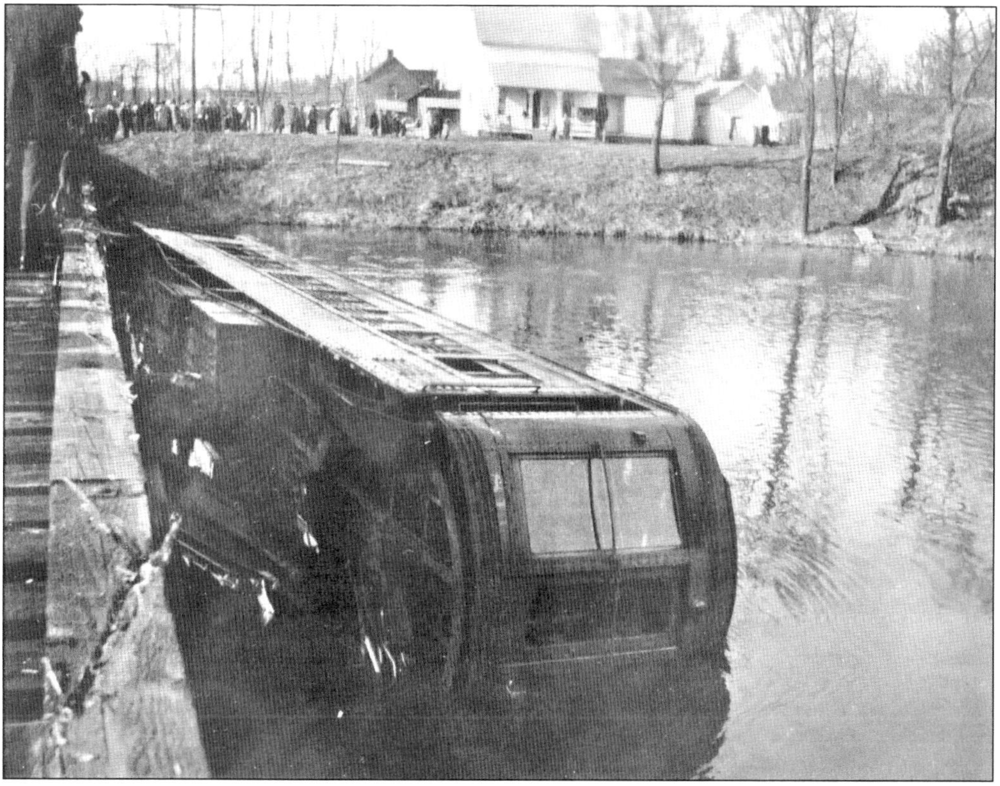

Electric interurban railcars, similar to streetcars, ran between cities along the Kalamazoo River, such as Battle Creek and Kalamazoo. Most interurbans were gone by 1930 but were a very popular mode of travel in their heyday. The interurban pictured here derailed on one of its many trips over the Kalamazoo River. (Sandy Stamm.)

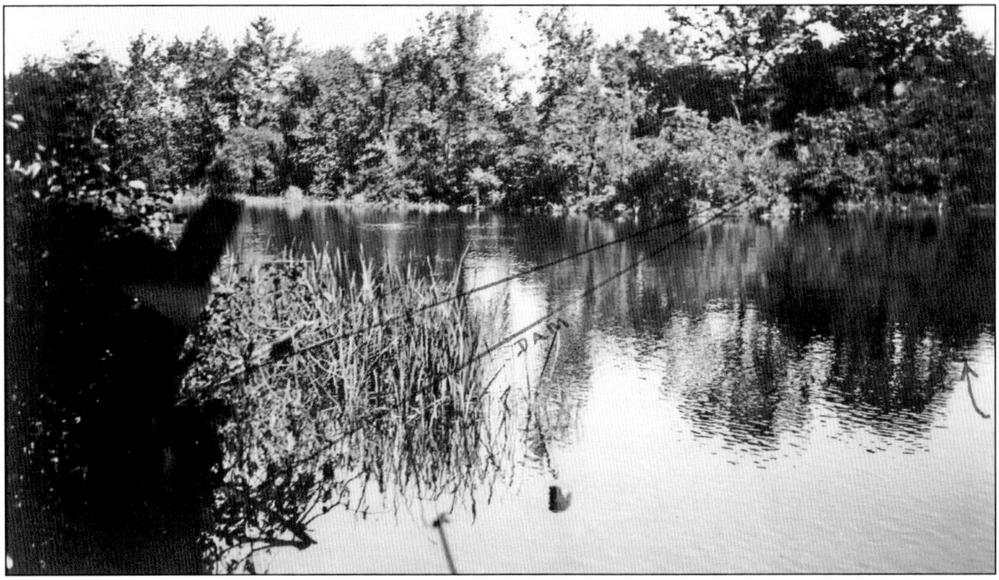

This is the site of an early sandstone dam along the Kalamazoo River near the city of Kalamazoo. These photographs, taken in 1933, show where the dam was located in 1835. The below photograph shows the glacial dyke that divides the river into a north and south channel. The north channel was used as a race bed. The dam indicated on both photographs was a four-foot sandstone dam built to divert water from the south channel into the north race bed to help with log transportation. After a six-foot dam was built closer to town, this one was dismantled and the sandstone was removed and used as building stone. (Both photographs by E.W. Roberts, WLBC.)

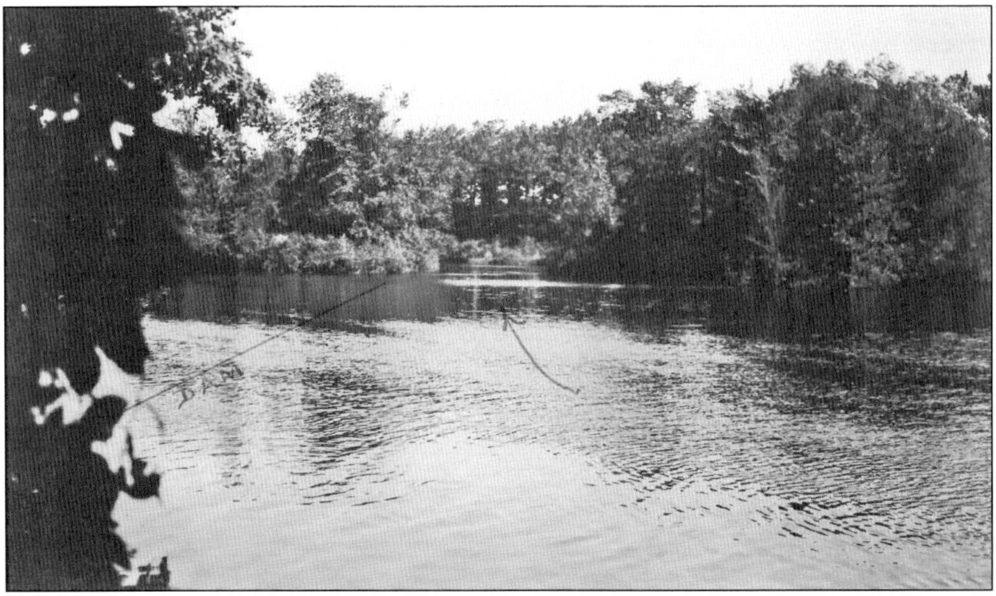

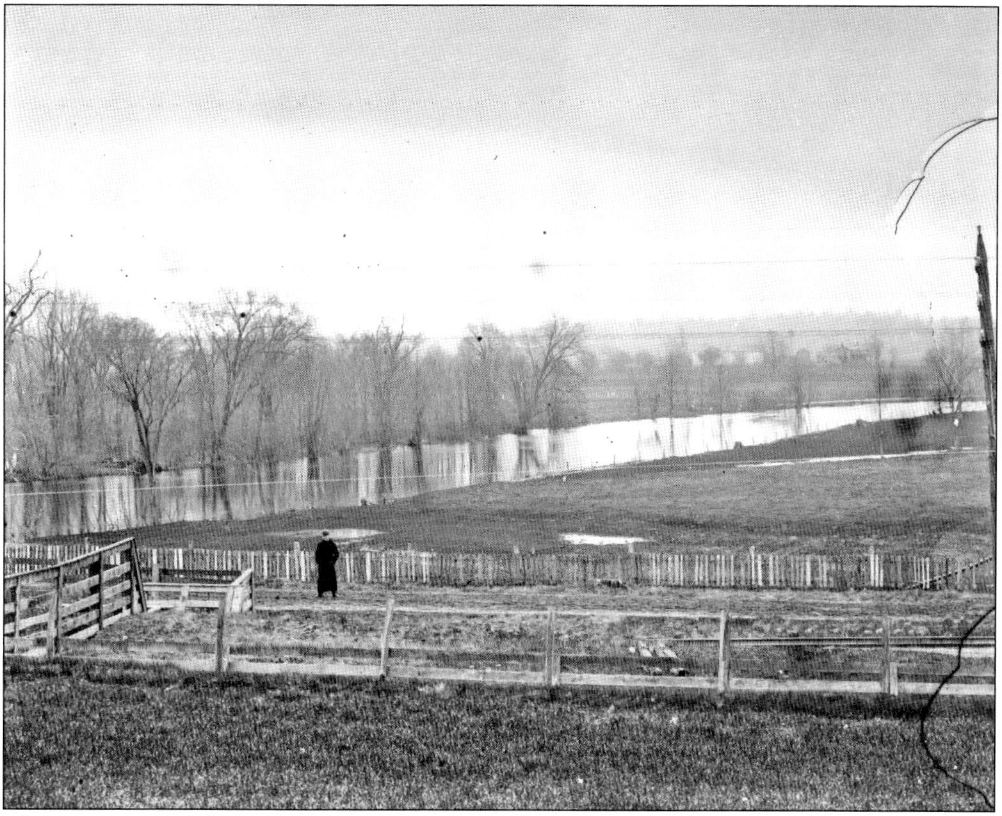

This 1800s view of the Kalamazoo River shows a house and outbuildings in the background. In the foreground, fences, a road, and railroad tracks can be seen. It appears that this might have been a spring day, as the man is wearing a heavy overcoat and hat and the river is swollen. (KPL.)

Surveyors always used monuments, or markers, when surveying land before it went into private ownership. These monuments indicated the corners for each parcel. Here, monuments can be clearly seen in the floodwaters of the Kalamazoo River. The flooding indicates that this is not a suitable area for constructing residences or commercial buildings. (Photograph by Joseph P. DeKorn, WMU.)

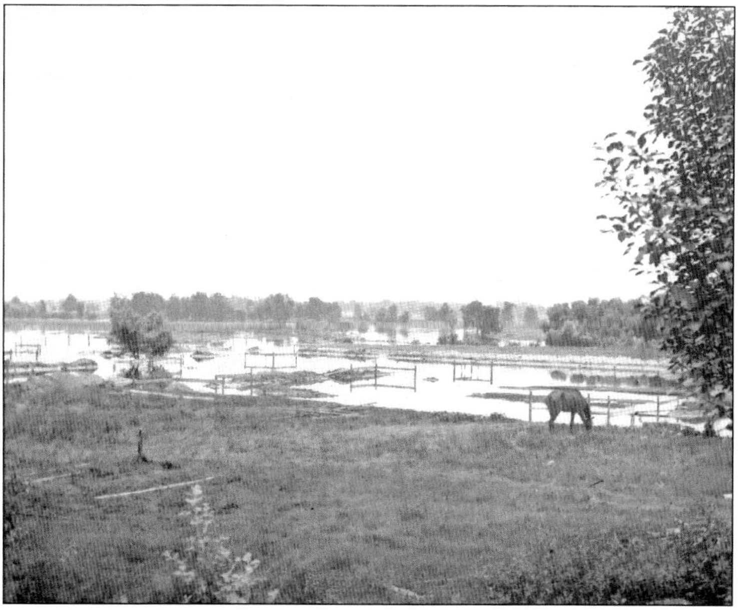

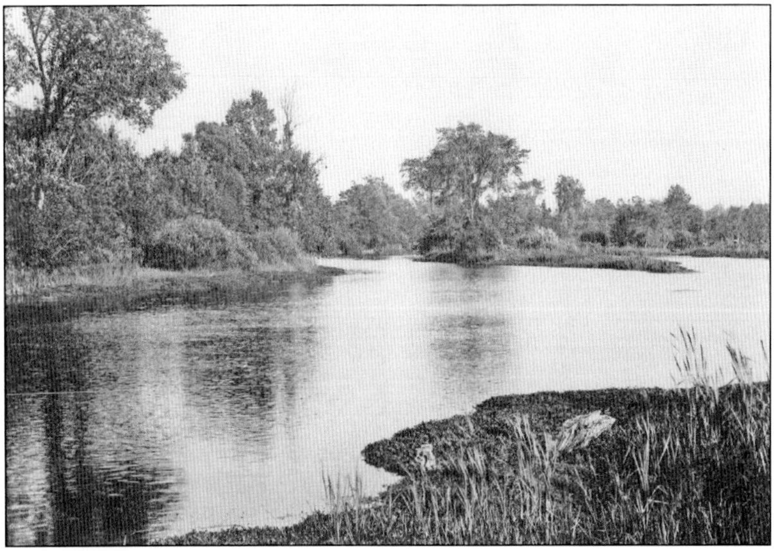

The calm Kalamazoo River winds its way through the landscape. An island sits serenely as the river flows around it. Pieces of driftwood lie in the foreground of this 1894 photograph. The meander of the river in this location shows the power the river has to modify the landscape. (KPL.)

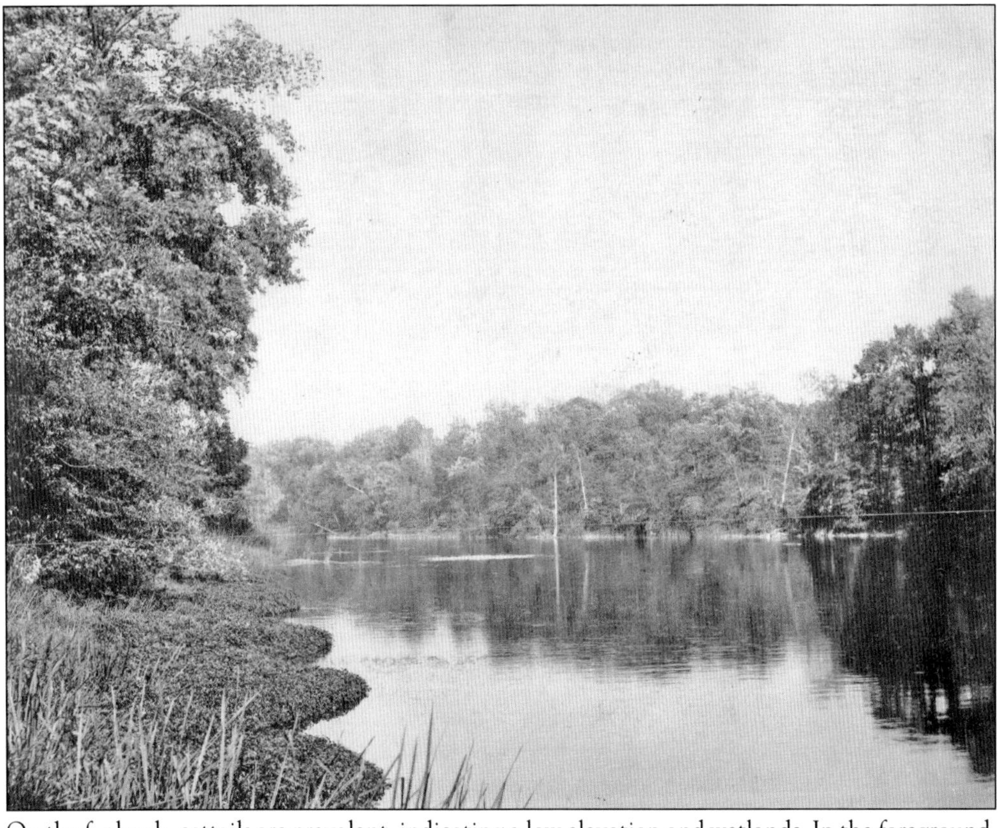

On the far bank, cattails are prevalent, indicating a low elevation and wetlands. In the foreground, riverweed is floating on the water attached to the bank. People who walked along the river's banks needed to be careful that they did not fall into the water because there is not solid ground under the riverweed. The width of the river at these locations shows that the waterway is unconfined. The thick growth of mature trees indicates that the land immediately near the river is low in elevation and not good for building. (KPL.)

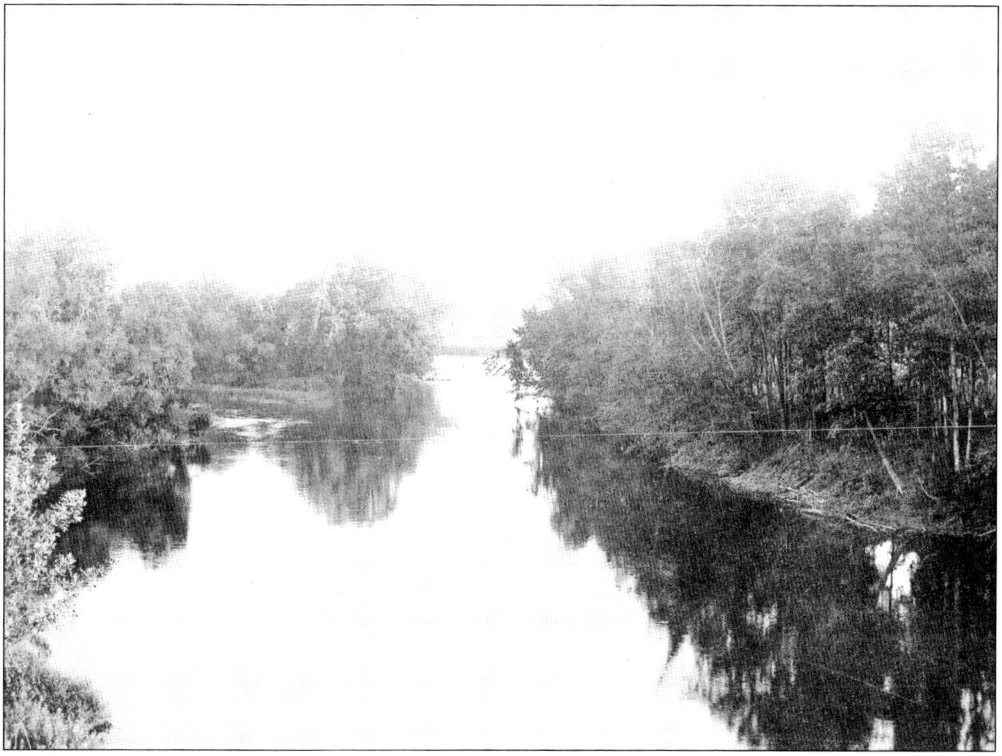

In this view of the Kalamazoo River, the water is flowing toward the viewer. The island in the middle of the channel splits the river into two smaller flows. The bank on the right indicates that the river was recently swollen, as the vegetation has been matted, lying in and near the water. (KPL.)

This view of the far bank indicates that changes are occurring. There are cut trees lying on the ground and stumps sticking up. It appears that an area is being cleared just behind the selected uncut trees along the bank to make room for potential new construction. (KPL.)

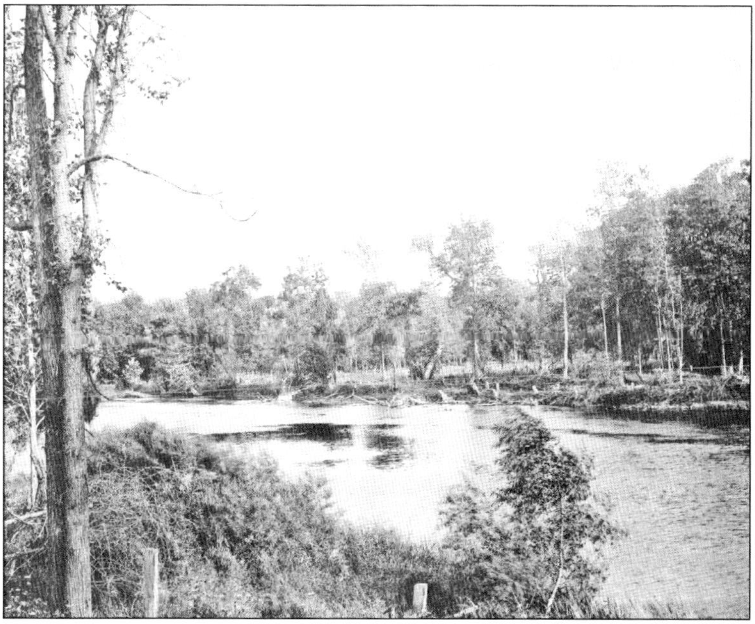

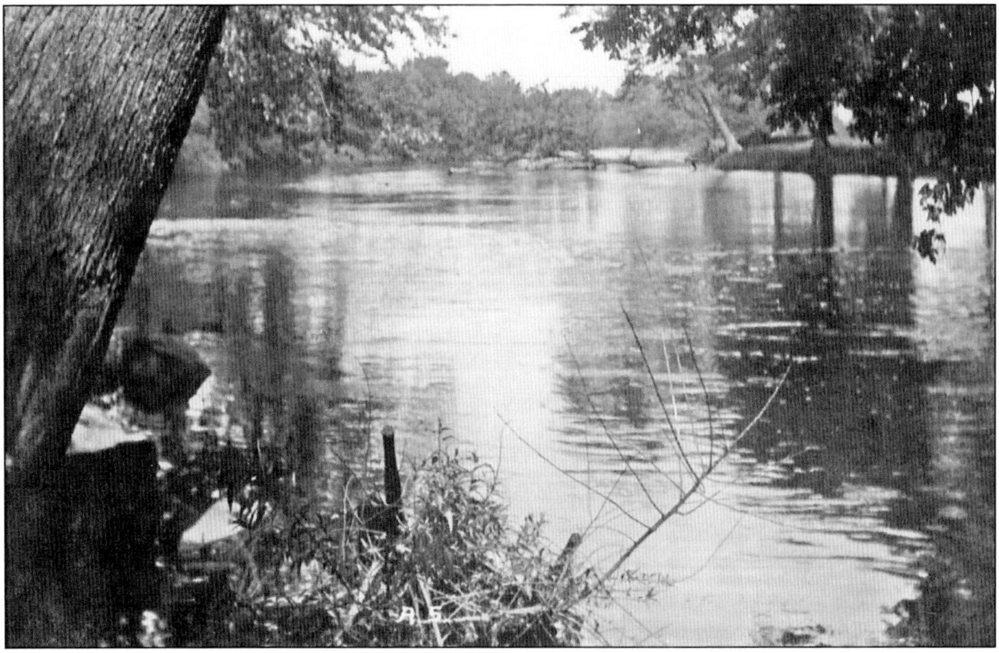

Some areas of the Kalamazoo River have changed drastically over time. However, this location along the river near Augusta still looks similar to how it did in this photograph from 1908. The tree in the river probably landed there after a strong storm rolled through the area, based on the extreme lean of the tree on the right bank. (Keith Martin.)

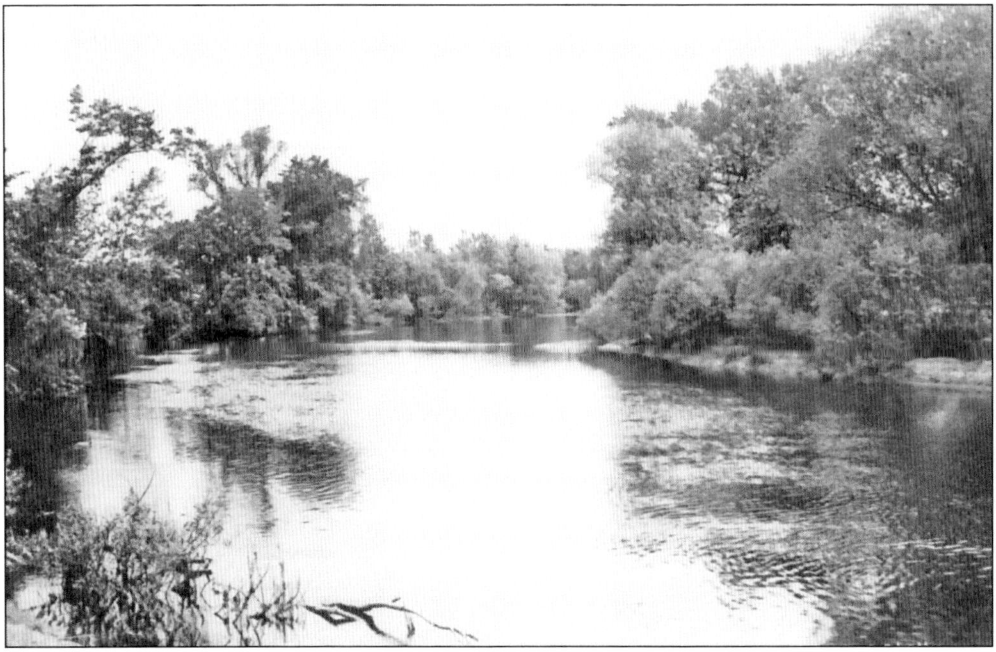

This scenic view of the Kalamazoo River from 1911 is near Augusta. This is one of the wider sections of the river, which was good for canoeing. The presence of ripples in the water suggests that the water level is a bit low and is flowing over rocks in the channel. Mature trees on the banks provide a shady spot for visitors to enjoy the scenery. (Keith Martin.)

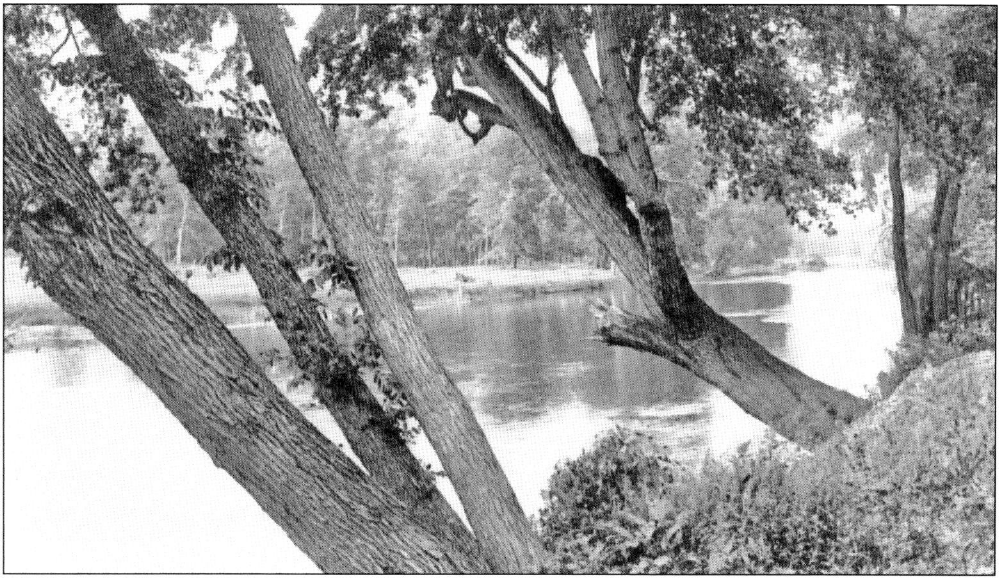

This peaceful riverbank is the perfect place to picnic and enjoy the lazy days of summer. The water is calm and flowing smoothly. The far bank is clear of trees and brush. The trees along the near bank are slowly falling into the Kalamazoo River due to bank erosion. (Keith Martin.)

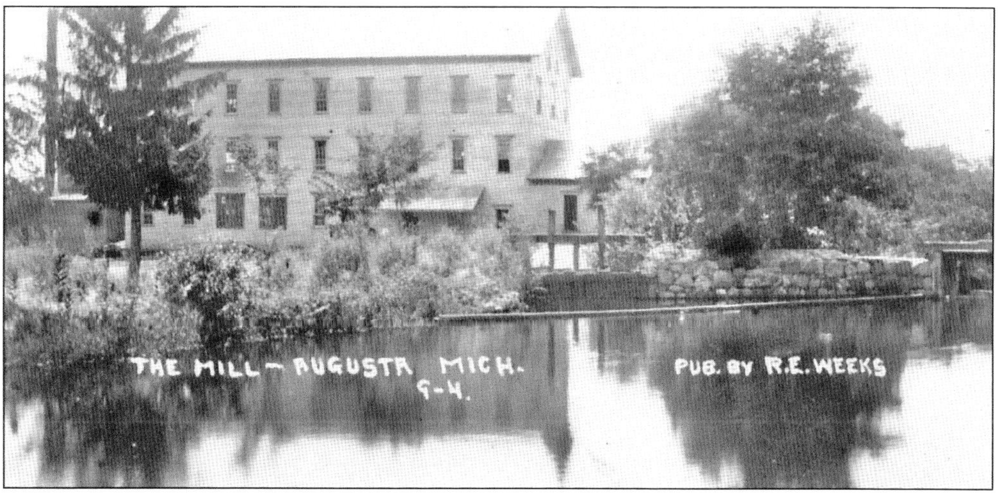

Originally known as the Augusta Milling Company, Knappen Milling was and still is located along a millrace that flows into the Kalamazoo River. This mill started as a specialty flour mill for the growing cereal industry in nearby Battle Creek. Today, it processes flour and bran for cereal, snack food, and wheat-based industries. (Keith Martin.)

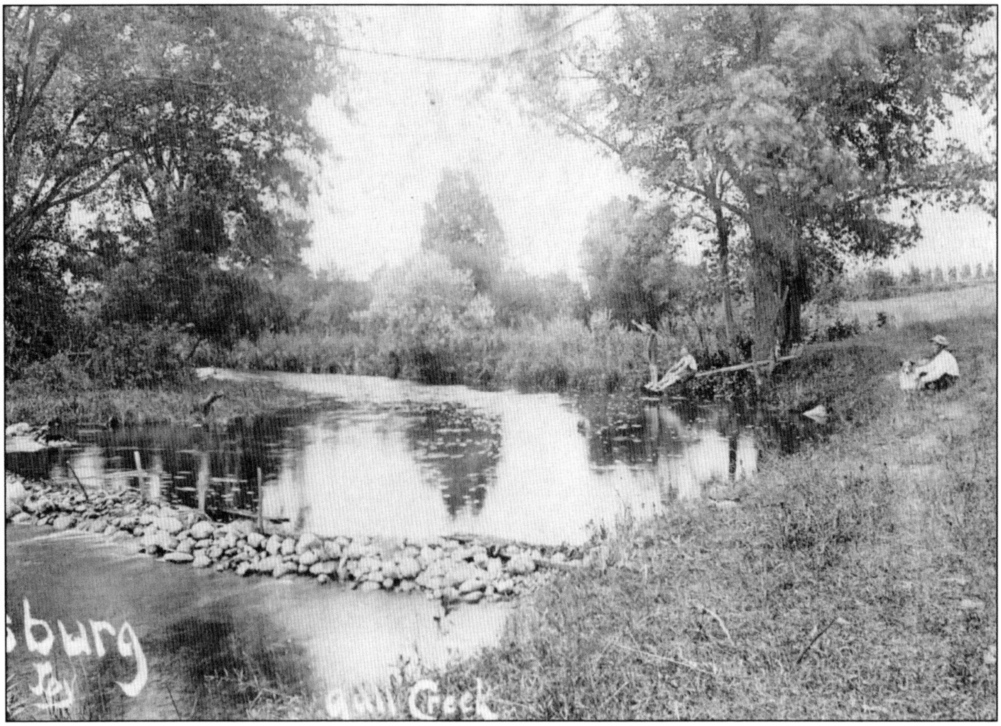

Gull Creek is a tributary of the Kalamazoo River. The stone dam allows water to be a bit deeper behind it, making it an ideal place for fishing and swimming. Three young men and a dog take time out to enjoy the peacefulness here. (GHS.)

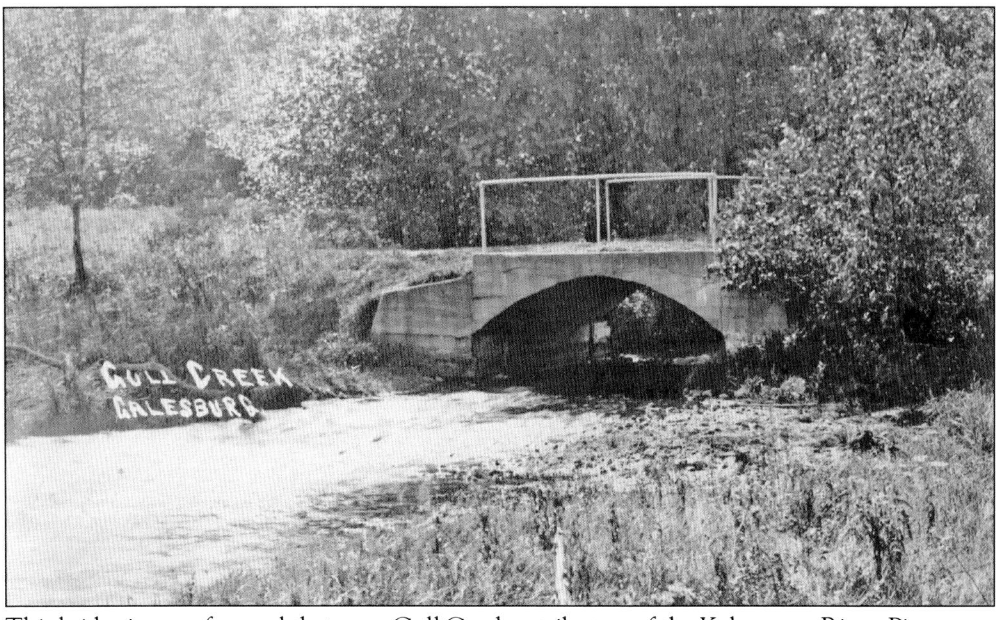

This bridge is one of several that span Gull Creek, a tributary of the Kalamazoo River. Pipes were used to construct the rails on either side of the bridge, providing a bit of safety for cars traversing the structure. Water is channelized as it goes under the bridge, evidenced by the rapid rush of water seen in the center of the photograph. (GHS.)

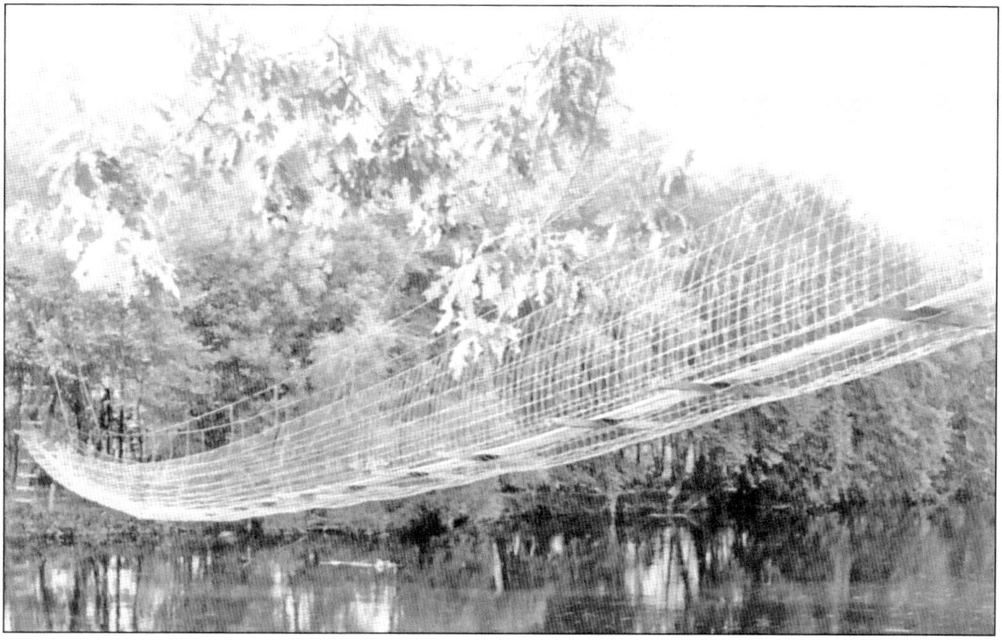

The swing bridge in Galesburg allowed pedestrians to cross the Kalamazoo River. It was made of strands of wire running lengthwise with a small wooden walkway at the bottom. It had a 184-foot span and held a record for holding 19 high school boys at one time. People using this bridge had to cross carefully and keep their balance. Note the ladder at far left (above), which was used to get up to and down from the bridge. The swing bridge was a favorite way for Murray Martin (right) to cross the Kalamazoo River in the late 1910s. When using these bridges, hanging on to the wire was essential, as the bridge would swing as the person walked over it. (Above, GHS; right, Keith Martin.)

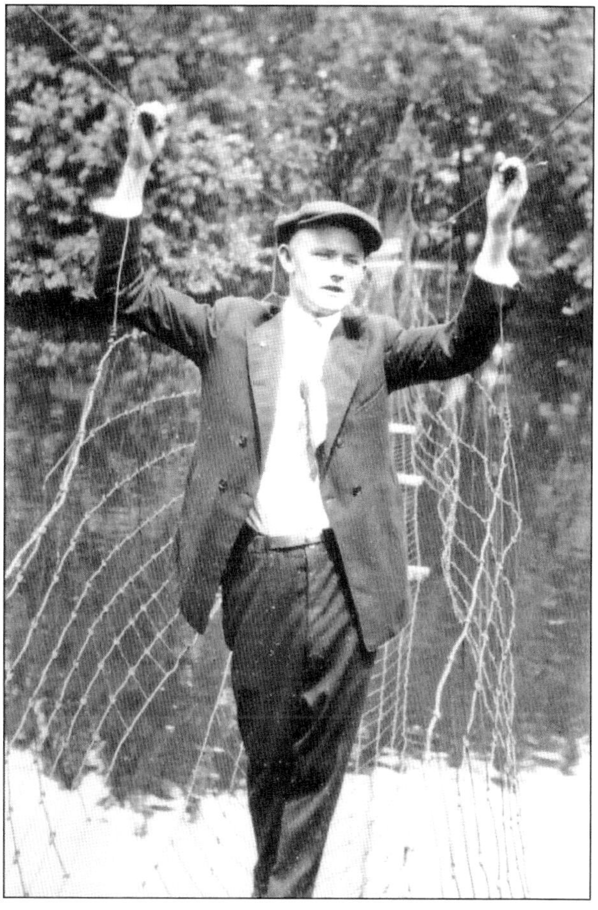

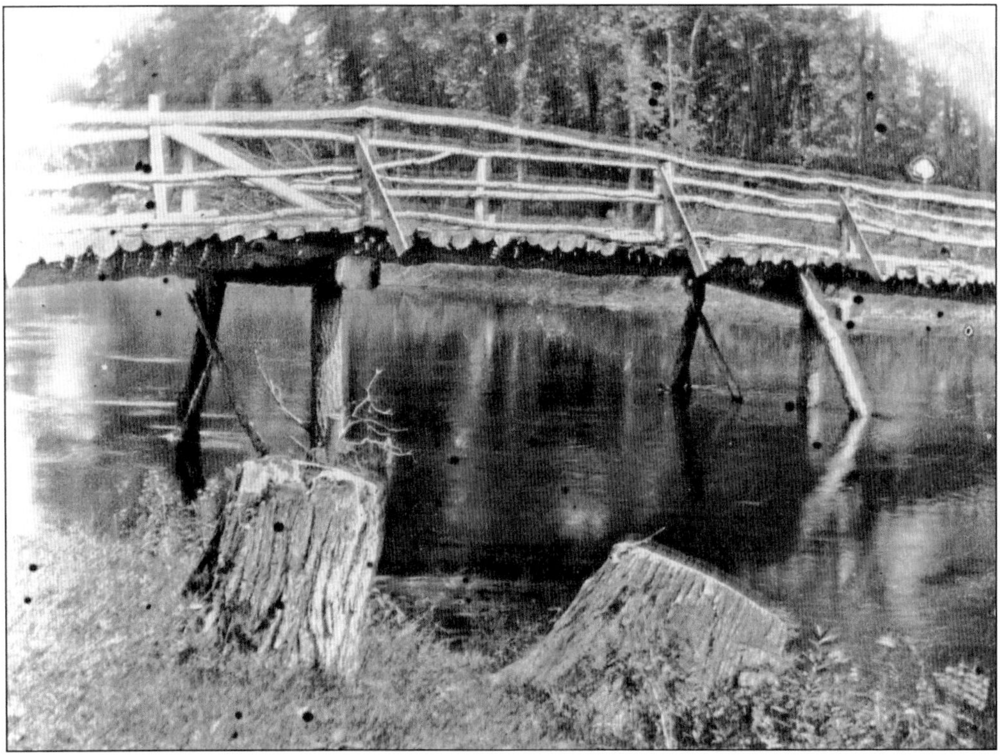

This old bridge once stood over the Kalamazoo River behind the mill in Galesburg. It was made completely of wood. The photograph illustrates how trees were simply cut and used, not planed into boards. Supports for the bridge still have their bark intact. (Photograph by Harry Streator, GHS.)

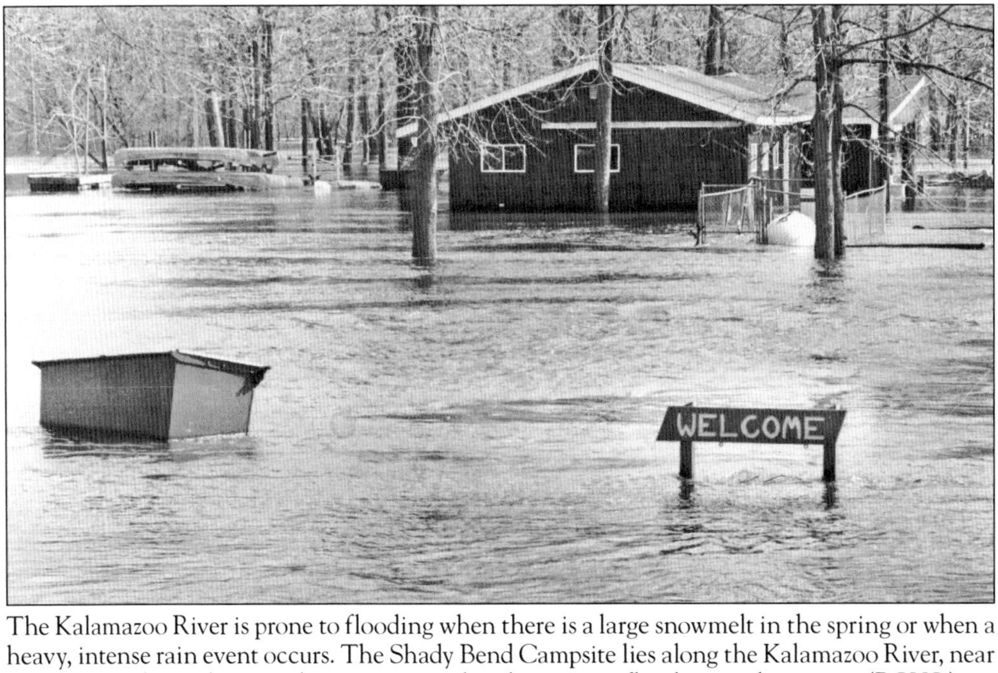

The Kalamazoo River is prone to flooding when there is a large snowmelt in the spring or when a heavy, intense rain event occurs. The Shady Bend Campsite lies along the Kalamazoo River, near Augusta. In the mid-1980s, the campsite endured extensive flooding in the spring. (BCHS.)

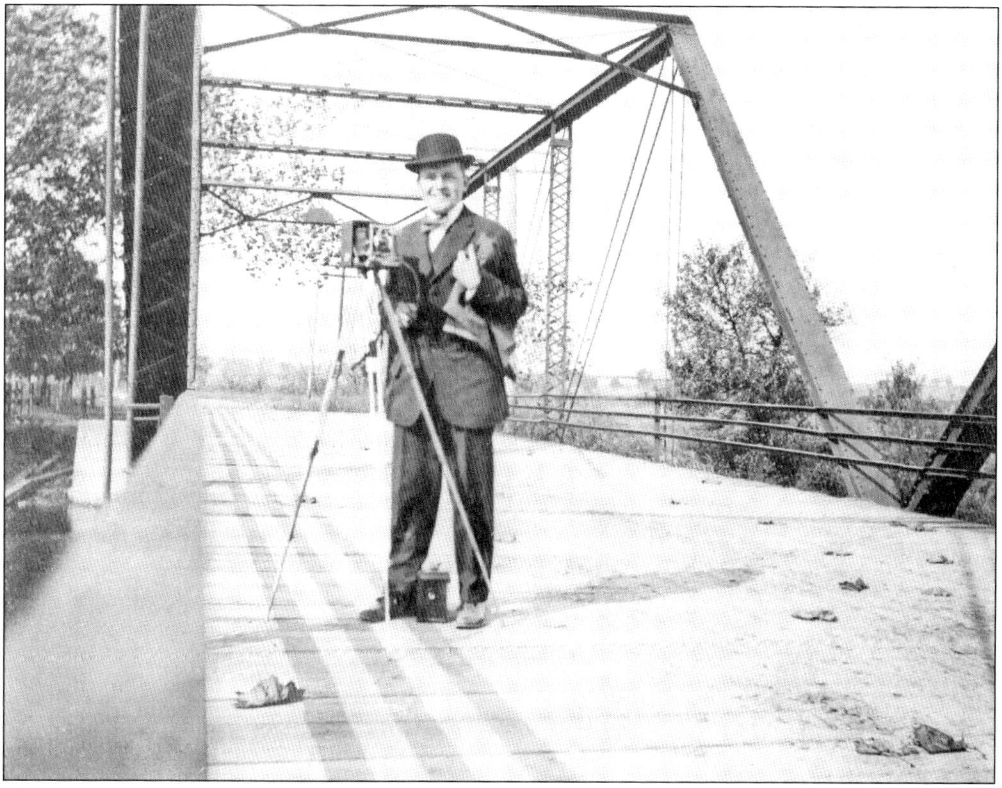

Photography at this time was an expensive endeavor. This man set up his tripod and camera on the iron bridge in Galesburg to take photographs of the Kalamazoo River and surrounding area The presence of a second camera at his feet and his clothing indicates that he may have been one of the wealthier citizens in this river town. (GHS.)

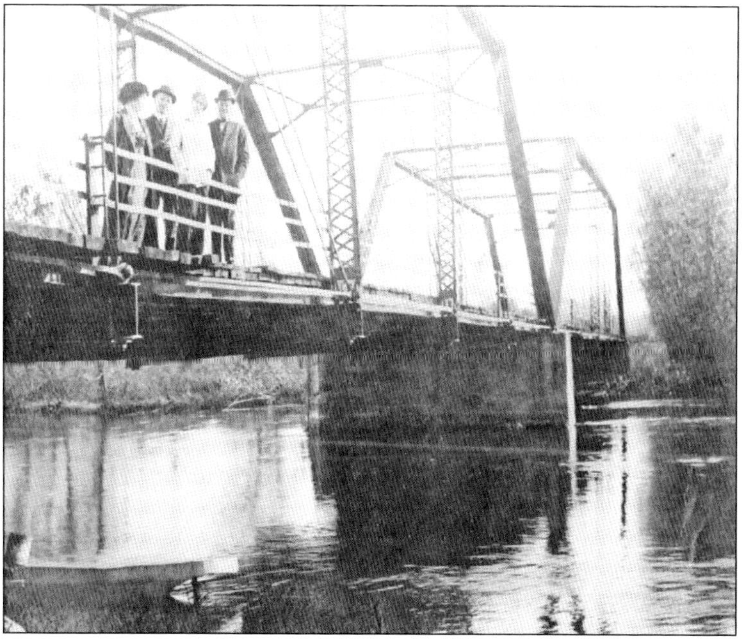

On day of this photograph, Veronica, Sam, Mae, and Paul (last names unknown) stand on the wooden plank bridge in Galesburg taking in the scenery. The wooden planks appear to be three feet wide. There is also a second row of planks to help reinforce the structure. (GHS.)

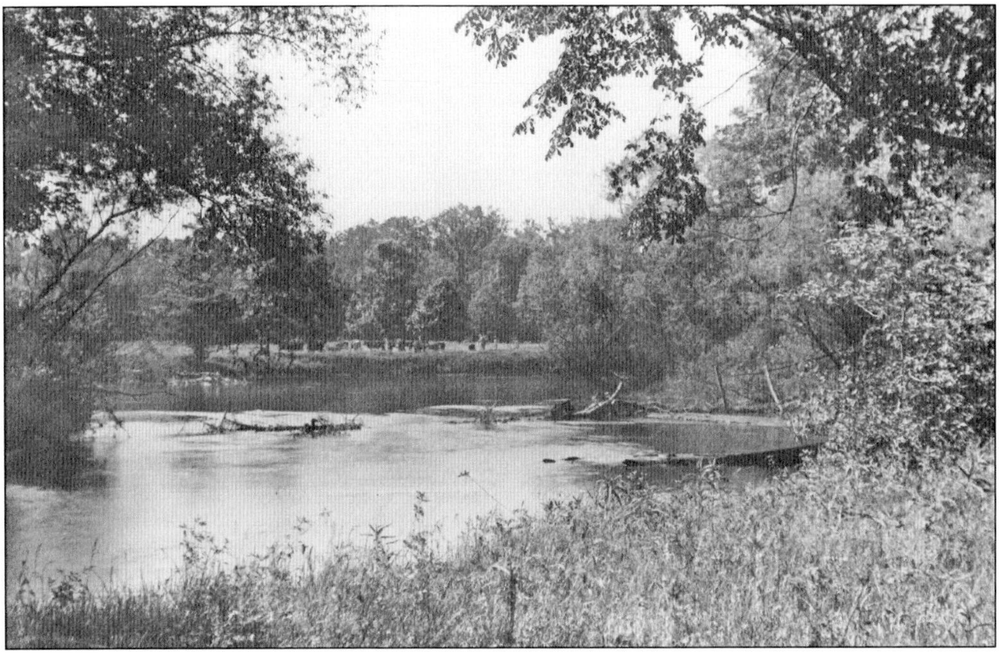

Farming was a livelihood for people living along the Kalamazoo River. Floodwaters would deposit a fertile layer of silt over land, creating lush vegetation for cattle to eat. Above, cattle line the fenced-in far bank outside of Galesburg. It appears that the river is swollen from recent rains and runoff. Fallen trees can also be seen floating in the river. (GHS.)

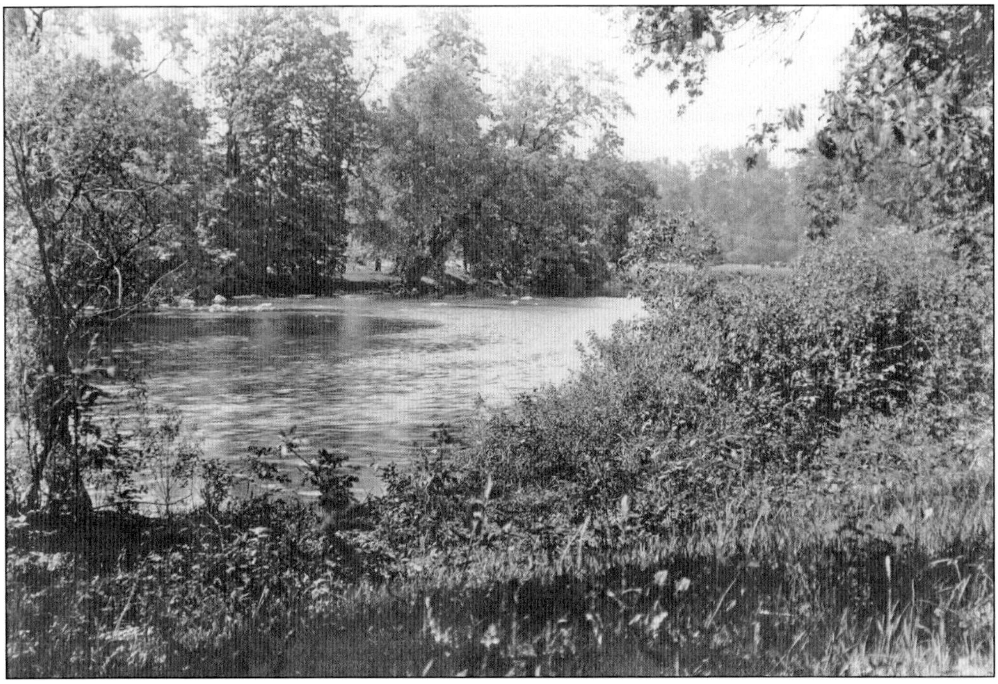

The Kalamazoo River winds around boulders as well as other natural high points in the water. The river is running swiftly around these boulders, creating eddies near the bank. The far bank appears to be mowed, indicating that a park or private residence is located close by. (GHS.)

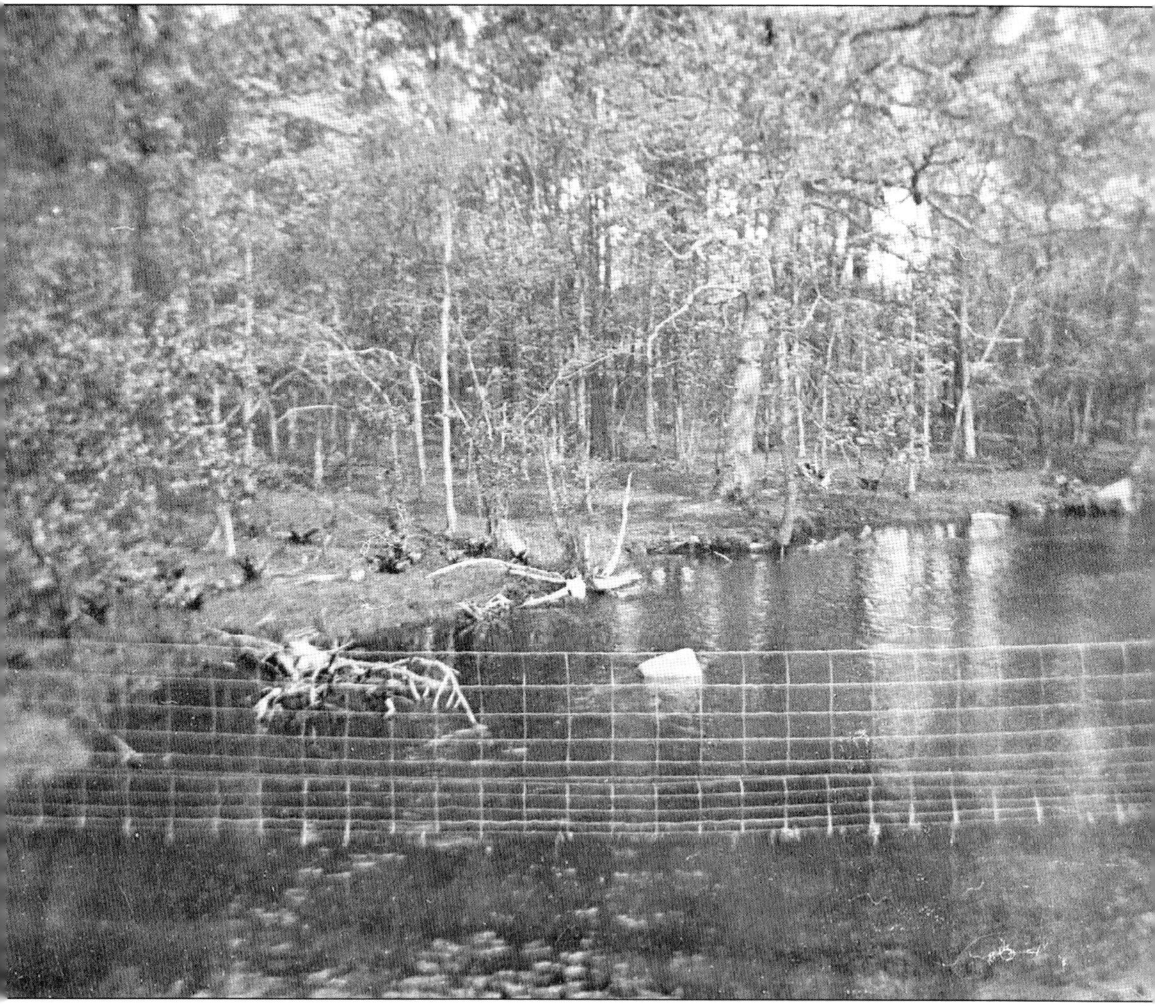

Many farmers tried to fence in their property because they knew that the river flow would change and they could not use it as a stable boundary. In the photograph, a wire fence spans a shallow part of the Kalamazoo River. The reflection of the fence in the water makes it appear as though it is a wire pedestrian bridge. (Photograph by Joseph DeKorn, Luanne Castle.)

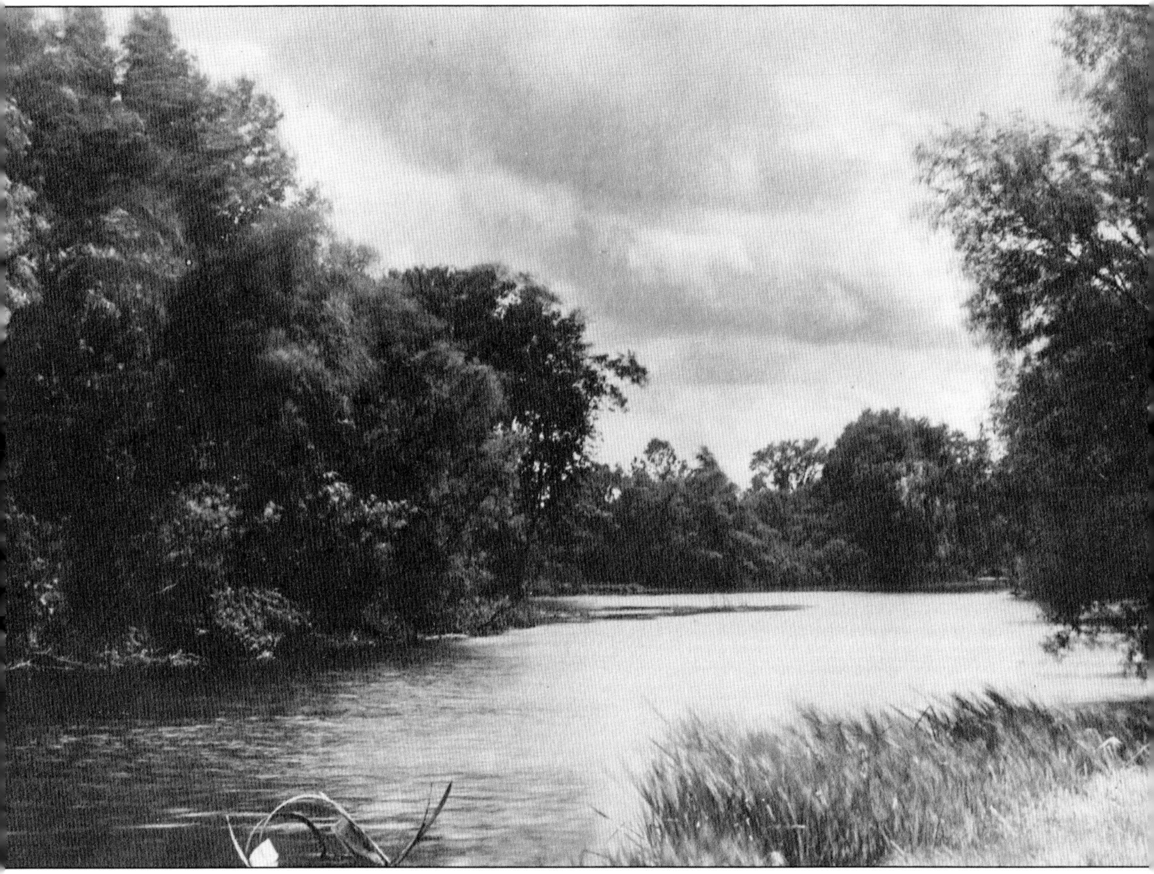

The scenic beauty of the Kalamazoo River near Galesburg was disturbed by the floating trash in the foreground. This was not an unusual occurrence prior to the 1970s, before conservation action and activities were popular. This trash appears to be close to the bank, so the photographer may have pulled it out after this image was taken. (GHS.)

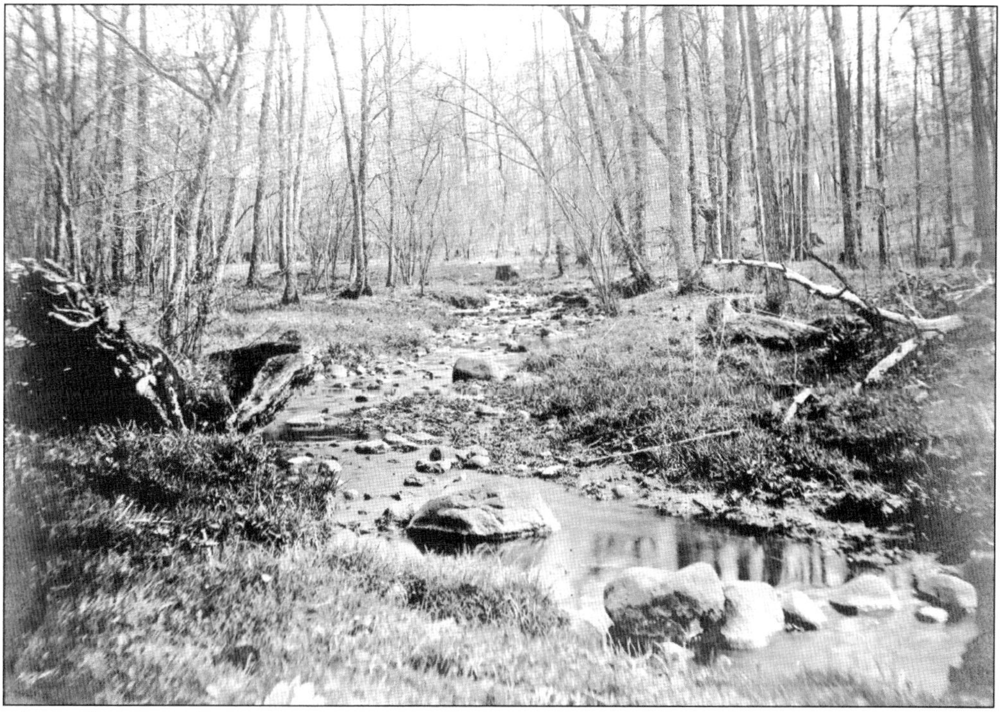

This Galesburg tributary of the Kalamazoo River appears to be at its low stage, as evidenced by the rocks and boulders scattered along its channel. In the foreground, a line of rocks across the channel act as a stepping stone bridge when the tributary is full of water. (GHS.)

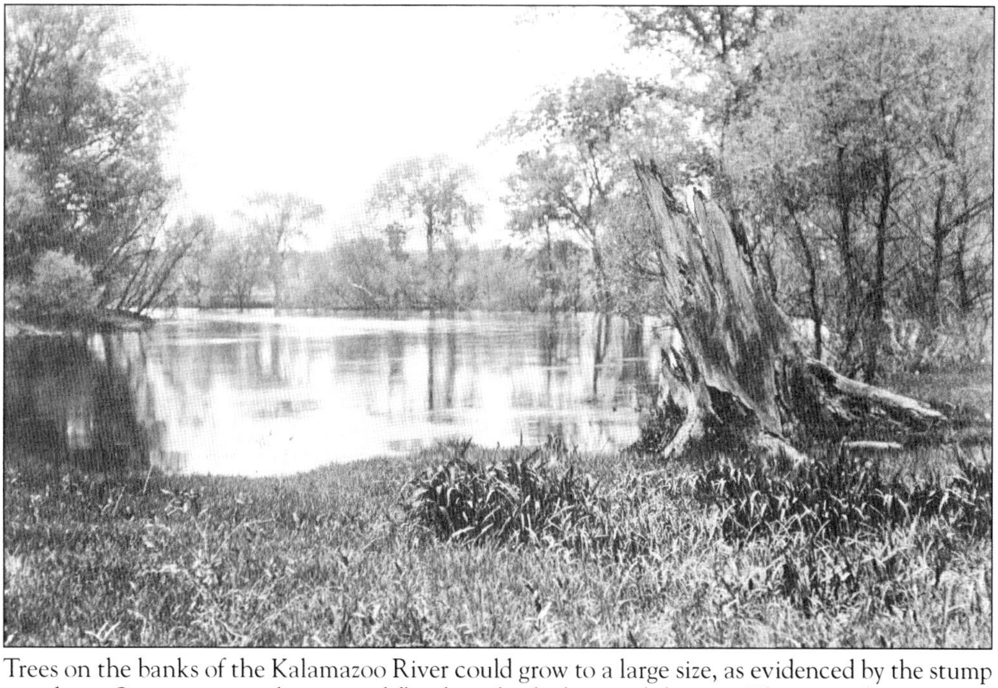

Trees on the banks of the Kalamazoo River could grow to a large size, as evidenced by the stump seen here. Over time, weathering and flooding slowly damaged the tree. The stump leans toward the river and, presumably, the top half has floated downstream. (GHS.)

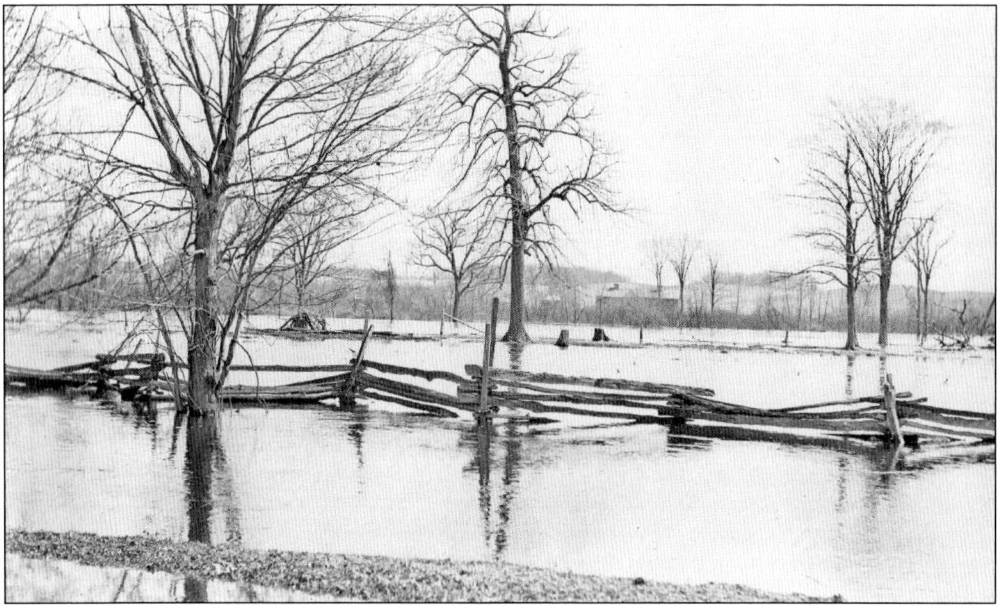

Spring flooding was a common occurrence in towns and cities all along the Kalamazoo River. This person's property suffered quite a bit of damage from this flood outside of Galesburg. The fence needed to be fixed to be effective once the floodwaters subsided. (Photograph by Virginia Burge, GHS.)

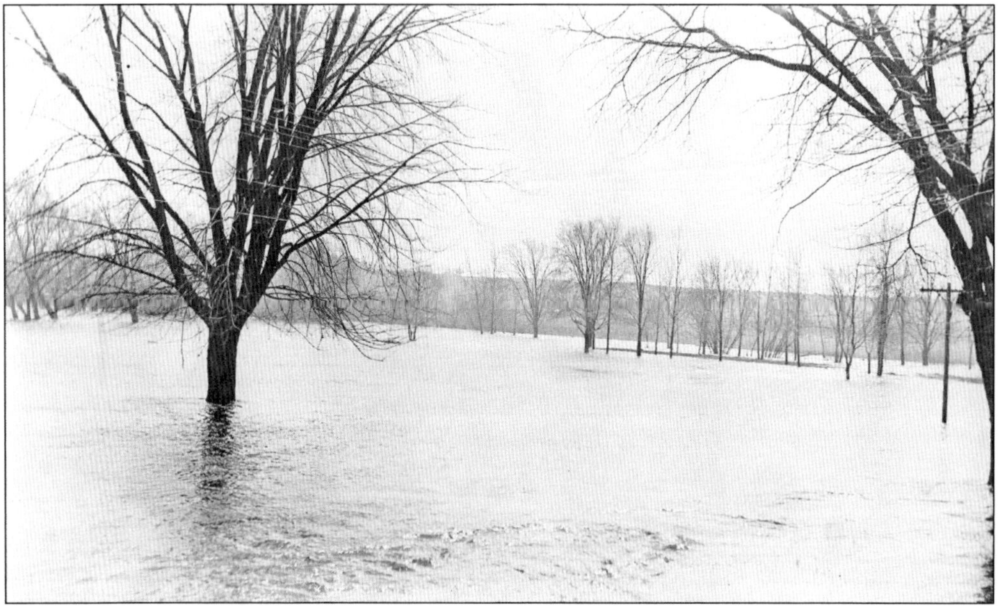

Galesburg sits along the banks of the Kalamazoo River and is subject to flooding on a regular basis. This photograph of a spring flood show just how much water can overflow the river's banks. The swiftness of the floodwater can be seen in the foreground between the two trees. (Photograph by Virginia Burg, GHS.)

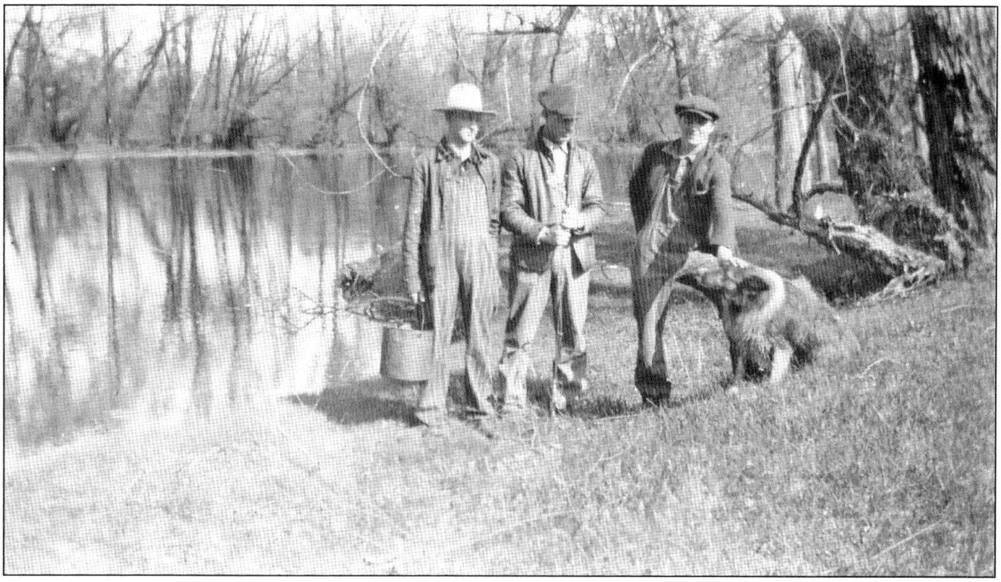

The banks of the Kalamazoo River were places men would go to fish and have a good time. From left to right, Roy Struble, Leo Root, and Robert Struble enjoy a sunny afternoon of fishing with their dog. The river on this day was perfect for fishing because it was flowing but not swiftly and was not swollen. (GHS.)

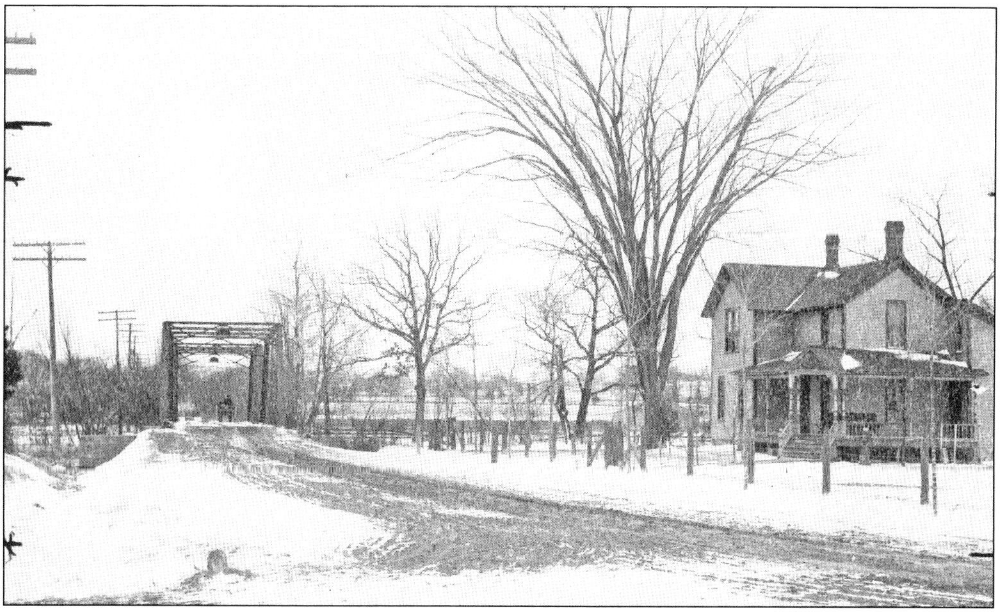

The East Iron Bridge was a major bridge that allowed people to cross the Kalamazoo River in Galesburg. In this photograph, the man with his horse and wagon traversing the bridge had to travel dirt roads to cross the wooden plank bridge. Concrete reinforcement walls constructed under this bridge help ensure it does not collapse in a large flood or spring snowmelt running into the river. (GHS.)

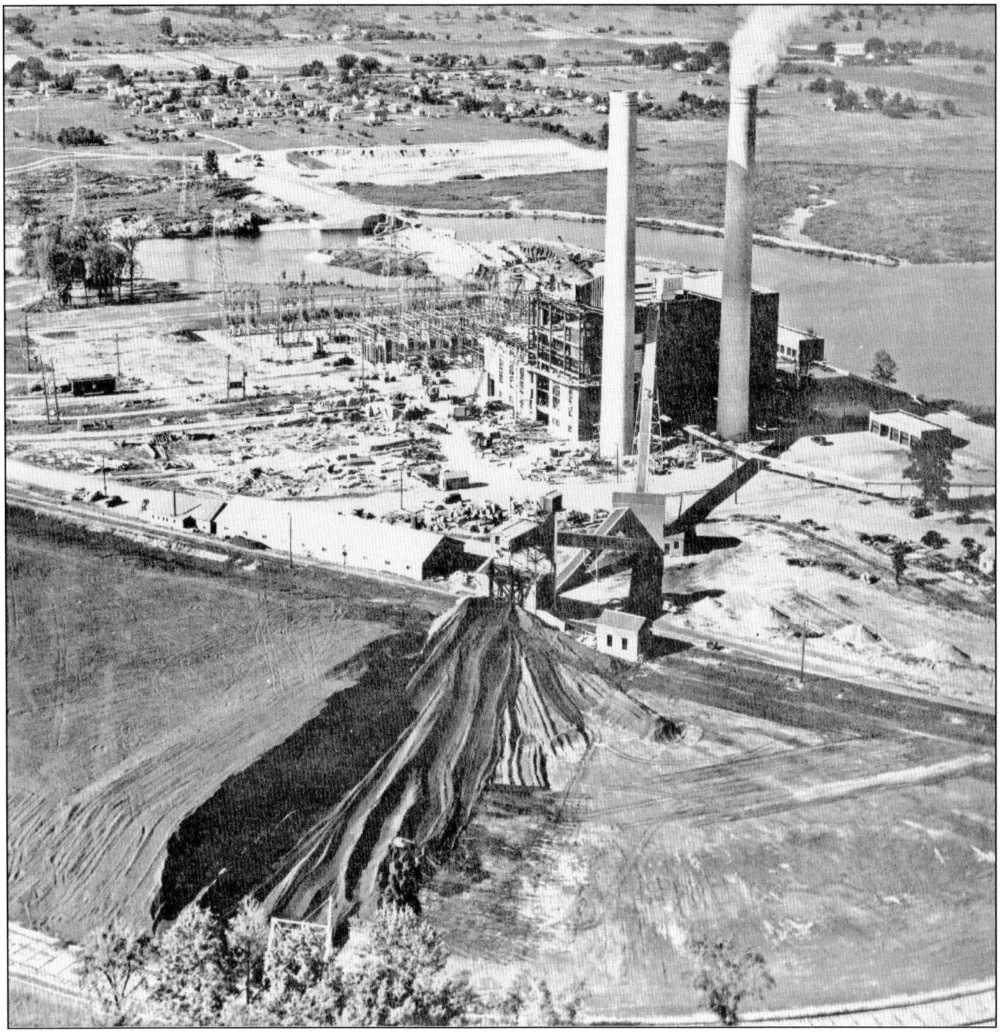

The Morrow Dam is on the Kalamazoo River in Galesburg. The dam created Morrow Lake, which was used to power the hydroelectric plant. This photograph from 1957 shows the Morrow Power Plant with the lake and river in the background. Coal in the foreground was dumped here by the railroad and then shoveled into the plant for processing. (Kalamazoo Valley Museum.)

Four

West to Kalamazoo

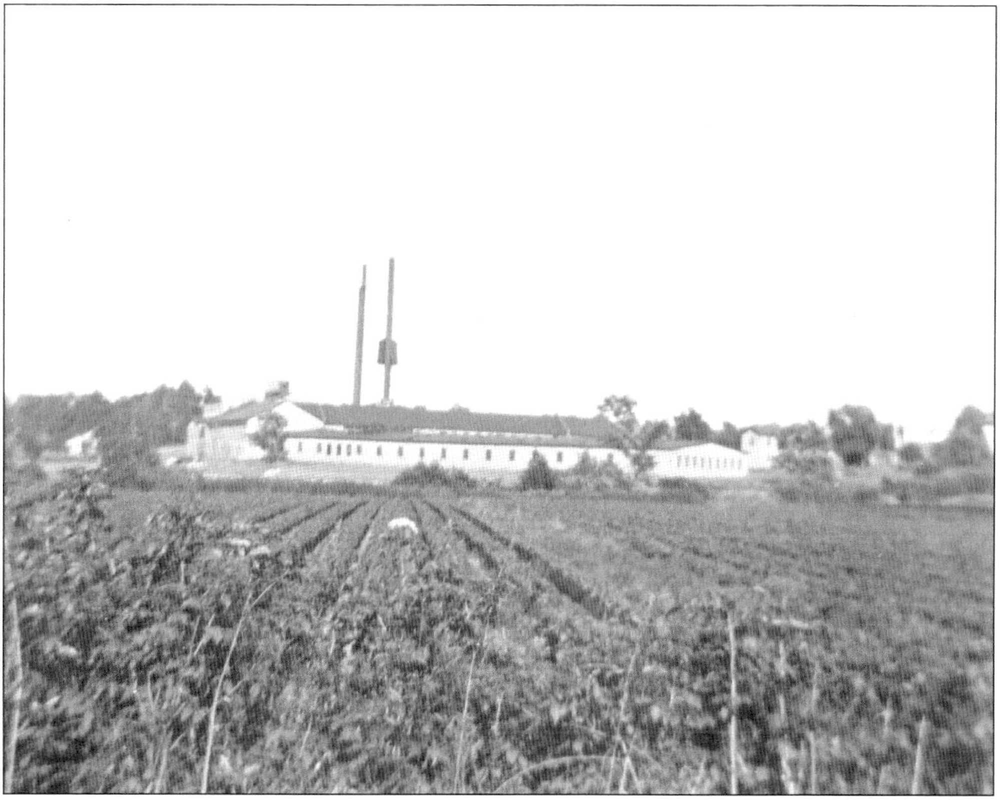

The Monarch Paper Mill sat along Portage Creek, a tributary of the Kalamazoo River. Behind the mill was a large celery field. The river regenerated the field during times of flooding and supplied needed irrigation water in the summer. It was also used as transportation for shipping the product to other towns along the river. (Photograph by Joseph P. DeKorn, WMU.)

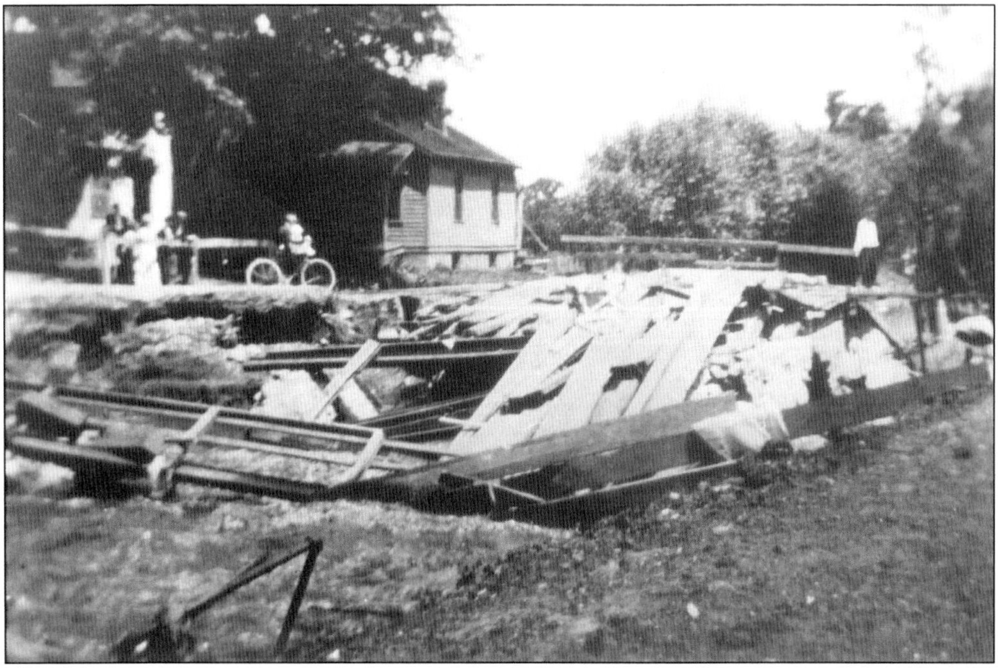

The Monarch Paper Mill was one of many mills in the city of Kalamazoo. It was damaged during the June 1916 flood when the Monarch Dam broke. The only part of this mill still in operation is the Monarch Millpond, which is upstream from Milham Park. (Photograph by Joseph P. DeKorn, WMU.)

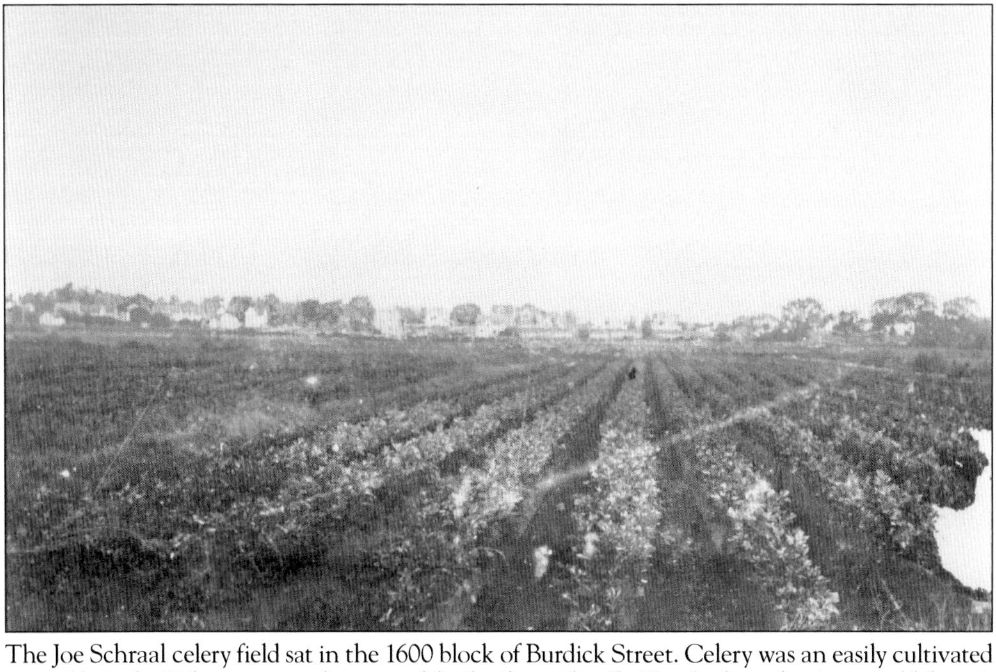

The Joe Schraal celery field sat in the 1600 block of Burdick Street. Celery was an easily cultivated vegetable in the Kalamazoo area because of the fertile muck soils. Floods along the river would deposit nutrient-rich sediment, regenerating these fields. Celery was such a cash crop that Kalamazoo was dubbed the "Celery City" in its heyday. (Photograph by Joseph P. DeKorn, WMU.)

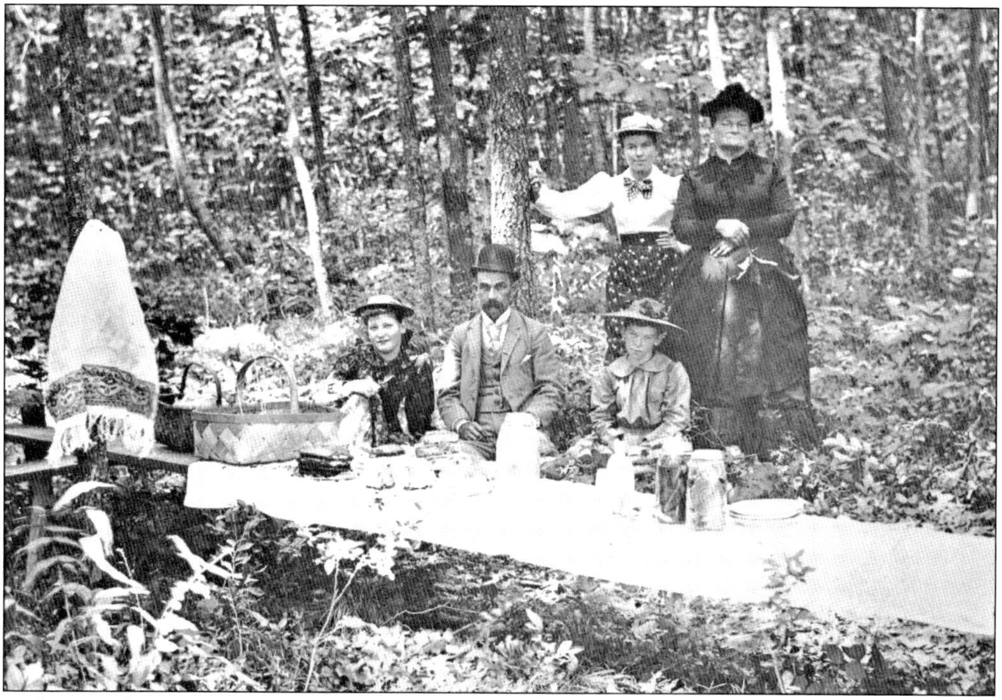

Milham Park, near East Kilgore Road and Lover's Lane, lies on Portage Creek, a tributary of the Kalamazoo River. This park has always been a popular spot for people to enjoy nature, do some picnicking, and give children a place to play. The above photograph, from the late 1800s or early 1900s, shows a family picnicking at the park. Everyone is dressed up, including hats, which is very different from what is seen today at Milham Park. The photograph below, taken in 1939, shows the playground at the park. There were lots of swings, and the slide was popular. The parents look happy that their children are playing off some of their energy. (Both photographs by Maime L. Austin, KPL.)

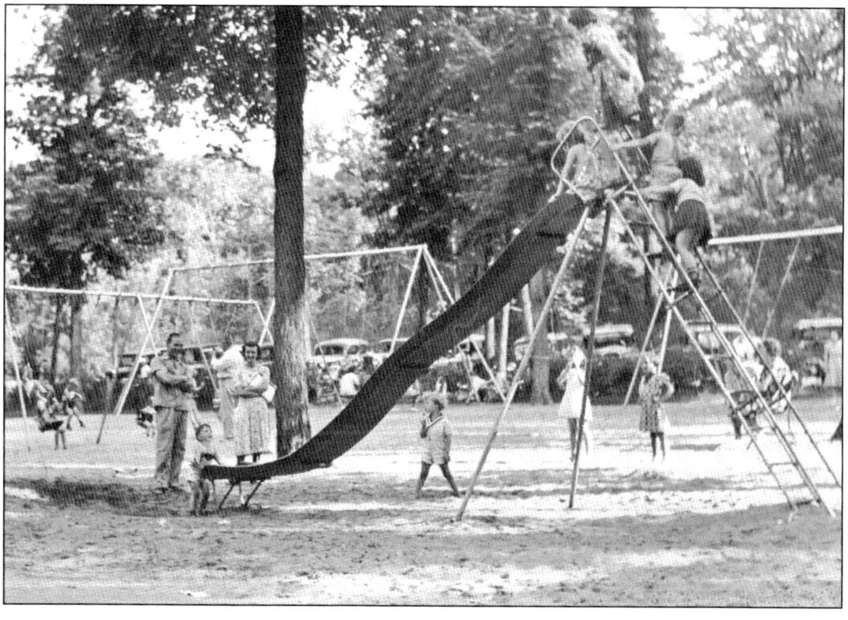

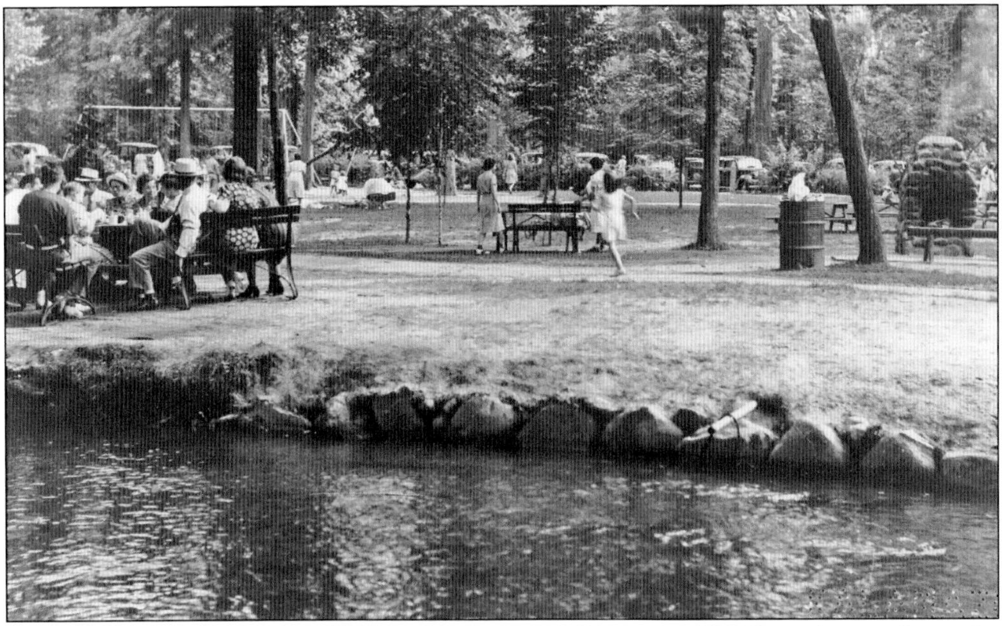

When it was opened in 1910, Milham Park consisted of 60 acres, and 5,000 people visited it on the first day. Milham Park, along Portage Creek, was and still is a true recreation spot for the residents of both Kalamazoo and Portage. It has expanded over the years and now encompasses approximately 120 acres with a playground, many picnic shelters and grills, and softball/T-ball fields. The above photograph shows people in 1939 enjoying picnic area, with Portage Creek in the foreground. The photograph below, taken in 1941, shows Portage Creek flowing at center, with a footbridge spanning it and a picnic area in the background. For over a century, Milham Park has drawn large crowds for outdoor recreational activities. (Both photographs by Maime L. Austin, KPL.)

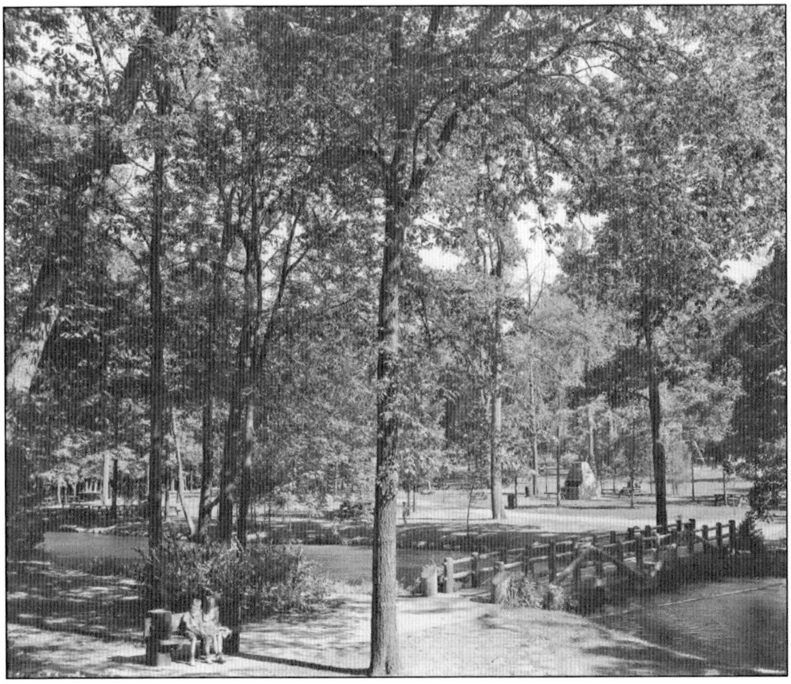

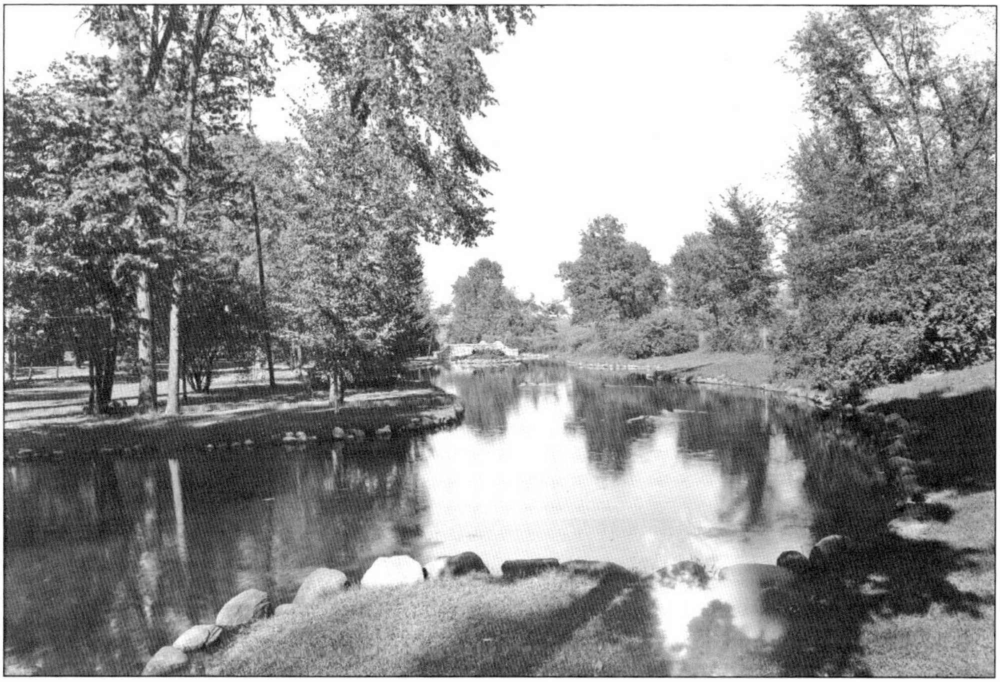

Like the Kalamazoo River, Portage Creek can be very picturesque. This photograph of the creek was taken from the back of Milham Park. Visitors to the park can traverse different areas and get a very different view of the creek. In the background, a stone bridge used by automobiles can be seen, giving the cars' occupants a serene view. (Photograph by Maime L. Austin, KPL.)

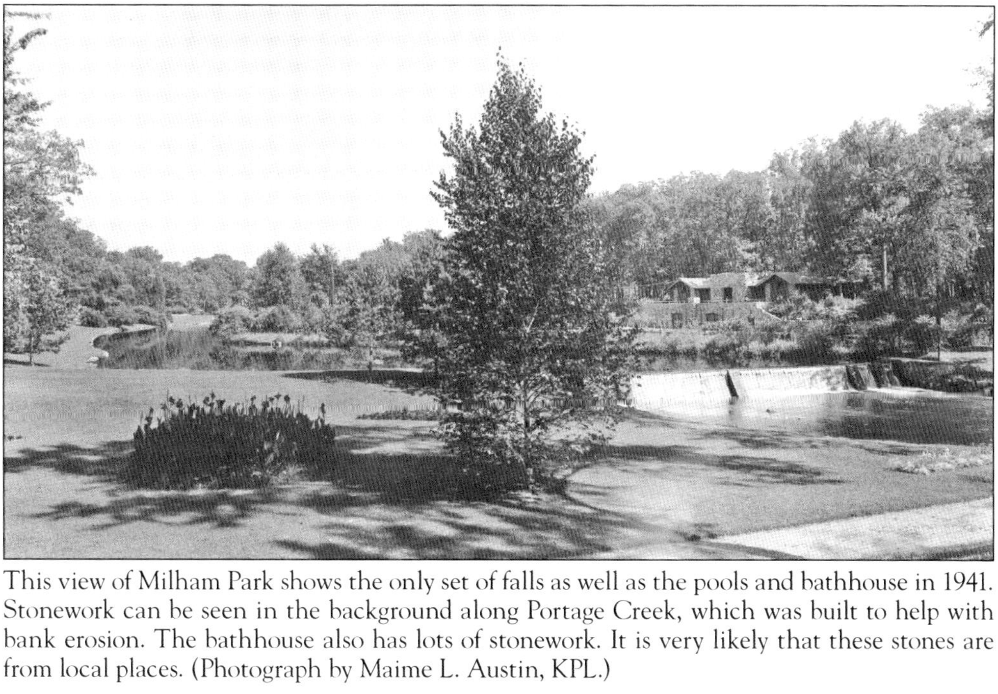

This view of Milham Park shows the only set of falls as well as the pools and bathhouse in 1941. Stonework can be seen in the background along Portage Creek, which was built to help with bank erosion. The bathhouse also has lots of stonework. It is very likely that these stones are from local places. (Photograph by Maime L. Austin, KPL.)

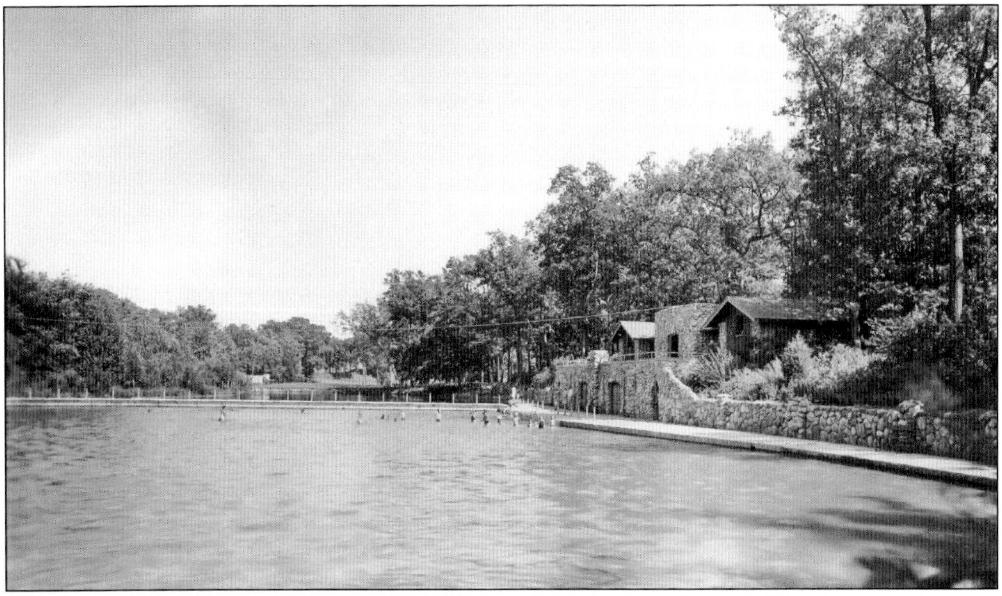

In the 1940s, Milham Park boasted a fieldstone bathhouse and pool. Children can be seen enjoying the cool water on a hot summer day. The Kalamazoo River flows by the pool in the center background. There were many mature trees around the pool and throughout the park that provided shade. (Photograph by Maime L. Austin, KPL.)

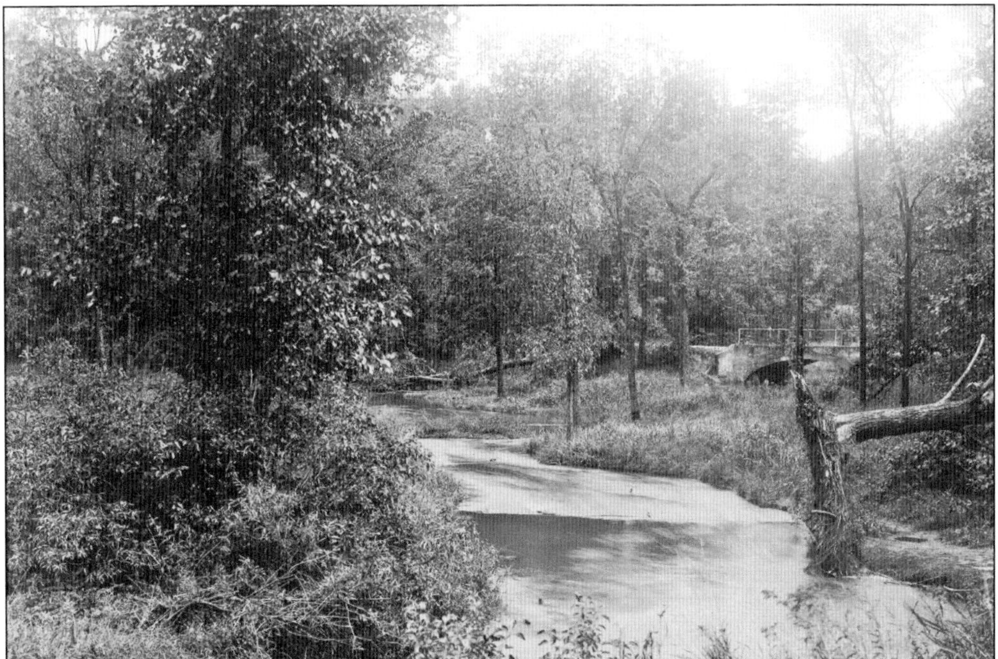

Water flows swiftly throughout Milham Park as the creek meanders its way to the Kalamazoo River. At the back right of the photograph, taken around 1940, a stone bridge with wooden railings crossing Lover's Lane allowed people to safely cross over the water. (Photograph by Maime L. Austin, KPL.)

The Kalamazoo River Valley Trail (KRVT) is a 22-mile, paved, nonmotorized trail leading recreationists from D Avenue, east of the town of Cooper, to South Thirty-Fifth Street in Galesburg. People enjoying the trail can experience wildlife and entertainment along the way to several parks: the Arcadia Creek Festival Place, many shops and restaurants in downtown Kalamazoo, and the Kalamazoo Nature Center. (Authors' personal collections.)

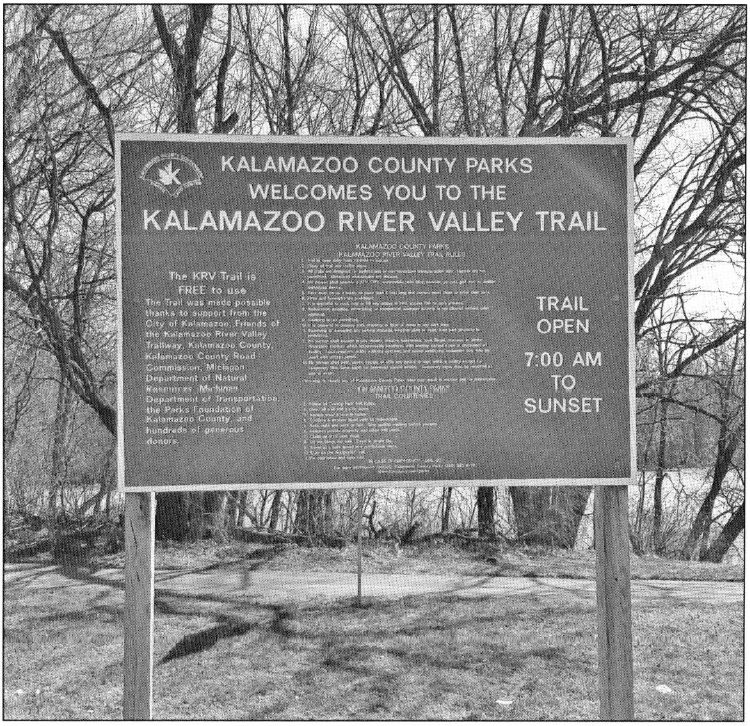

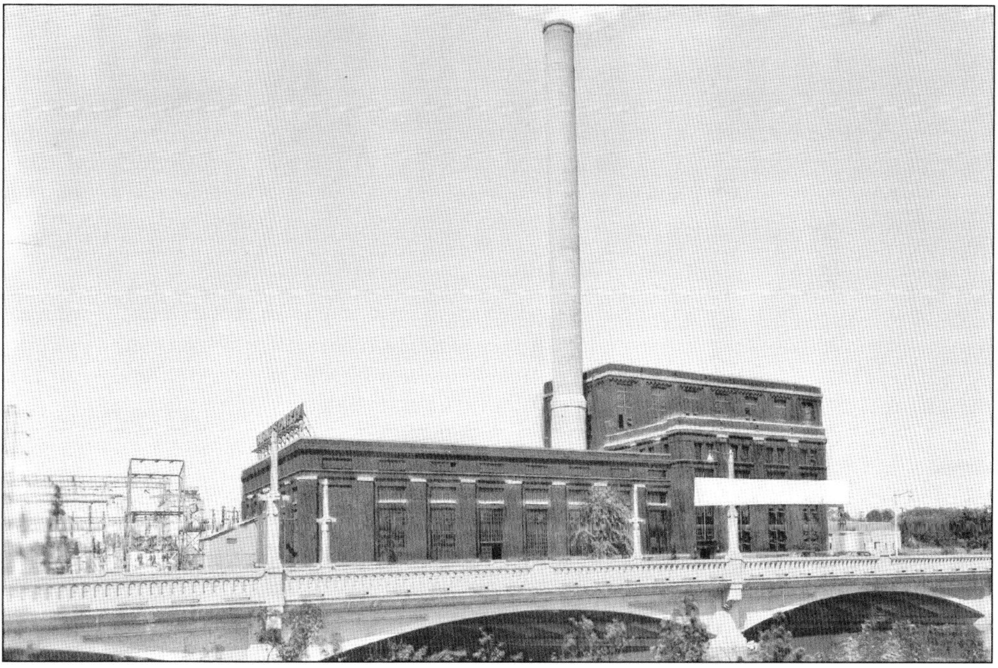

Consumers Power Company lies in Comstock, east of the city of Kalamazoo, along the Kalamazoo River. At the time of this photograph (around 1936), the power company was supplying electricity to homeowners and to manufacturing plants that were using electric to run their machinery. The East Michigan Avenue Bridge is in the foreground, providing a route over the Kalamazoo River (Photograph by Maime L. Austin, KPL.)

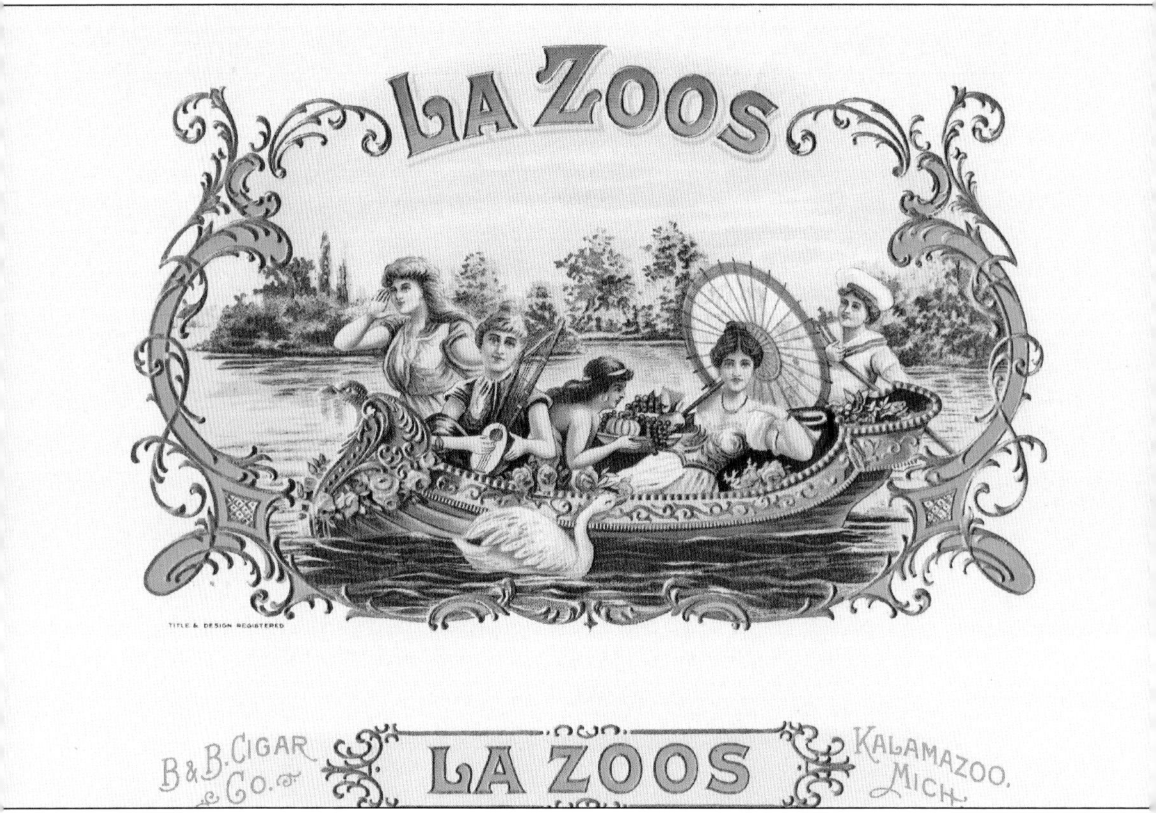

Cigar making in Kalamazoo was a big business between 1861 and 1969. The largest cigar manufacturing company was Lilienfelds, or Lillies. La Zoo cigars were created in 1916 by the B&B Cigar Company. Tobacco for cigars may have been shipped to the city via the Kalamazoo River. During the peak of production, 38 different companies, employing over 500 cigar makers, produced 150,000 cigars a day. (Jeff Weisman.)

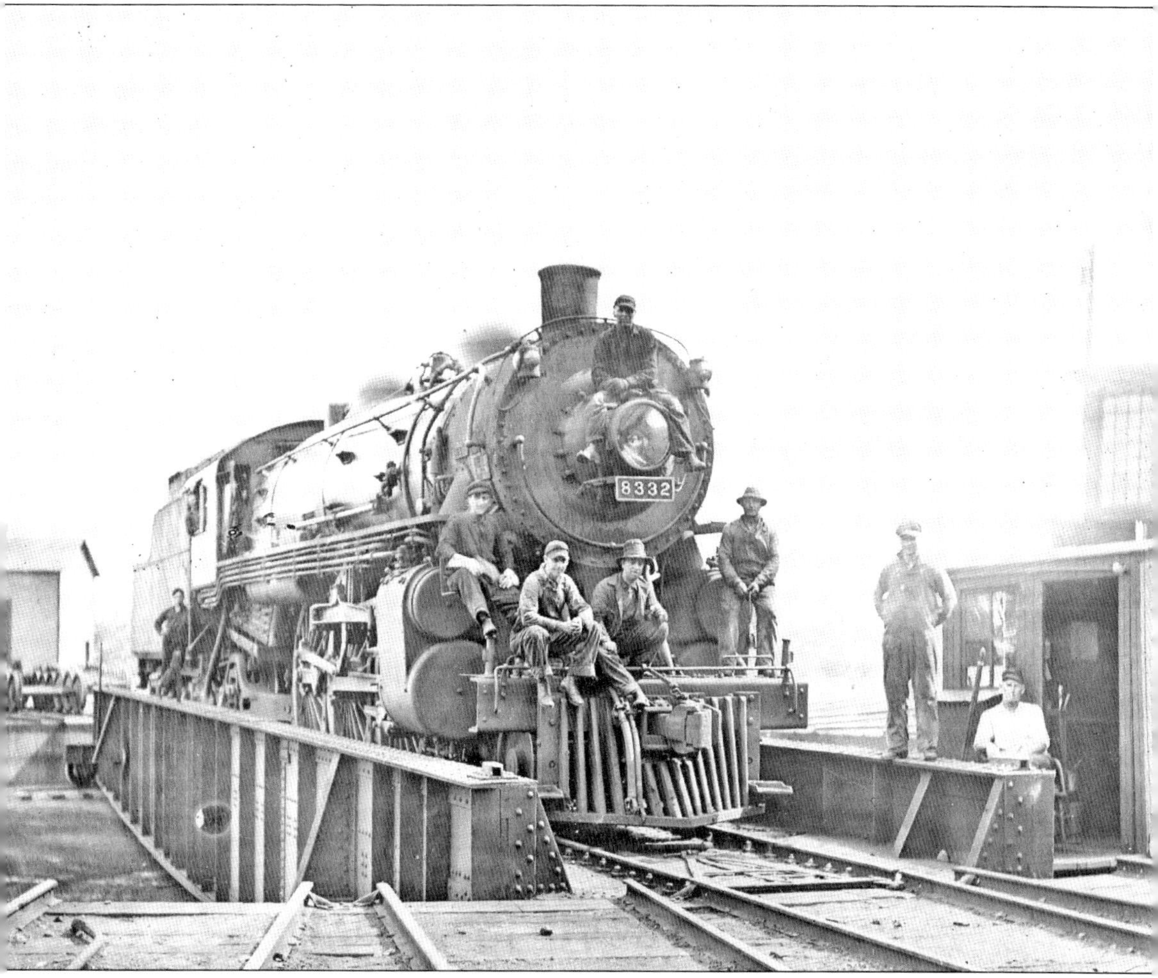

The Michigan Central Railroad, which ran along the Kalamazoo River in some places, completed a rail line from Kalamazoo to Chicago in 1950. This made the city of Kalamazoo the transshipment point for villages and towns seeking access to Detroit or Chicago. Seen here in June 1921, these men are taking a break after turning the train engine in the roundhouse. (KVM.)

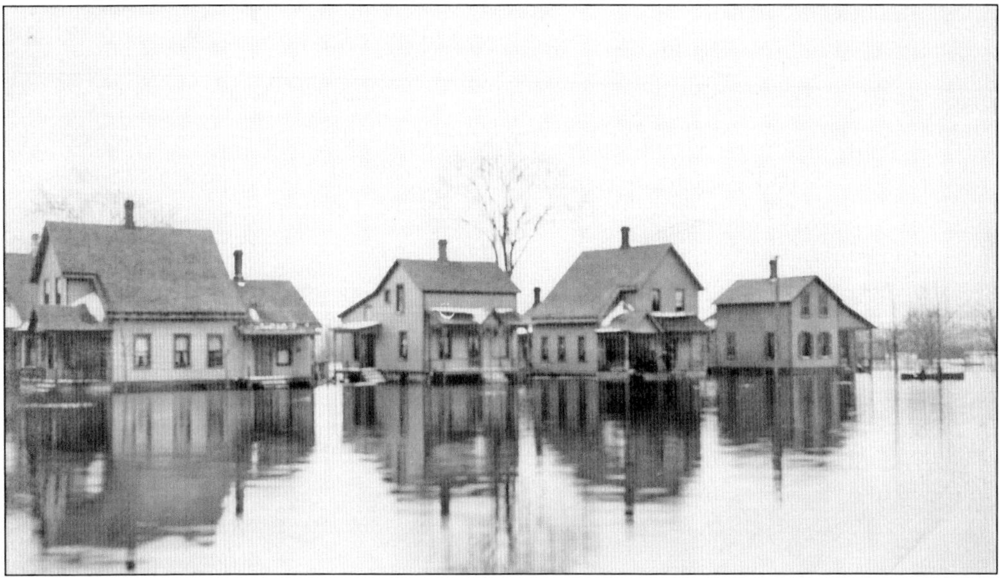

In March 1904, parts of the city of Kalamazoo experienced flooding due to snowmelt after 110 days of snow. This area near Jasper, Dutton, and Vine Streets experienced significant flooding because Portage Creek, which is nearby, and the Kalamazoo River, farther downstream, could not handle the quick influx of water. (Photograph by Maime L. Austin, KPL.)

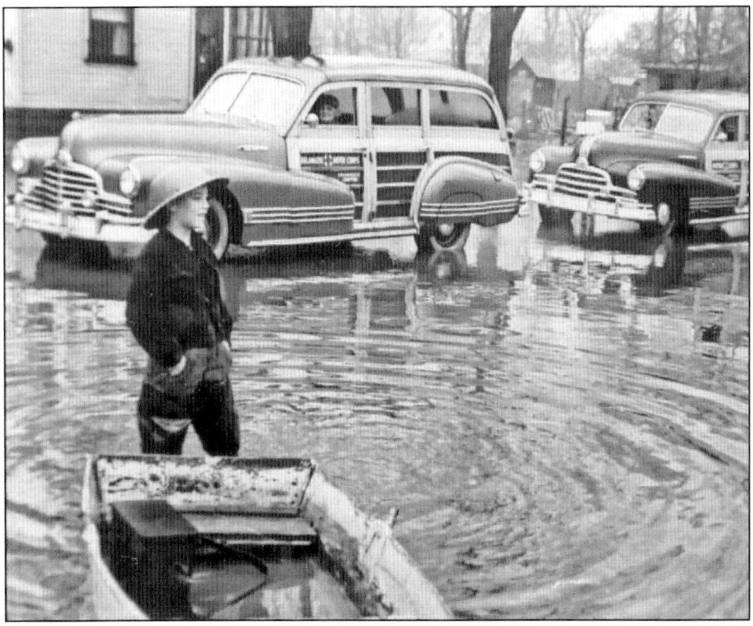

In 1946, the Kalamazoo River flooded this 10-year-old boy's home near the Kalamazoo County Fairgrounds. He went outside to survey the damage. Note that the tires on the cars in the background are not very deep in the water compared to where the water comes up to on the boy. (Allen Marr.)

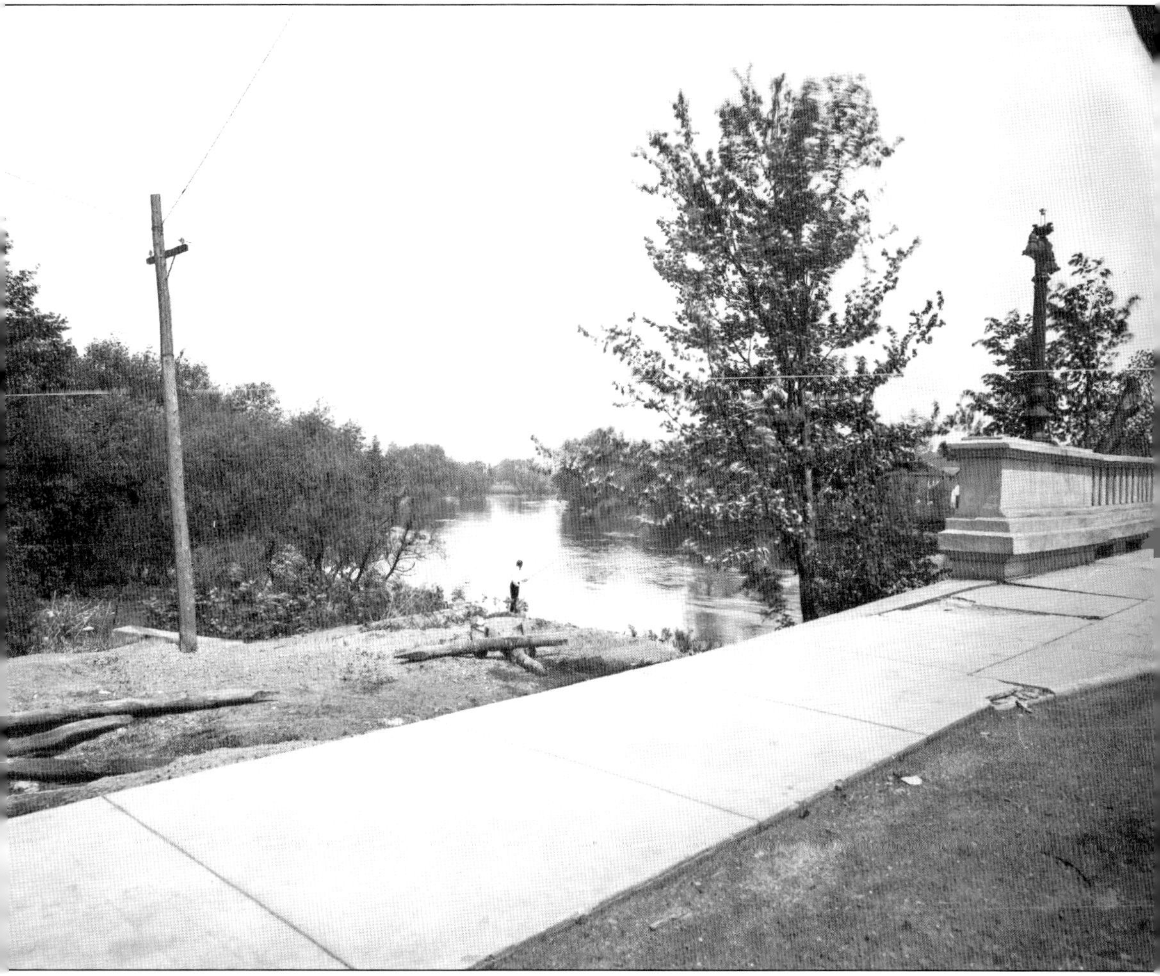

Gull Bridge crosses the Kalamazoo River on Gull Road, between Cave Court and Ray Street. A fisherman is visible in the center of the photograph on this beautiful afternoon. The Kalamazoo River winds its way past the man on its way toward the center of town. (KPL.)

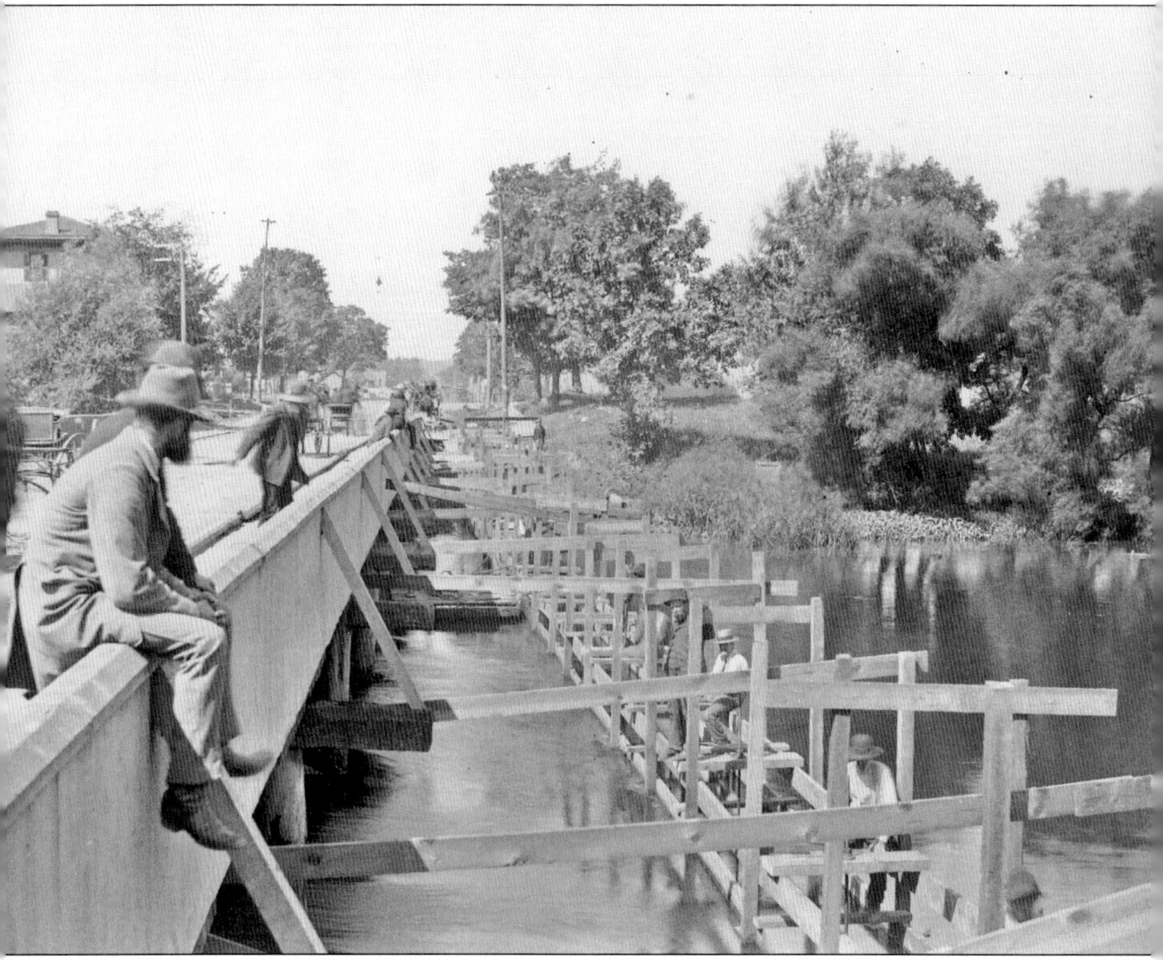

These men are working on the construction of a sanitation line that crosses the Kalamazoo River next to the bridge in the city of Kalamazoo. Even in the late 1880s, city engineers had the forethought to keep the sanitation and storm systems separate. The City of Kalamazoo purchased its first electric streetlights in 1866. One can be seen in the center background. (KPL.)

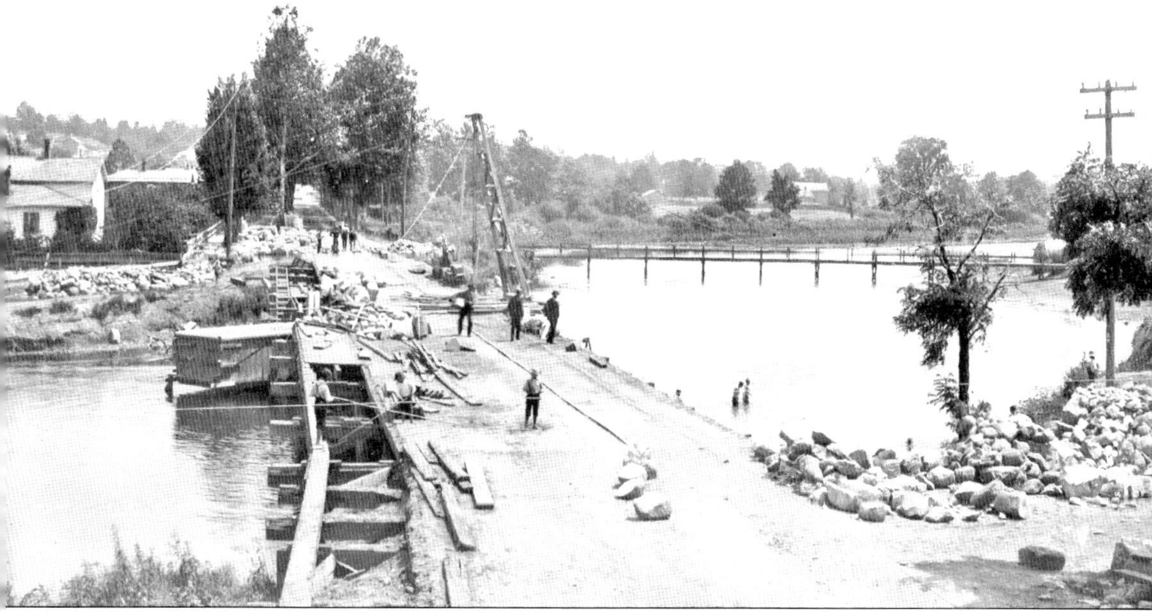

Here, workers are laying a little bridge over the Kalamazoo River, west of the East Main Bridge, sometime between 1870 and 1890. The piles of boulders on each end were used to stabilize the riverbanks and create a foundation for the bridge. These boulders would have been locally quarried for this project. (KPL.)

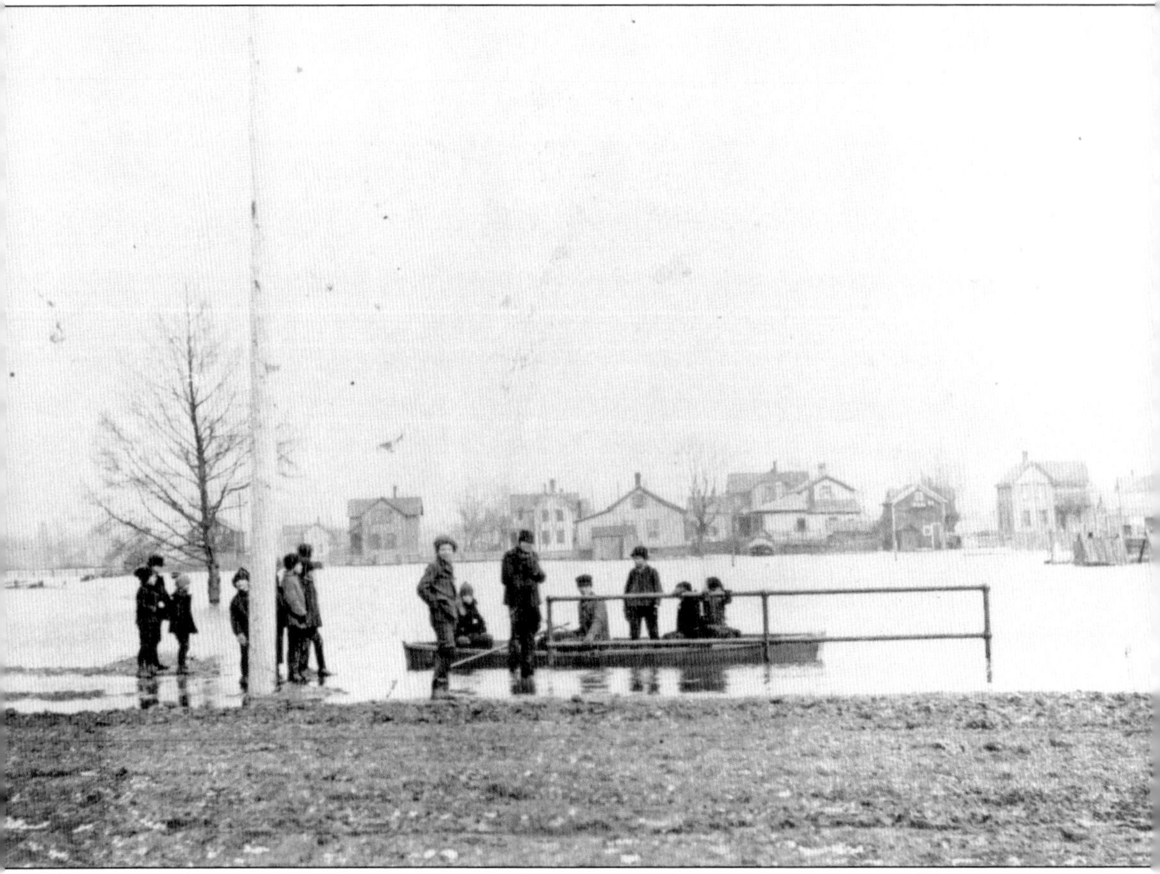

Pictured here is Burdick Street at Wall Street in Kalamazoo. Fourteen children, some in a rowboat, survey the flood damage at the Waterworks Bridge. After this photograph was taken, the floodwaters rose another six inches. (Photograph by Joseph P. DeKorn, WMU.)

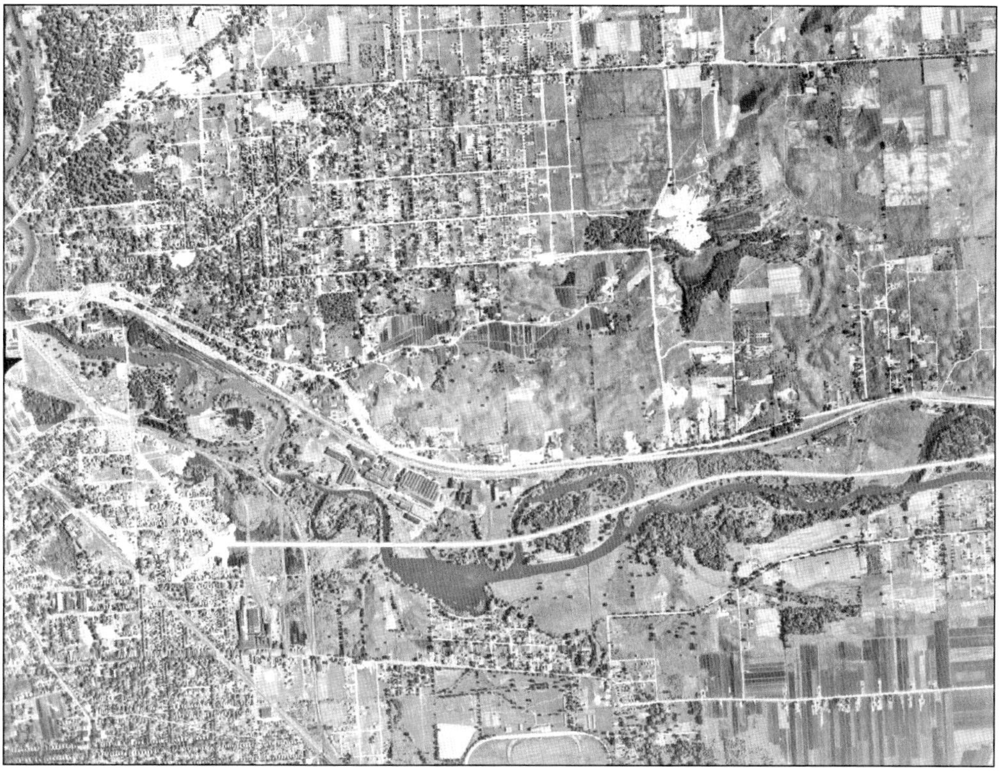

Above is a 1938 aerial photograph of east Kalamazoo (the city). Several oxbow lakes can be seen. Some are man-made while other are naturally occurring. Much of the rich, fertile, black muck adjacent to the river was cultivated for celery. At center is the Kalamazoo Paper Company, located northwest of the widest part of the Kalamazoo River. The paper company was strategically located to take advantage of the water resource and, later, a major highway. Below is a 1964 image of this same area. The widest part of the river in 1938 was filled by paper mill waste product. The plant is no longer in existence, but its footprint can still be seen in the landscape. (Both, Upjohn.)

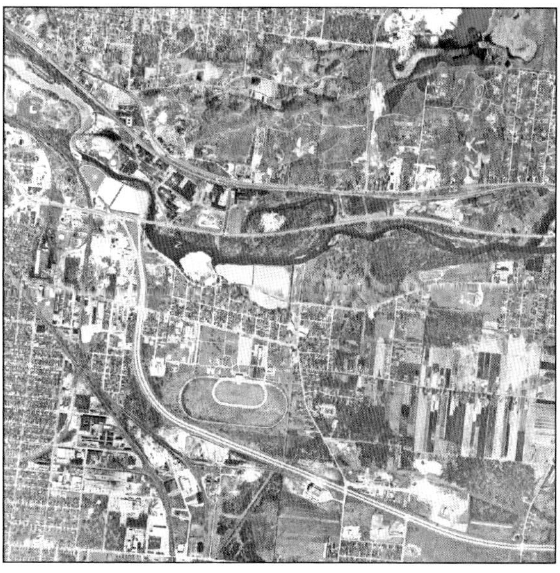

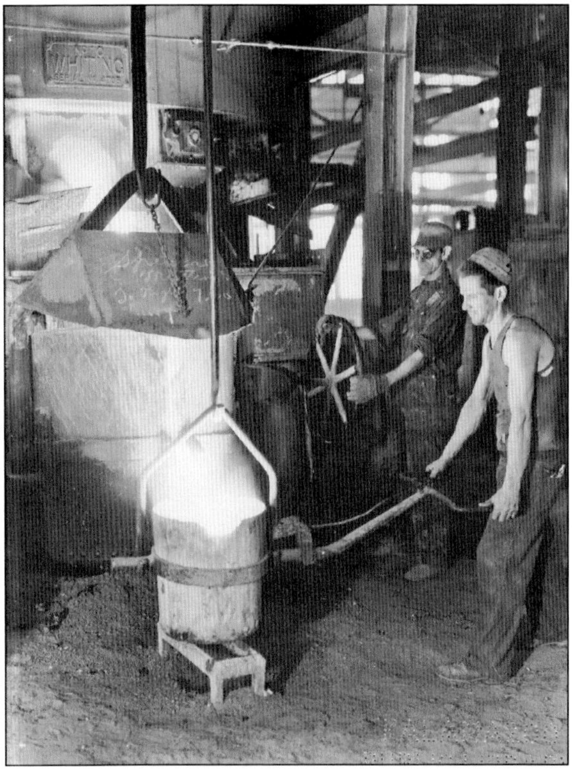

The Kalamazoo Stove Company was in operation from 1902 to 1954 and sat along Portage Creek, a tributary of the Kalamazoo River. Raw materials, such as iron and steel, were needed and were shipped up the river to the foundry. The photograph at left provides a look at the extreme conditions some men worked under. The man with the protective eyewear is controlling the flow of the molten iron into the pour bucket, which is being held in balance by the second man. Note the handle that he is holding on one side of the smaller bucket. The image below shows two men controlling the flow of the melted pig iron as it is poured into molds for a stove. (Both photographs by Maime L. Austin, KPL.)

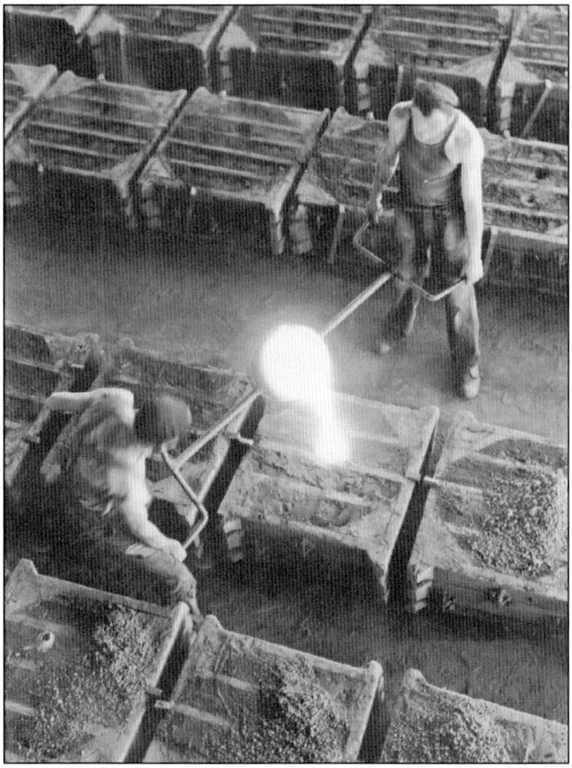

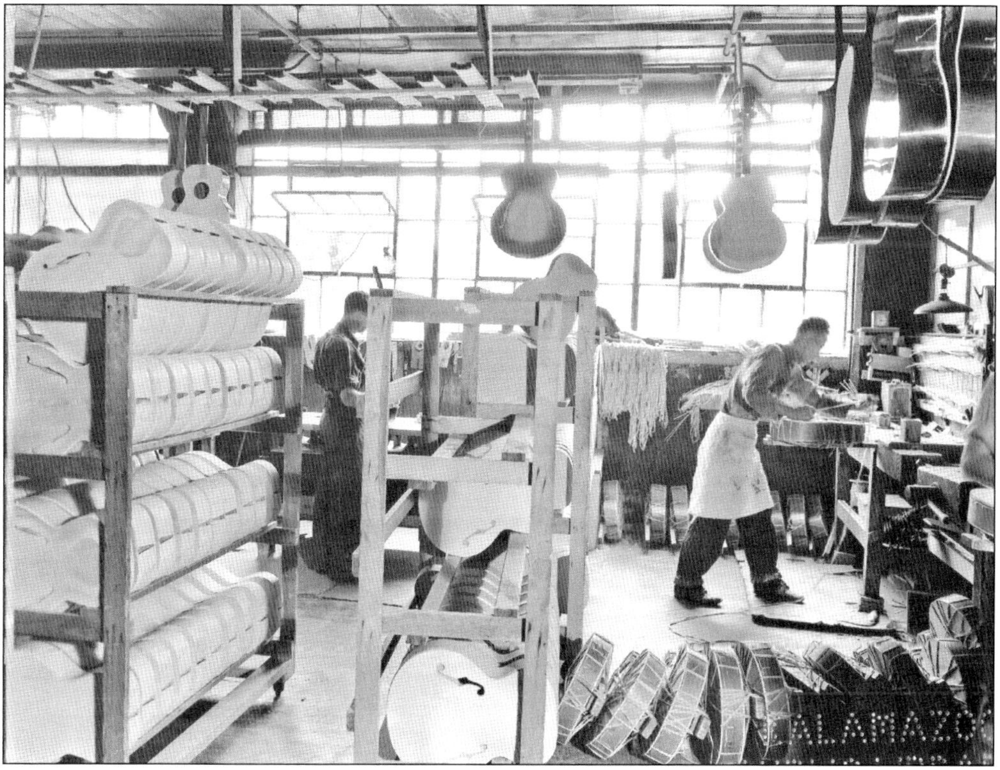

The Gibson Guitar Corporation established its headquarters in Kalamazoo in 1902, although Orville Gibson, the owner, had been selling mandolins from his one-room workshop since 1894. Early on, workers had to rely on the Kalamazoo River to transport the finished product to distant markets. The company produced mandolin-family instruments, most notable the iconic Gibson guitar. Gibson's first electric guitar shipped from Kalamazoo in 1936. Above, in 1936, is the gluing department, where the binding is glued to the edges of the bodies of the instruments. The image below shows one section of the general assembling room in 1936. Both photographs indicate that this was a large operation even then, as many guitar bodies are on racks or hanging from the ceiling. (Both photographs by Maime L. Austin, KPL.)

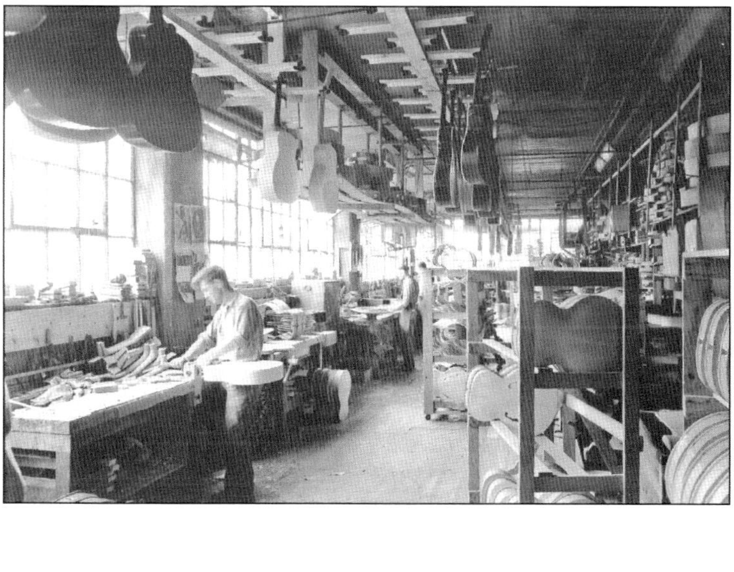

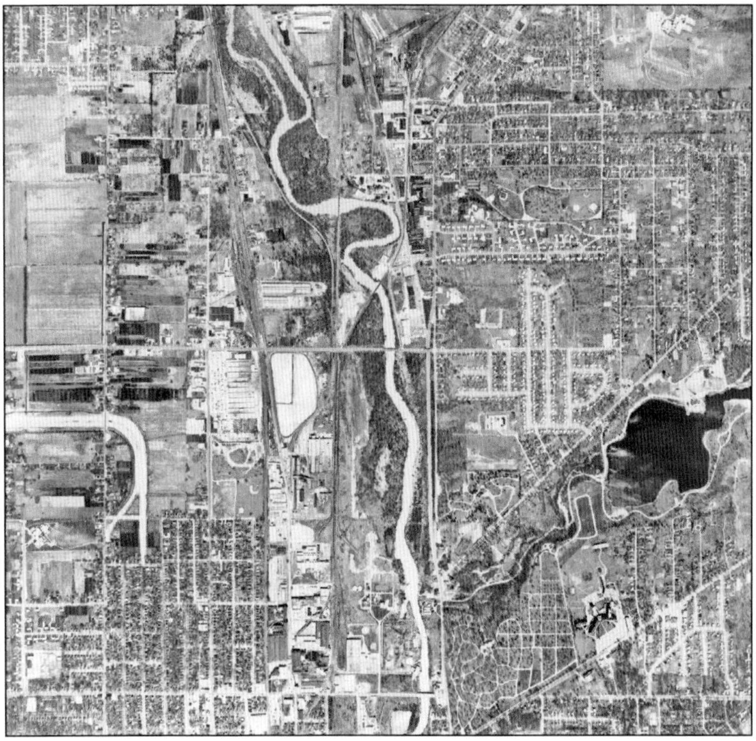

The water treatment plant (lower center) is located on the north side of the city of Kalamazoo, along the Kalamazoo River in this 1964 aerial photograph. Over the decades, this plant worked hard to decontaminate the river water. To this day, one could drink the river water coming out of the plant. (Upjohn.)

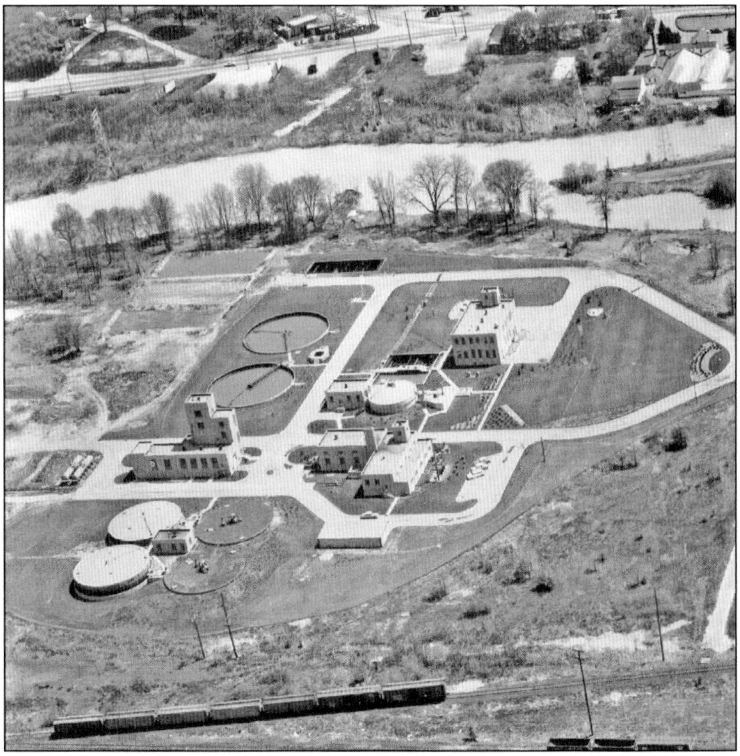

The Kalamazoo Sewage Treatment Plant sits on the banks of the Kalamazoo River. The plant, shown in this 1957 photograph, services more than 150,000 residents. Water that enters the plant goes through three treatments to remove debris and heavy grit; dissolved and finely divided impurities; and small, suspended particles and any carbon remaining from the other processes. (KVM.)

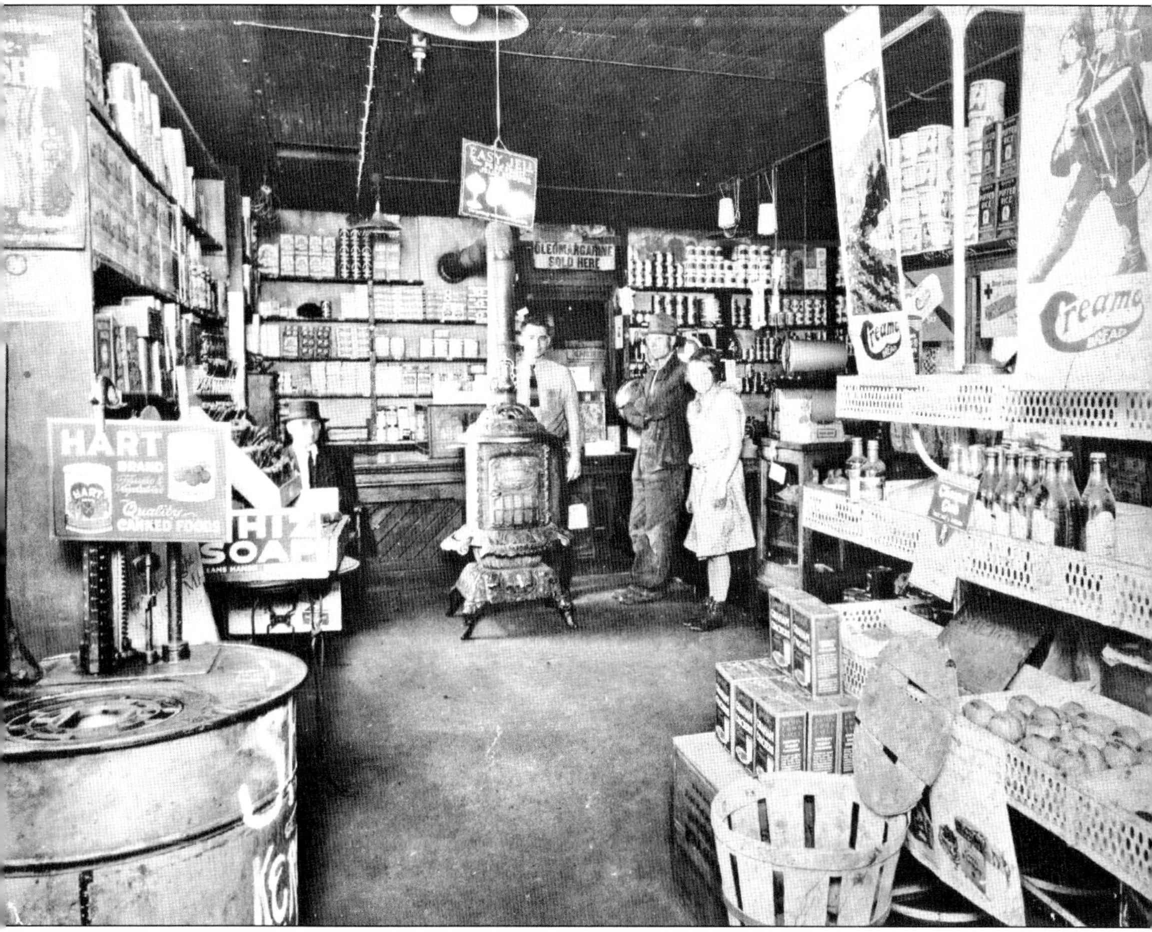

Pictured here is Charles Drummond's grocery store, sometime between 1910 and 1928. A stove from the Kalamazoo Stove Company can be seen at center. Many of the goods sold in this grocery store would have been shipped to Kalamazoo via the Kalamazoo River, especially the fresh, seasonal produce. (Photograph by Maime L. Austin, KPL.)

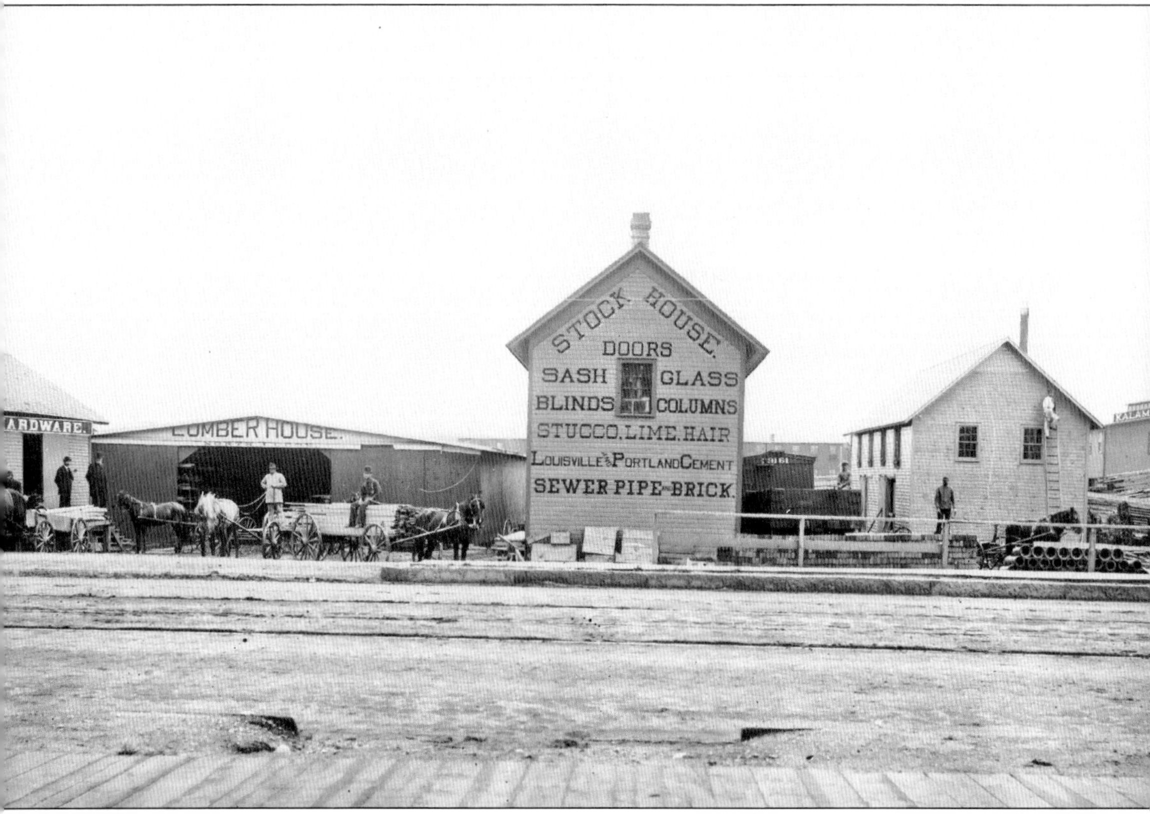

This photograph shows the North and Coon Lumber Company between 1890 and 1892. Portage Creek runs behind these buildings; its banks make the perfect place for a lumber company. Logs could be brought to the mill along the Kalamazoo River and up Portage Creek. Note the buggy in front of the lumber house loaded with planed wood. (KPL.)

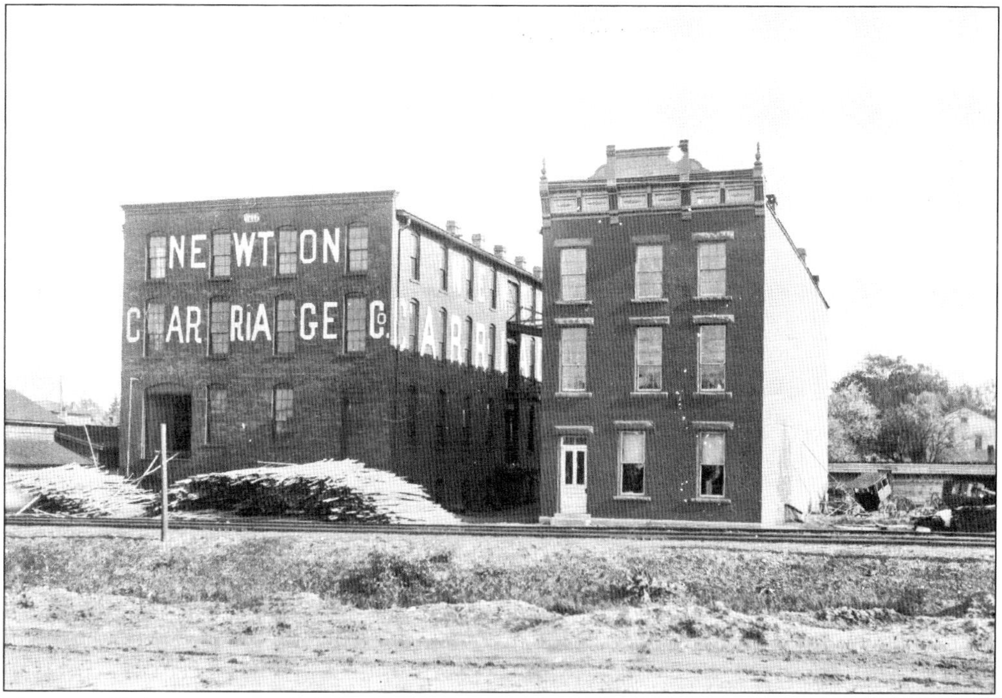

The city of Kalamazoo was a hub for making carriages and buggies. The Newton Carriage Company was situated on Arcadia Creek, a tributary of the Kalamazoo River in the city of Kalamazoo. This 1891 view (above) looks south from Willard Street. The Michigan Buggy Company was about a block west of the Newton Carriage Company. A photograph of the company (below) was taken in 1892 from the northwest. Railroad tracks are visible in both images, which eliminated the need to use the Kalamazoo River for transporting goods to and from the business. It is interesting to note that both businesses have the company name painted right on the building. Today, there would be a sign somewhere on the property to designate it. (Both, KPL.)

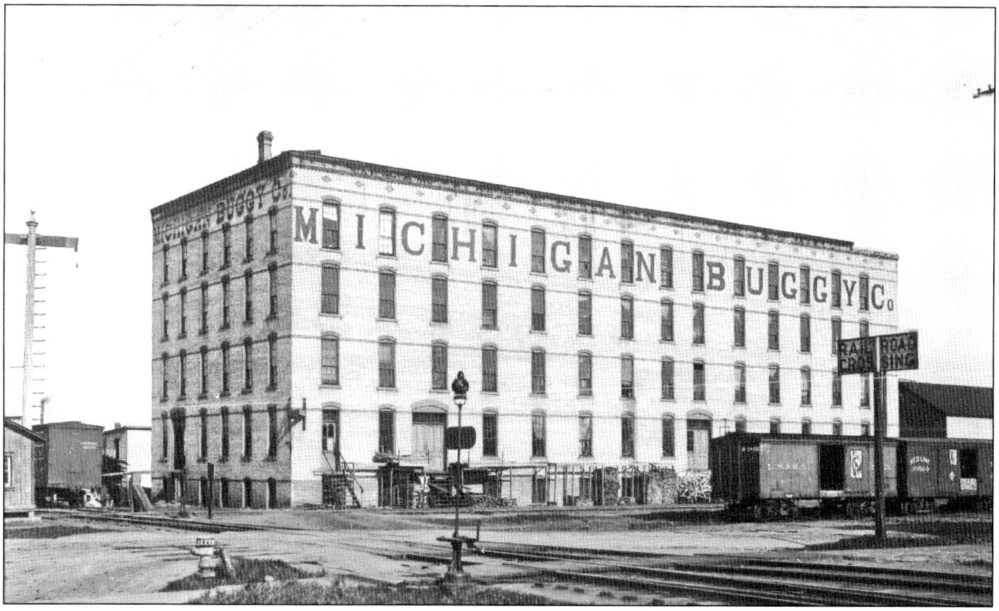

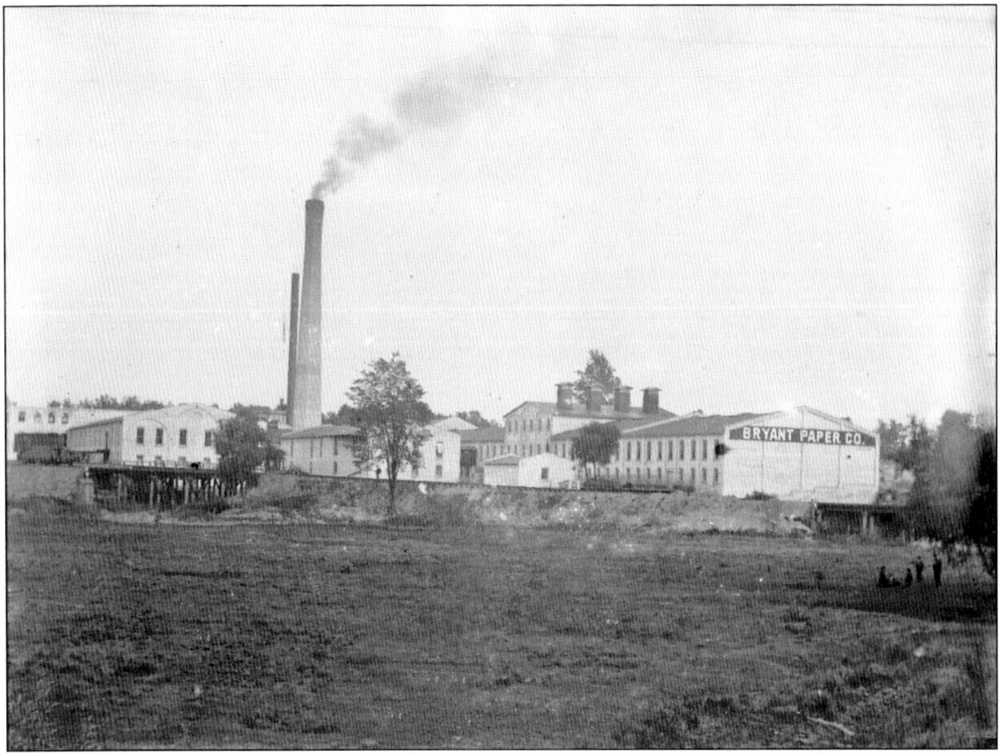

At least eight buildings comprised the Bryan Paper Mill complex that sat along the Kalamazoo River. The complex and the railway track sat on the Kalamazoo River floodplain and therefore had to be built up artificially so they would not flood and wash away. The lowland in the foreground was marshy because it is part of the river's floodplain. (Photograph by Joseph P. DeKorn, WMU.)

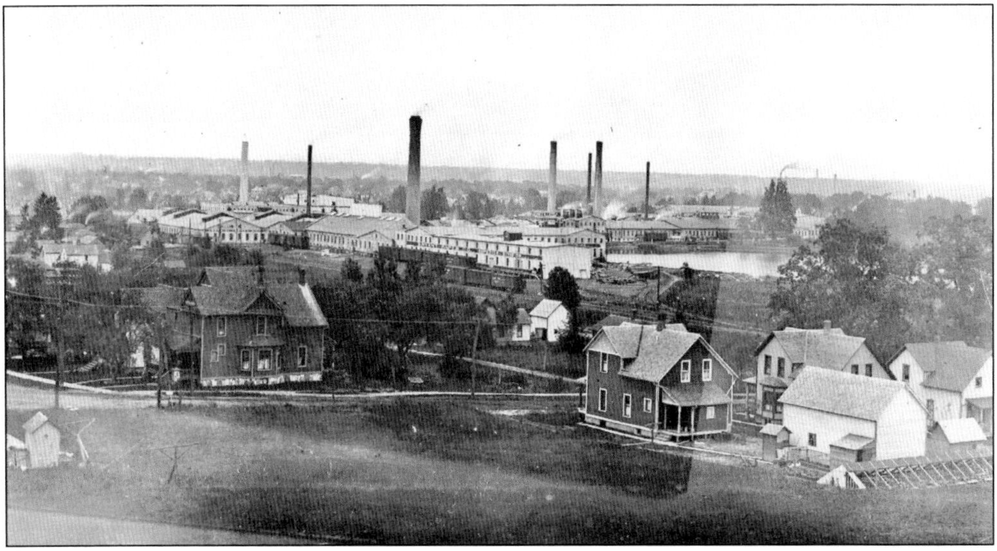

This photograph is most likely from the early 1900s and shows the paper plant as seen from the southwest. The Bryant Paper Company relied on Portage Creek, a tributary of the Kalamazoo River, to transport wood to the mill and paper to other places along the river. The millpond is also partially visible. (KPL.)

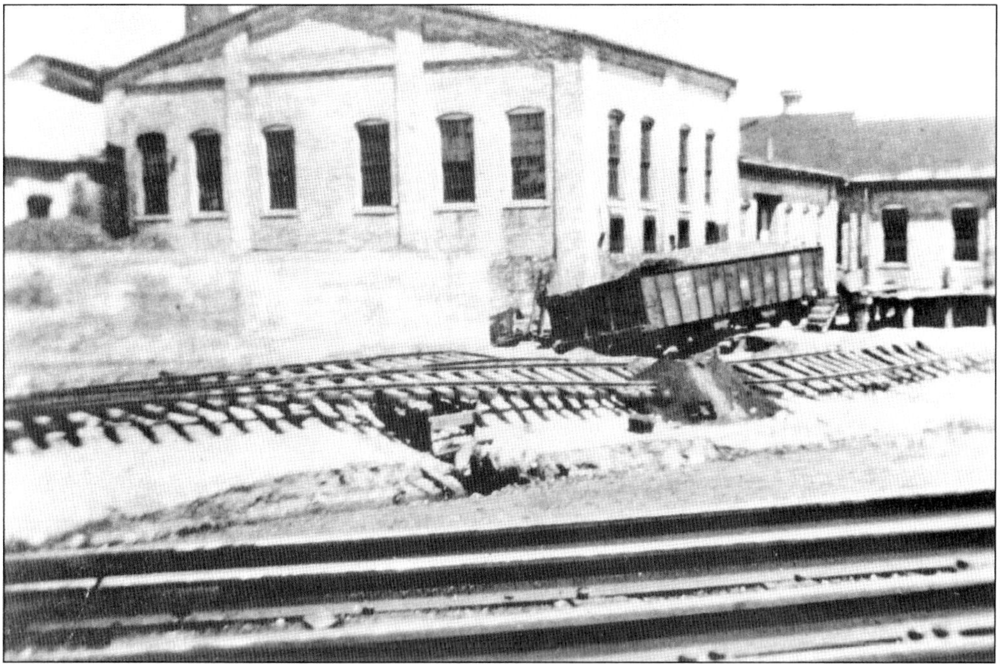

The Bryant Paper Mill complex suffered a lot of damage during the June 1916 flood event. The railroad tracks in the foreground were damaged when the ground beneath them washed out with the floodwaters. The loaded boxcar was washed off the tracks and deposited where it sits next to the building. (Photograph by Joseph P. DeKorn, WMU.)

In the foreground of this photograph, footings were being constructed to support new buildings. In the far distance, the Kalamazoo River can be seen. Next to the largest chimney is a large pile of planed lumber for the new buildings. The river was vital to shipbuilding and foundation material and as an energy source for the mill. (Photograph by Joseph P. DeKorn, WMU.)

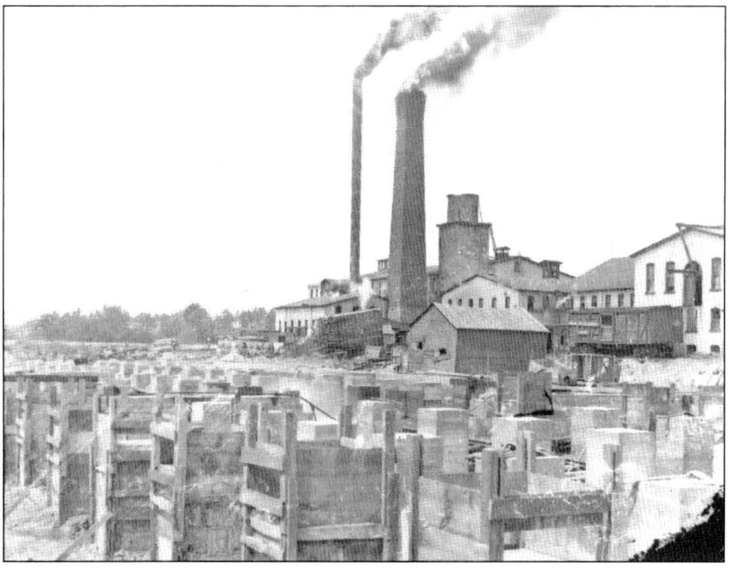

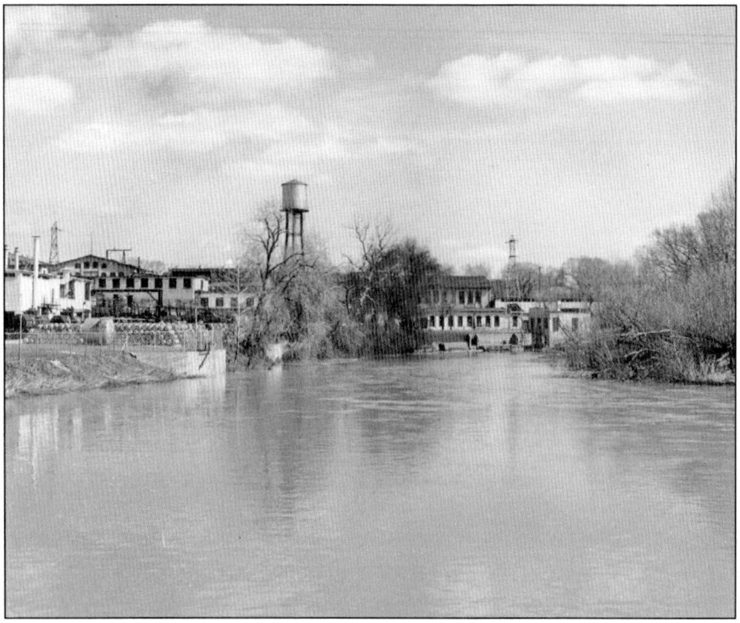

Jacob Kindleberger established the Kalamazoo Vegetable Parchment Company along the banks of the Kalamazoo River in 1909. As with many other paper companies in the area, this plant changed hands or was merged with other businesses over the year. Papermaking at this plant, shown here in 1955, ceased in 2000, marking the end of Kalamazoo Vegetable Parchment's papermaking industry. (KVM.)

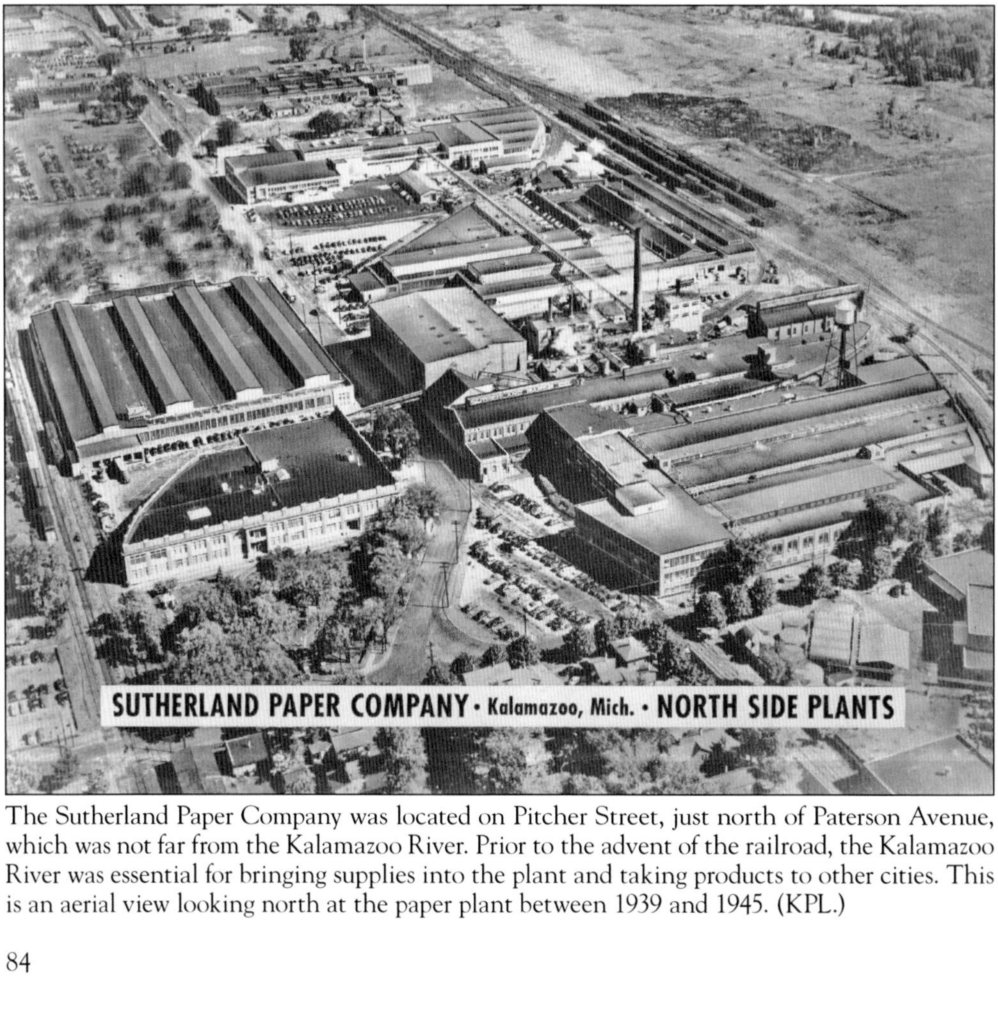

The Sutherland Paper Company was located on Pitcher Street, just north of Paterson Avenue, which was not far from the Kalamazoo River. Prior to the advent of the railroad, the Kalamazoo River was essential for bringing supplies into the plant and taking products to other cities. This is an aerial view looking north at the paper plant between 1939 and 1945. (KPL.)

Five

West to Plainwell/Otsego

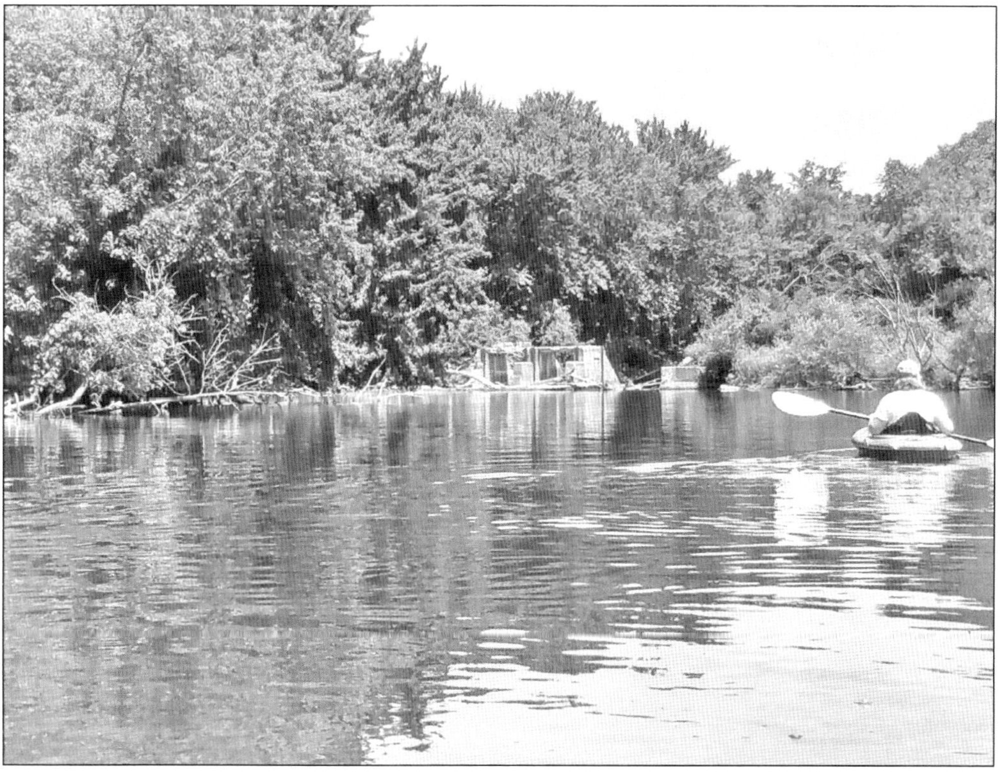

Kayaking is very popular along many stretches of the Kalamazoo River. It is a serene and relaxing way to see the river. Along the way, remnants of old dams can be seen and explored. Kayakers and canoers can shoot the rapids over some dams or take their boats out and portage around them; this dam lies at D Avenue between the cities of Kalamazoo and Plainwell. (Authors' personal collections.)

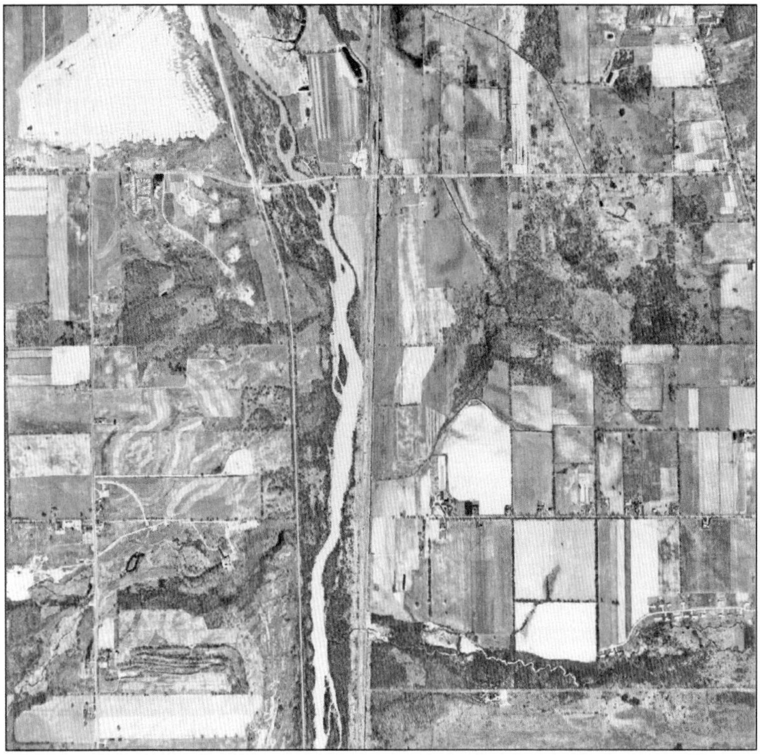

The Kalamazoo River runs through the middle in this 1964 aerial photograph, taken near Cooper. At left, train tracks follow the river. In the upper left corner, pulp from papers mills was unloaded from train cars and dumped on the farmland, with runoff going into the river. This brownfield site is now an industrial area. (Upjohn.)

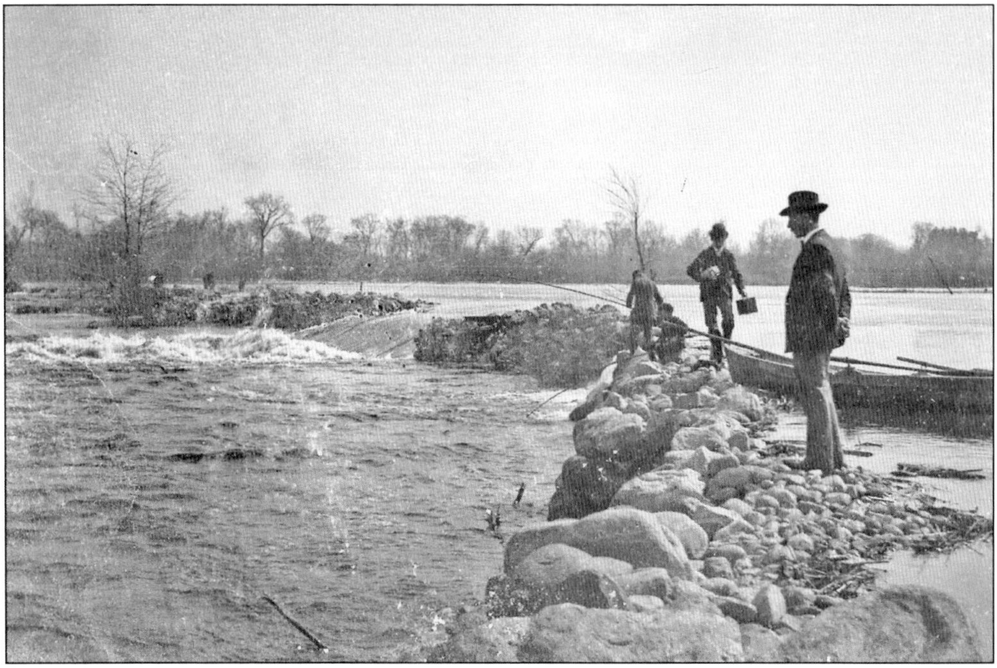

This stone dam separates the millrace at left with the Kalamazoo River at right. The millrace captures water from the river and channels it to businesses' waterwheels to generate power. Because the millrace is narrower than the Kalamazoo River, it is easy to see the swiftness of the water in the millrace. (*Union Enterprise*, RL.)

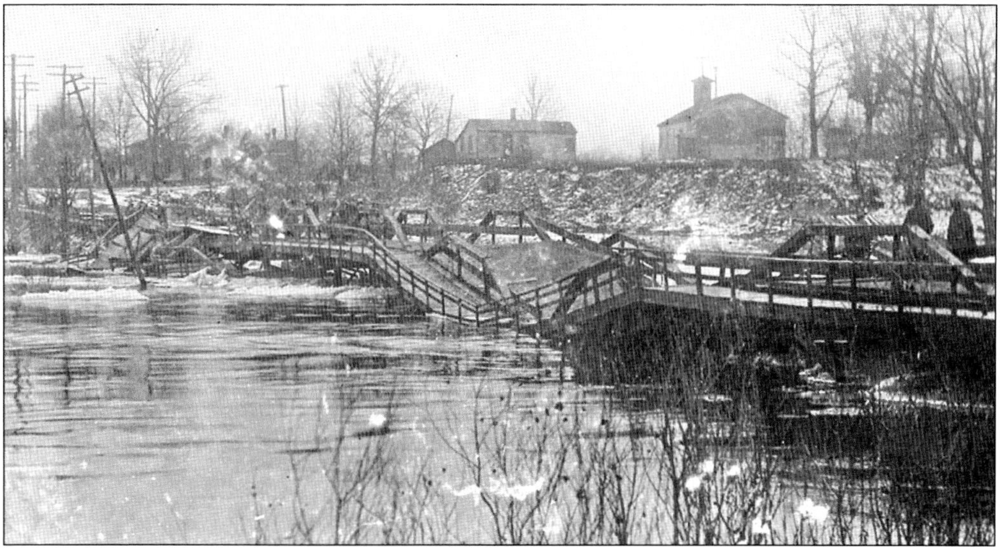

Plank Road began in 1852 to provide a thoroughfare between the cities of Kalamazoo and Grand Rapids. It was made from oak and walnut hardwood planks that were eight feet long and two inches thick. Travelers needed to cross the Kalamazoo River in Plainwell, which is approximately halfway between both cities. In 1853, Plainwell's first transportation and pedestrian bridge, the Plank Road Bridge, aided travelers across the Kalamazoo River and completed the Plank Road project. Plank Road was a toll road with a tollgate every six miles. In 1903, spring thaws caused flooding on the Kalamazoo River, and the bridge collapsed (above). The bridge was replaced by a concrete one. Large glass globe lights were mounted on tall pillars to light the bridge. The original concrete bridge was replaced in 1942. (Both, Sandy Stamm.)

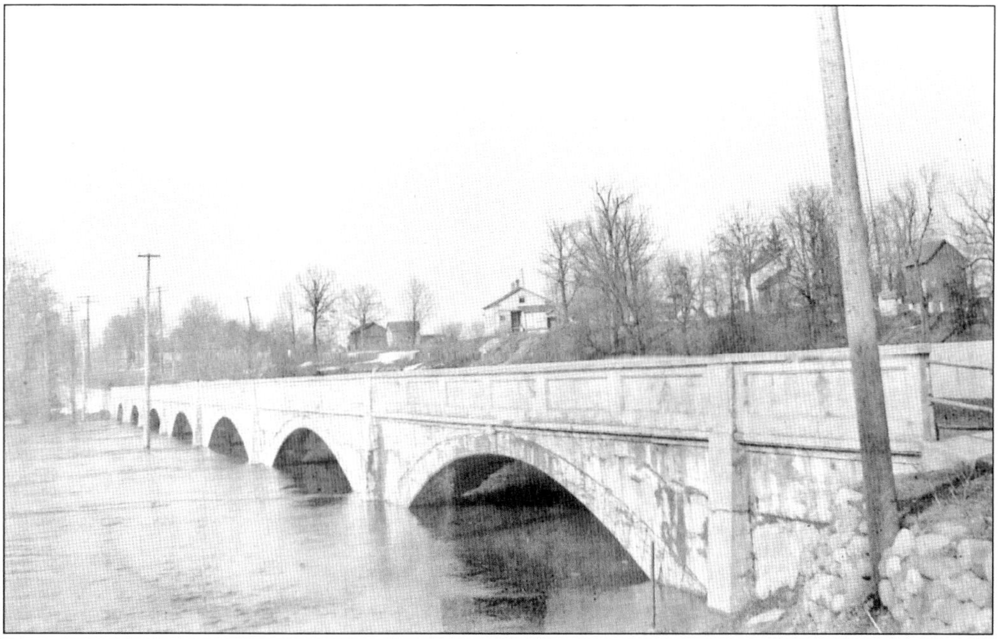

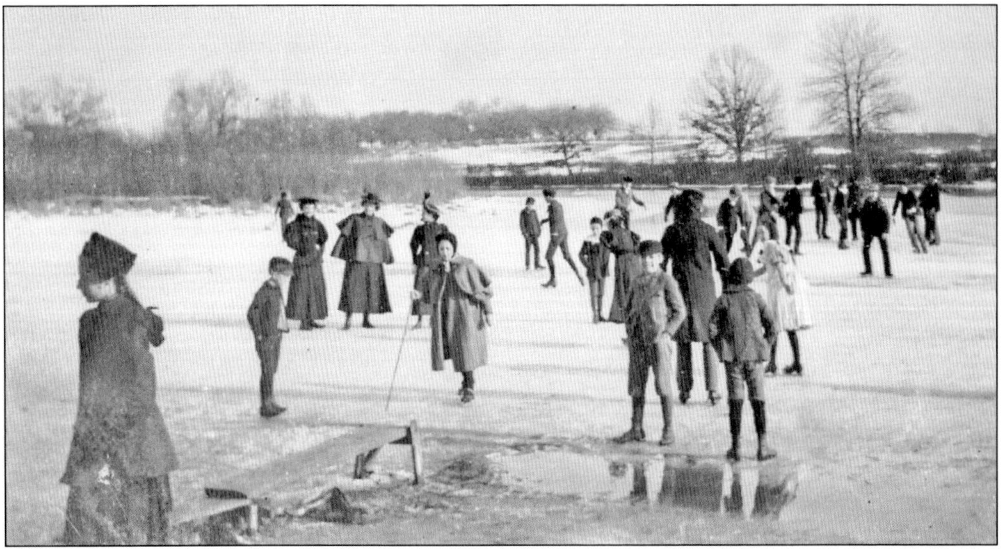

The frozen river and millrace provided an outdoor winter recreational area for residents in January 1887. Families enjoyed skating together and socializing with their neighbors. Some people were more daring on their skates than others. This is not a sight that can be seen today as neither the river nor the millrace freezes completely in winter. (*Union Enterprise*, RL.)

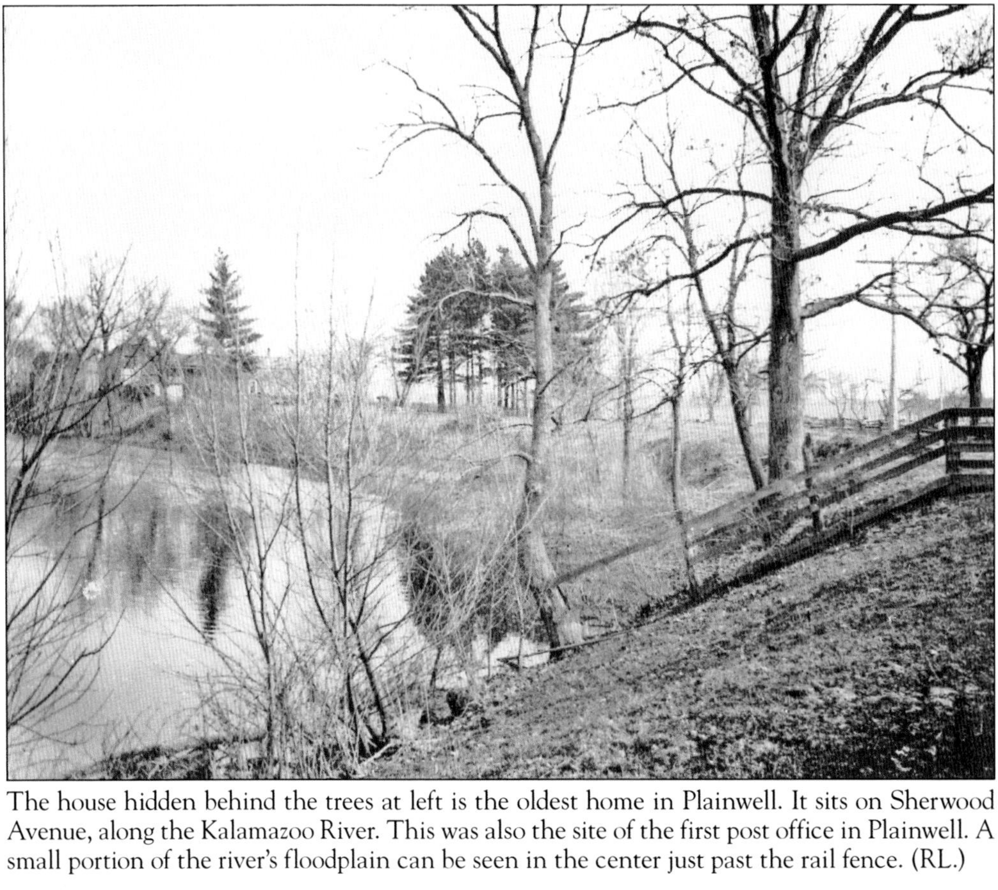

The house hidden behind the trees at left is the oldest home in Plainwell. It sits on Sherwood Avenue, along the Kalamazoo River. This was also the site of the first post office in Plainwell. A small portion of the river's floodplain can be seen in the center just past the rail fence. (RL.)

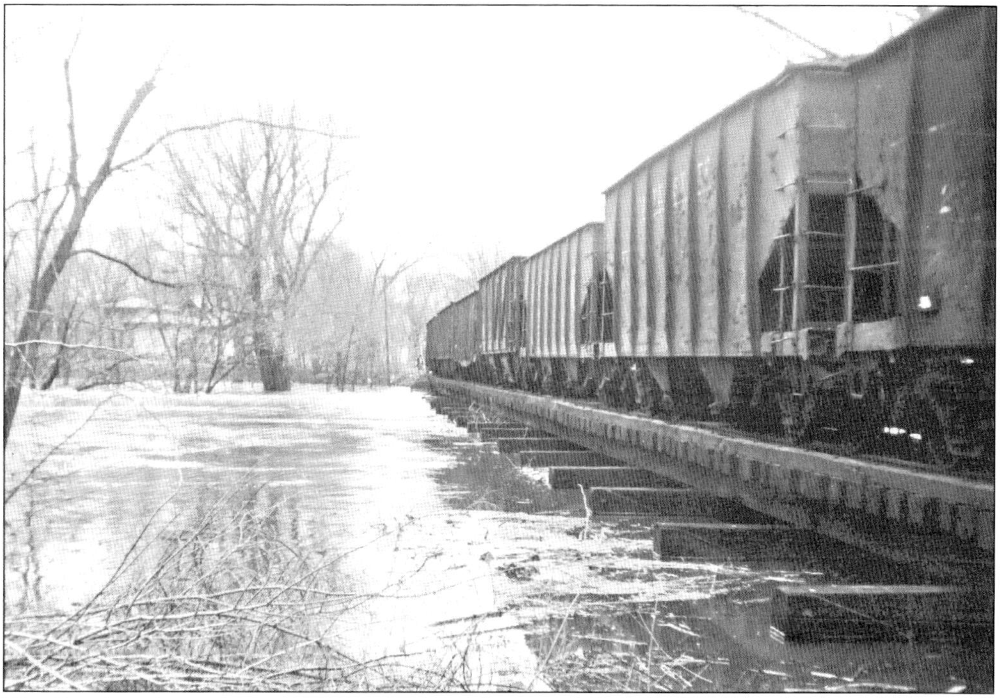

The flooding that occurred in 1947 devastated parts of Plainwell. This photograph, with a view looking west, shows just how high the water level was at the railroad trestle. The freight train, with five fully loaded railcars, was stopped on the bridge to help hold it in place. (RL.)

This railroad bridge in Plainwell was once used extensively to move goods to and from the Plainwell Paper Mill. The city council decided to preserve this piece of its history by turning it into a pedestrian bridge, which creates a shortcut over the Kalamazoo River to Dean's Ice Cream and Sherwood Park from downtown. (Authors' personal collections.)

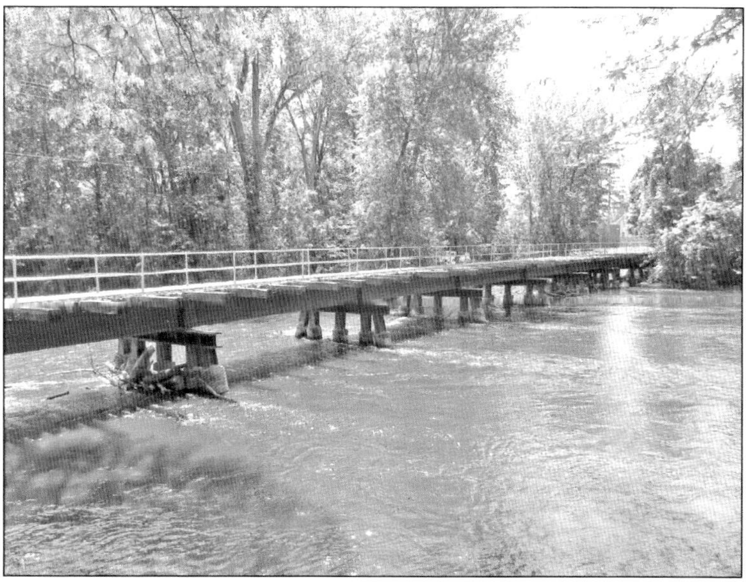

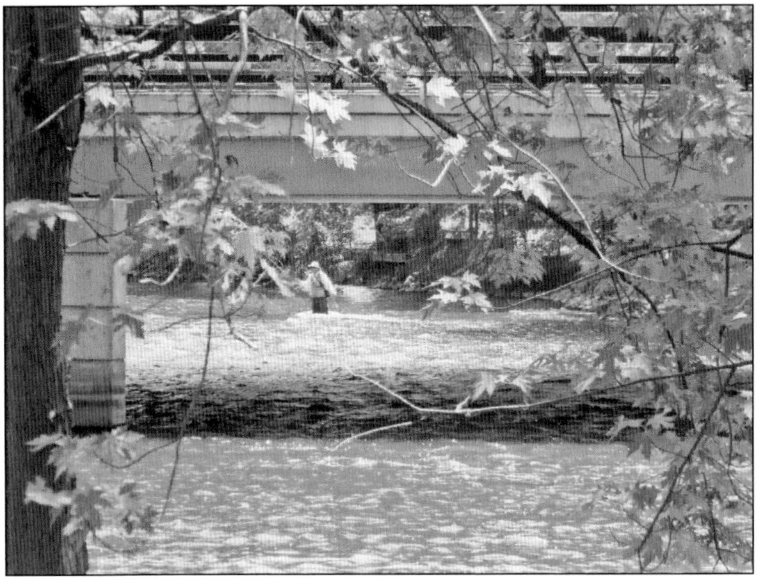

The Kalamazoo River is used for all types of recreation. When the water level is below average, fisherman can wade out and fly-fish. This angler tries his hand at catching one of the many species of fish found in the river, which include bass, catfish, carp, and panfish. (Authors' personal collections.)

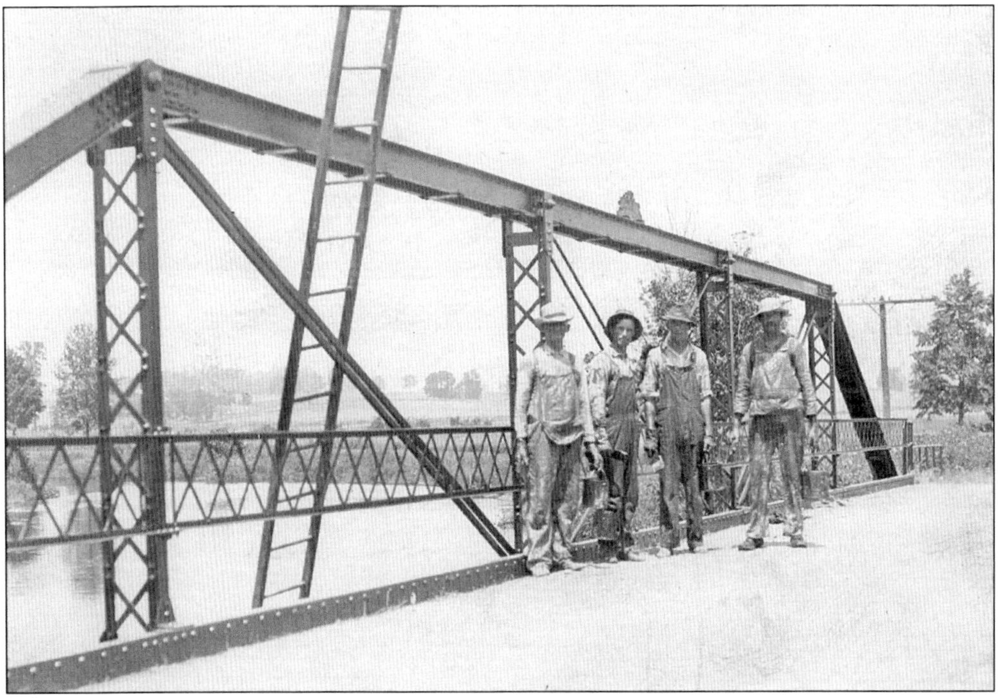

Plainwell is known as the "Island City" because the millrace that was dug from the Kalamazoo River to the Plainwell Paper Mill created the island. This iron bridge was built to help people cross from Plainwell (on the island) to the east side of the Kalamazoo River at East Bridge Street. (Sandy Stamm.)

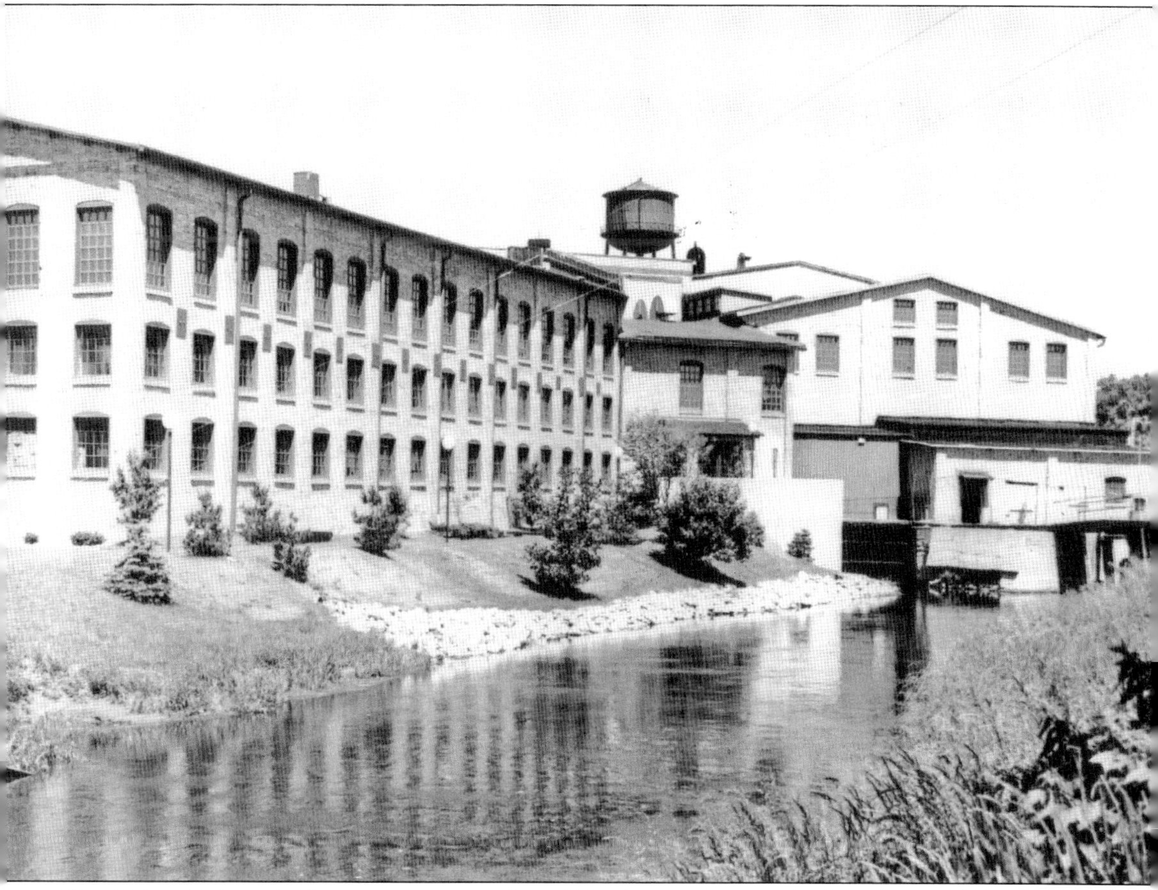

The Plainwell Paper Mill was in operation from 1872, known then as the Lyon Paper Mill, until 2000. This mill was also known as the Michigan Paper Company (1886–1956). In its heyday, the Plainwell Paper Mill produced 50 tons of paper a day. Some of the mill buildings have since been torn down and others renovated, such as the one that houses Plainwell City Hall. (Sandy Stamm.)

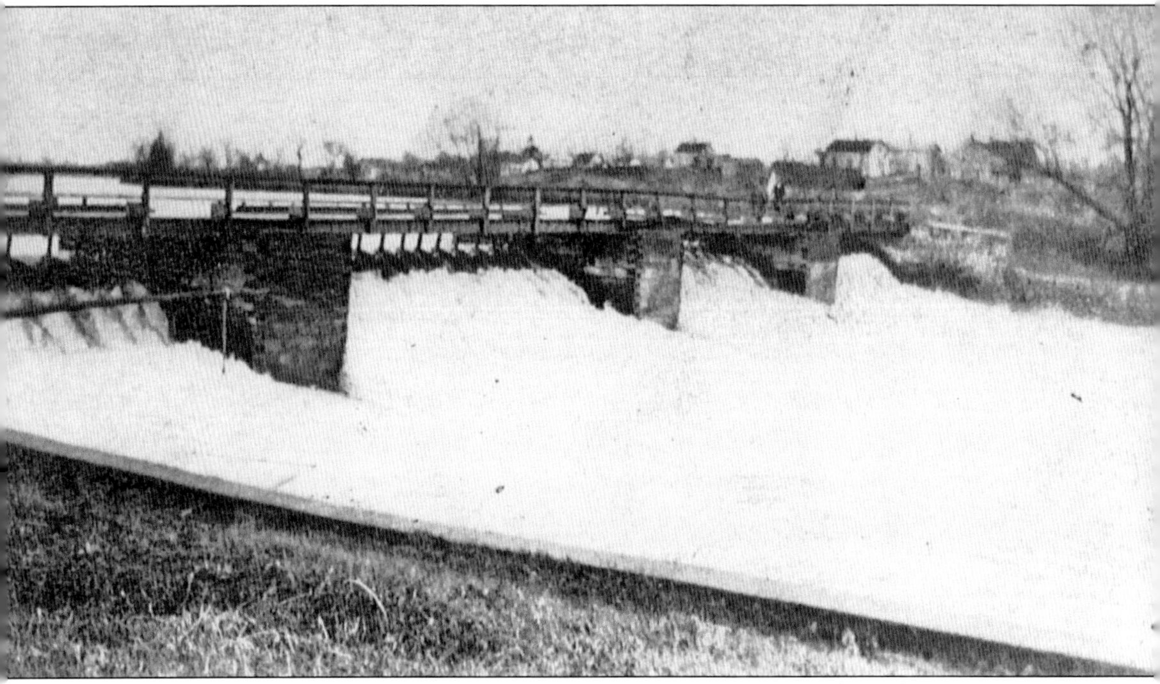

Two men are strolling across this dam in the Kalamazoo River, east of North Farmer Street in Otsego, in 1915. It appears that the floodgates are fully open as water is gushing downstream from the dam. Opening the gates was done to alleviate the growing water pressure upstream. (OHS.)

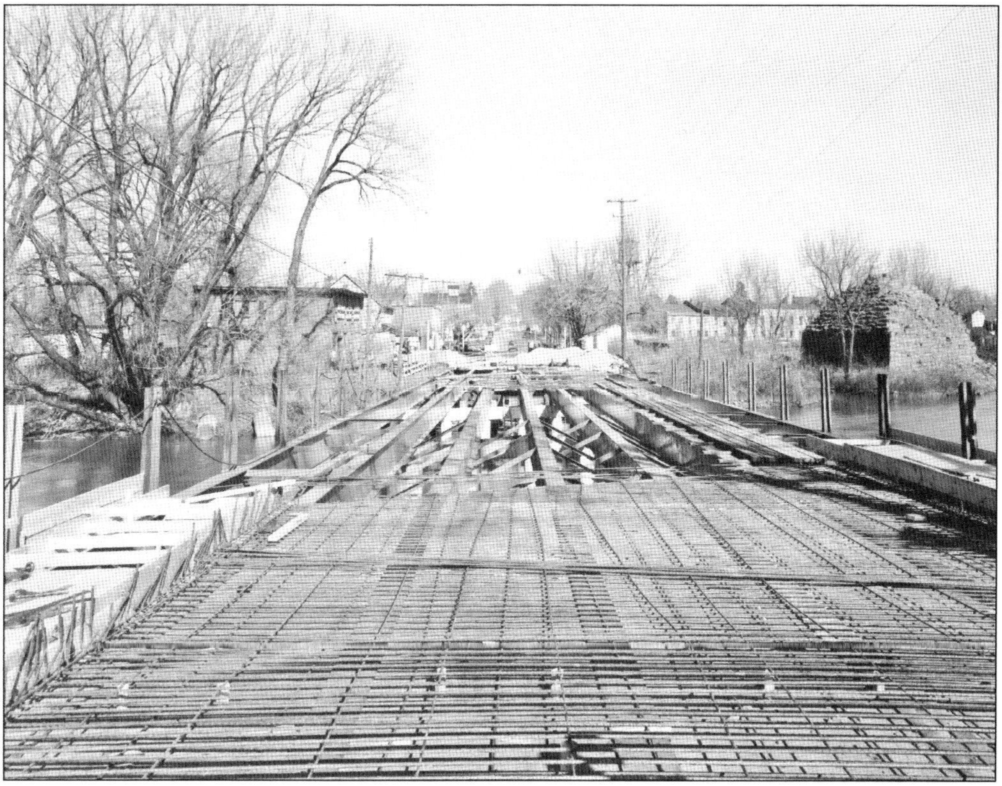

North Farmer Street in Kalamazoo was the main thoroughfare from one side of the Kalamazoo River to the other, especially for the paper mills. When the original bridge, built in the 1880s, need to be replaced and widened, it was not up for debate but had to be done. The photograph above shows the new bridge being built in 1938 using rebar, steel, and concrete. Below is the bridge after construction. This bridge included new sidewalks and guardrails to aid in a safe crossing over the Kalamazoo River for motorists and pedestrians. (Both, DDC.)

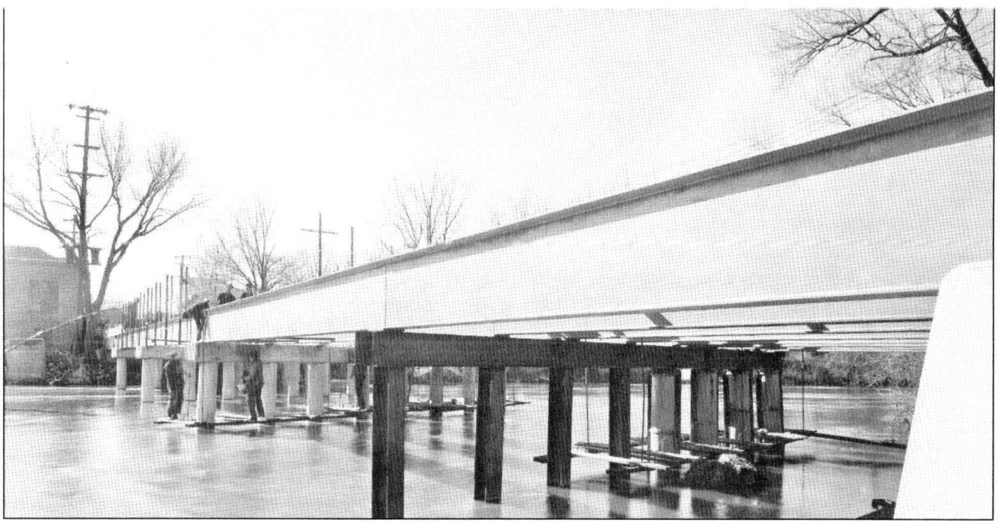

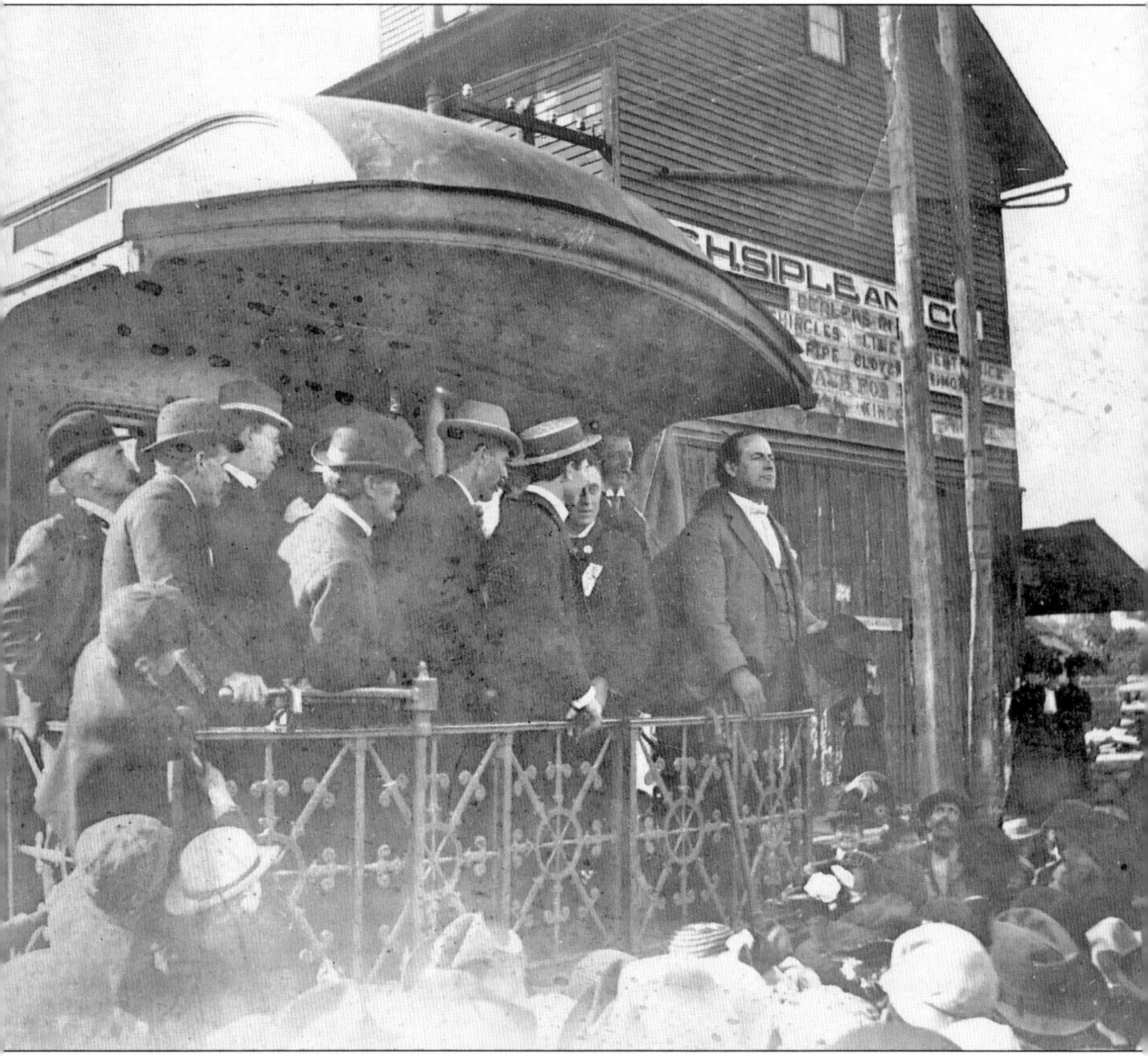

On October 9, 1900, at 1:15 p.m., presidential candidate William Jennings Bryan made a campaign stop in Otsego. He made his speech beside G.H. Siple and Company, which sold lumber and elevator equipment. The business was located at the corner of Farmer and River Streets along the Kalamazoo River. (DDC.)

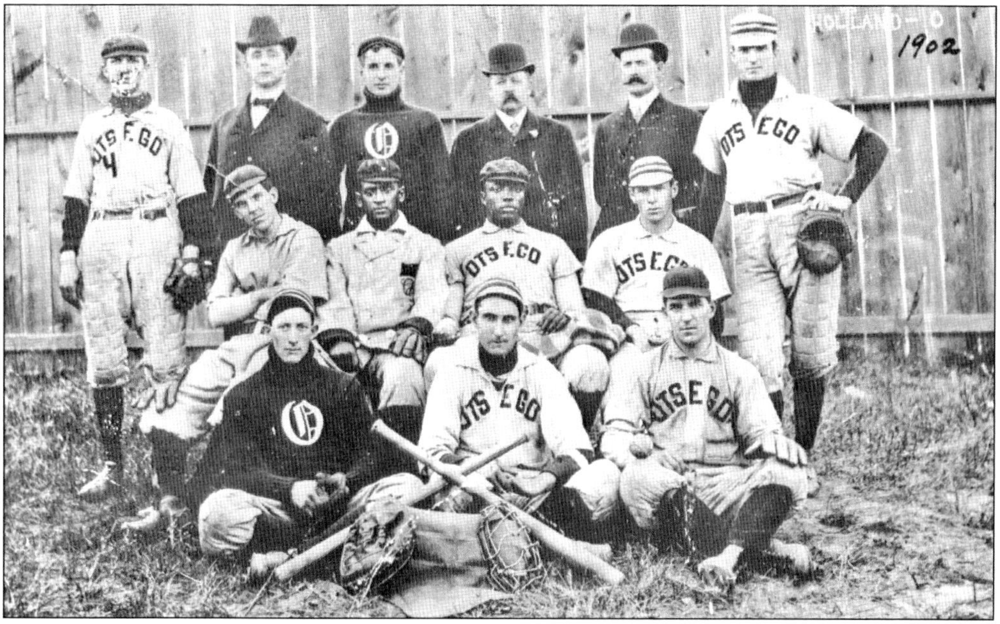

Business was not the only reason that Otsego was a prestigious city along the Kalamazoo River. Bardeen's Otsego Independents was a baseball team that provided entertainment for residents. One of the most famous players on this team in 1902 was Andrew "Rube" Foster, who was a pioneer executive in the Negro National League and elected to the National Baseball Hall of Fame in 1981. (OHS.)

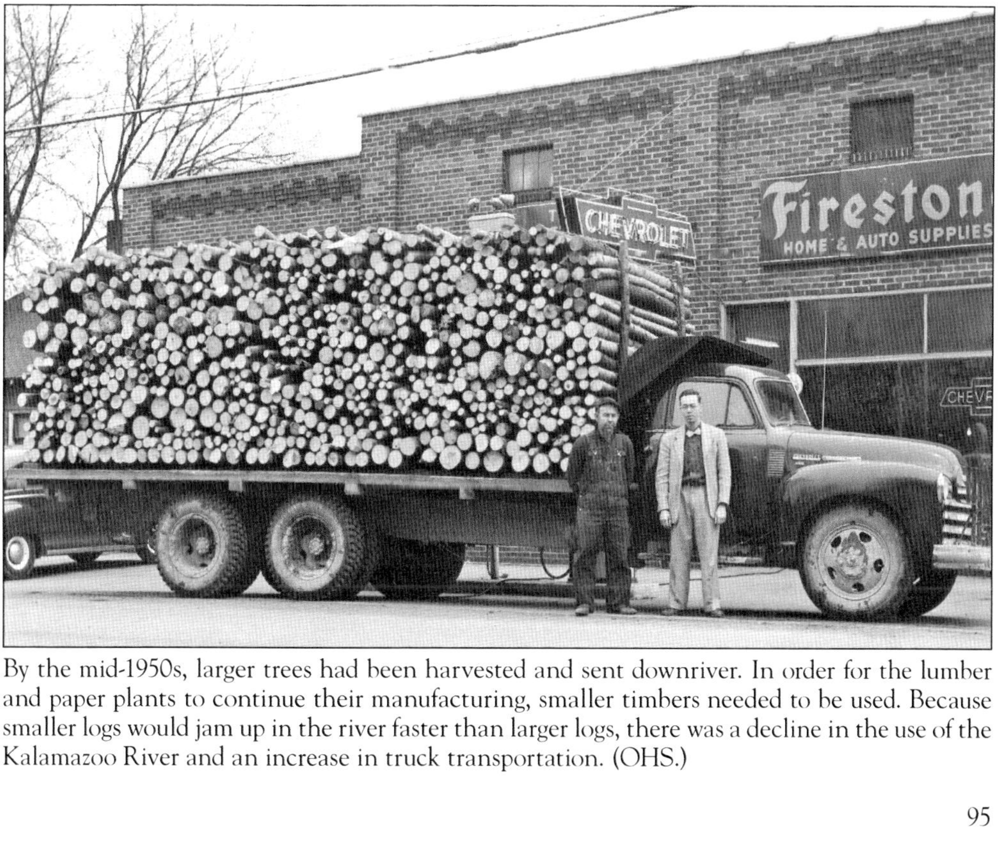

By the mid-1950s, larger trees had been harvested and sent downriver. In order for the lumber and paper plants to continue their manufacturing, smaller timbers needed to be used. Because smaller logs would jam up in the river faster than larger logs, there was a decline in the use of the Kalamazoo River and an increase in truck transportation. (OHS.)

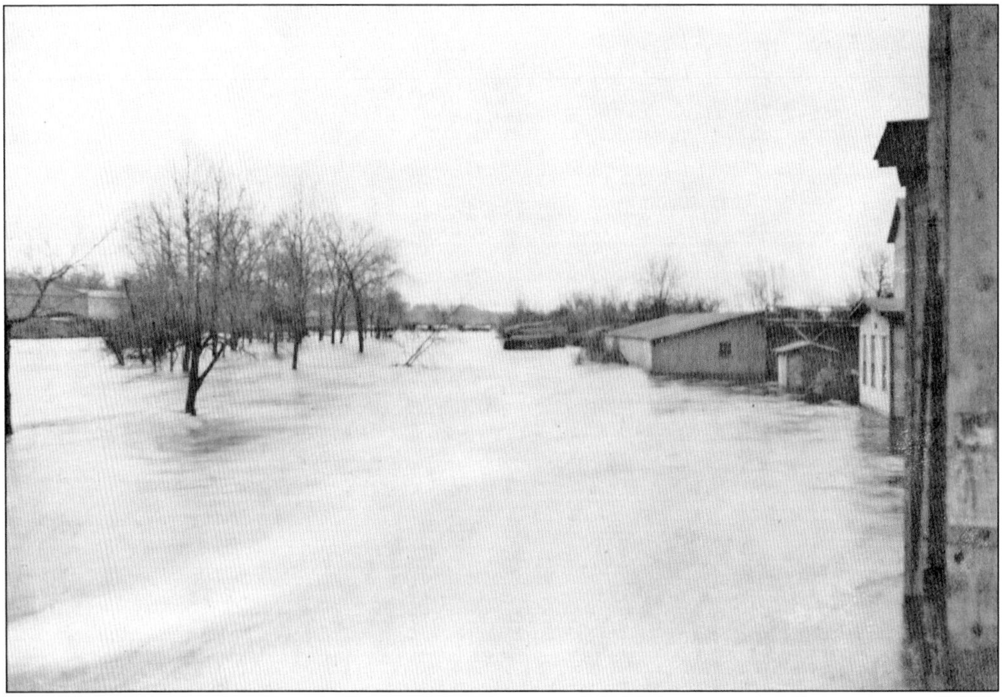

The Kalamazoo River floodplain is submerged due to the 1903 flood. Houses and businesses located on the riverbanks suffered damage from the floodwaters. At the time, floodplains were not understood as well as they are now and people built too close to the river, resulting in scenes like this one. (DDC.)

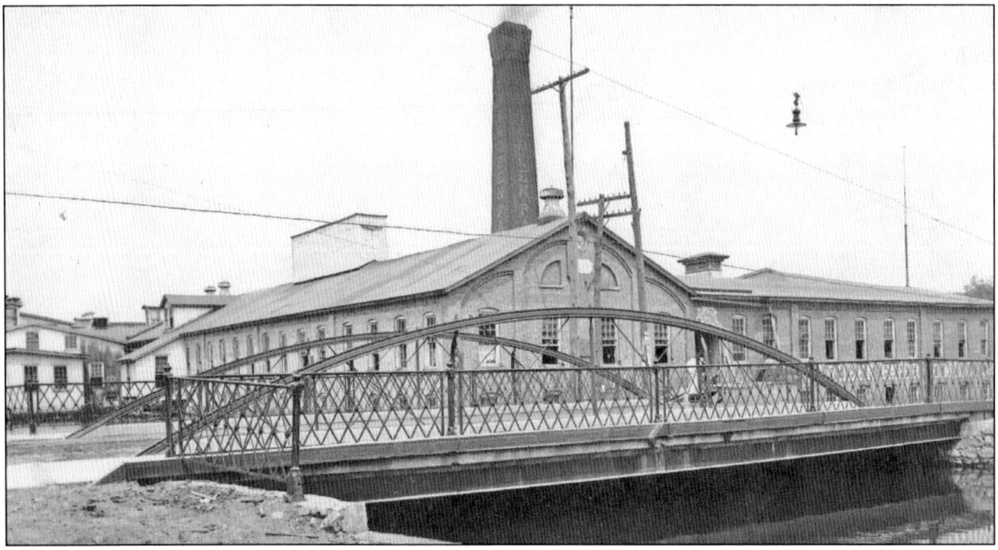

George Bardeen established the first paper mill in Otsego in 1887. This mill was one of the best employers in Otsego at the time, paying workers $7 a week. The Bardeen Paper Company mill was located across Farmer Street from the Otsego Mineral Springs Bath House. Paper production depleted the available spring water and effectively shut the bathhouse down. (OPL.)

The Bardeen Paper Company's mill no. 2 is in the foreground of this bird's-eye view looking west in Otsego. There is a millrace to the left of mill, and the Kalamazoo River flows on its right. The road in front of the mill is North Farmer Street. (OPL.)

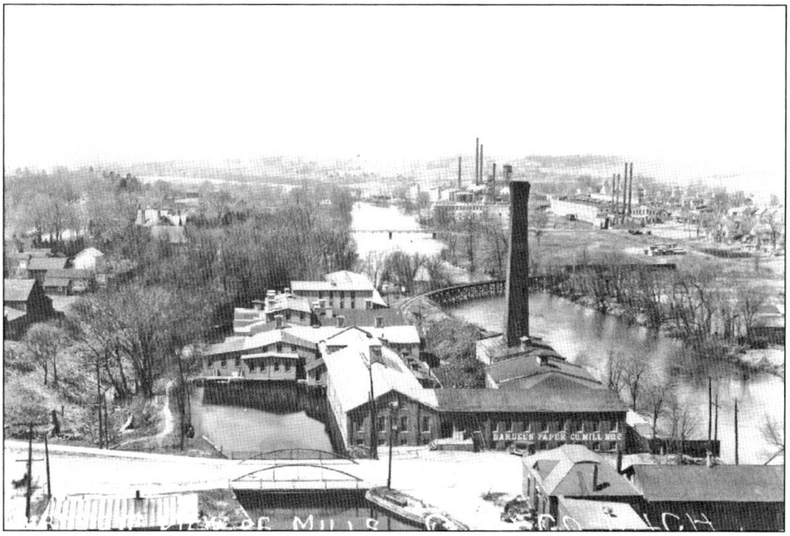

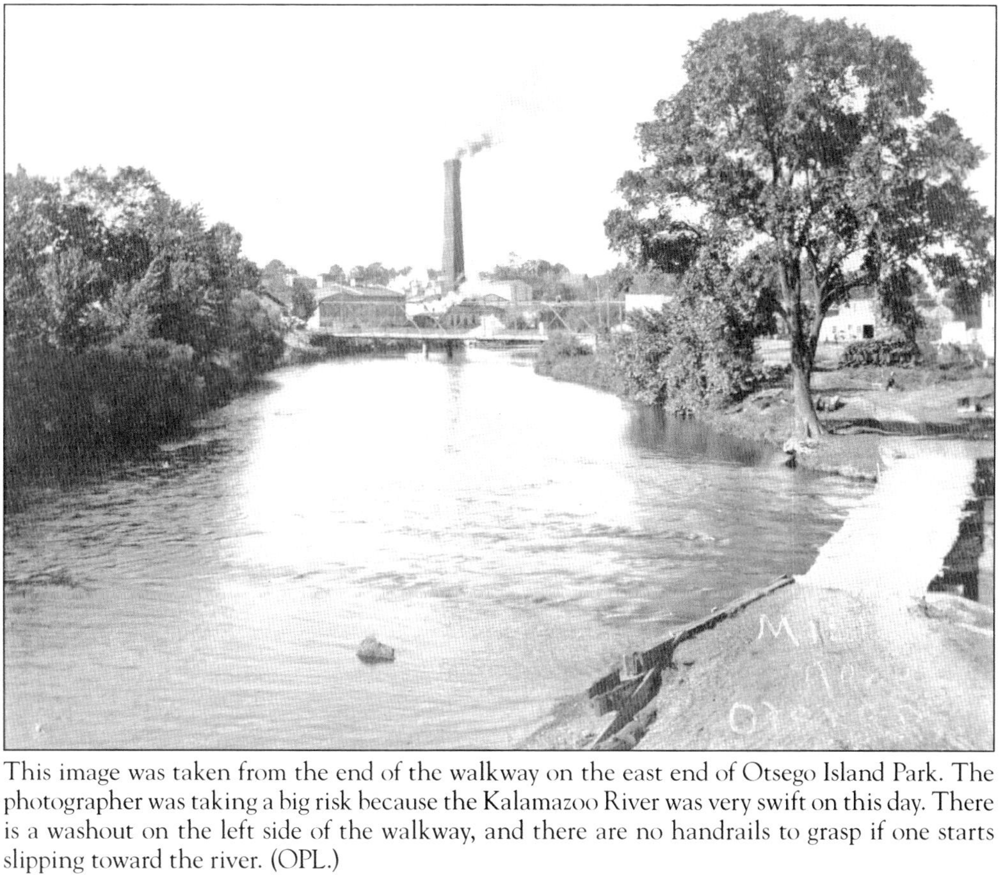

This image was taken from the end of the walkway on the east end of Otsego Island Park. The photographer was taking a big risk because the Kalamazoo River was very swift on this day. There is a washout on the left side of the walkway, and there are no handrails to grasp if one starts slipping toward the river. (OPL.)

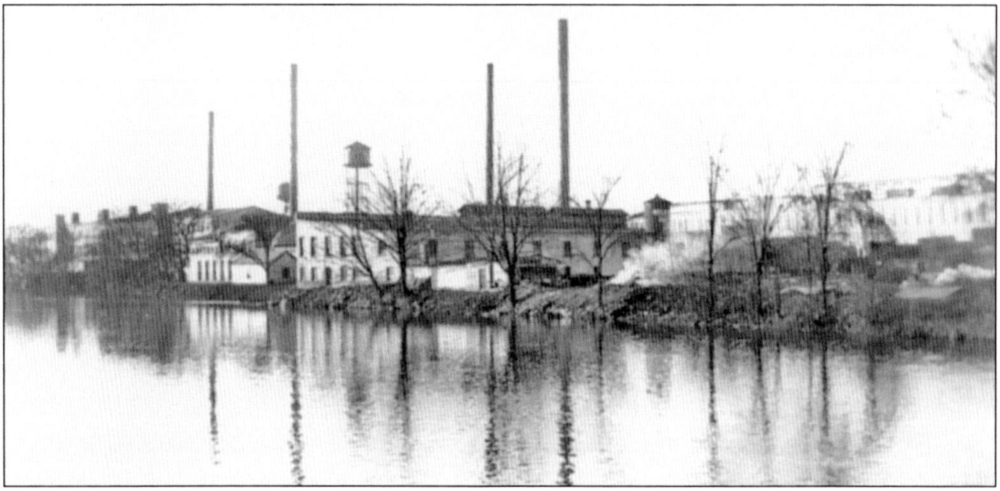

The MacSimBar Paper Mill sat along the banks of the Kalamazoo River in Otsego. It began operation in 1905 and included 20 beating and refining machines. It could produce 80,000 pounds of roofing and deadening felts, carpet lining, corrugated and perforated boards, and rag paper specialties. MacSimBar Paper Mill continued its operations until July 2004. (DDC.)

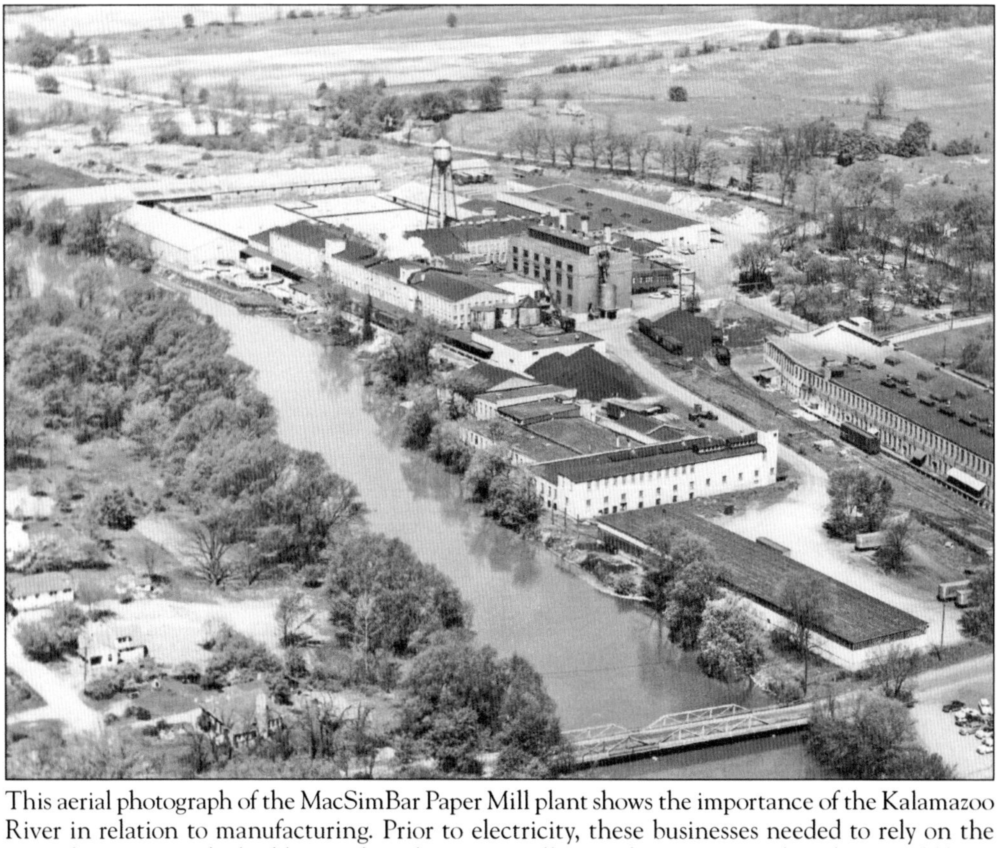

This aerial photograph of the MacSimBar Paper Mill plant shows the importance of the Kalamazoo River in relation to manufacturing. Prior to electricity, these businesses needed to rely on the water for powering the building and machinery as well as producing paper. They then would have used the river to ship their products to other towns and cities. (OHS.)

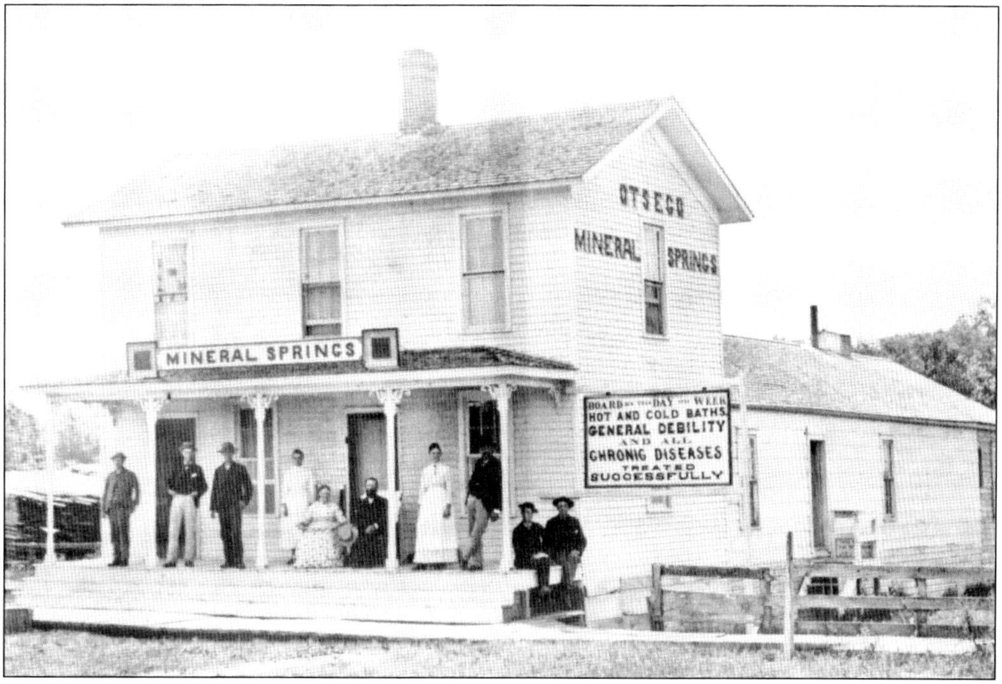

The Otsego Mineral Springs Bath House was built north of Farmer Street, which was frequently swampy due to natural springs. The bathhouse touted therapeutic waters and saw its heyday from the 1870s through the late 1880s. The Bardeen Paper Company, located across the street, had depleted the spring water so much that the bathhouse closed in 1887. (OHS.)

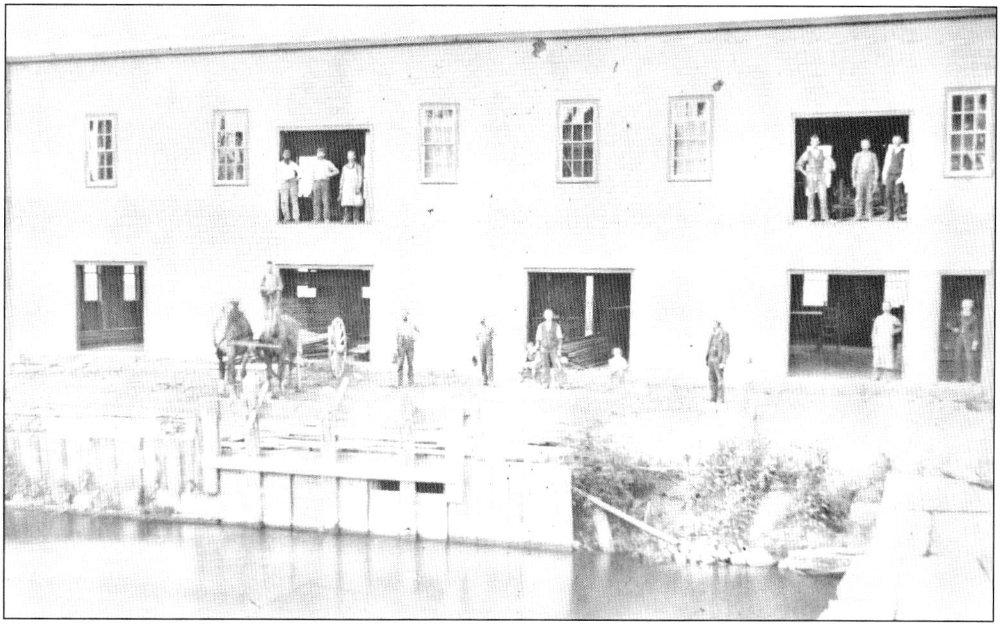

In 1873, the Empire Planing Mill in Otsego sat along the millrace of the Kalamazoo River. It provided planing, matching, and resawing services for sashes, doors, and blinds as well as storefronts, moldings, scrolls, and brackets. As seen in the photograph, customers could bring their products by horse and buggy or by boat to be worked on. (DDC.)

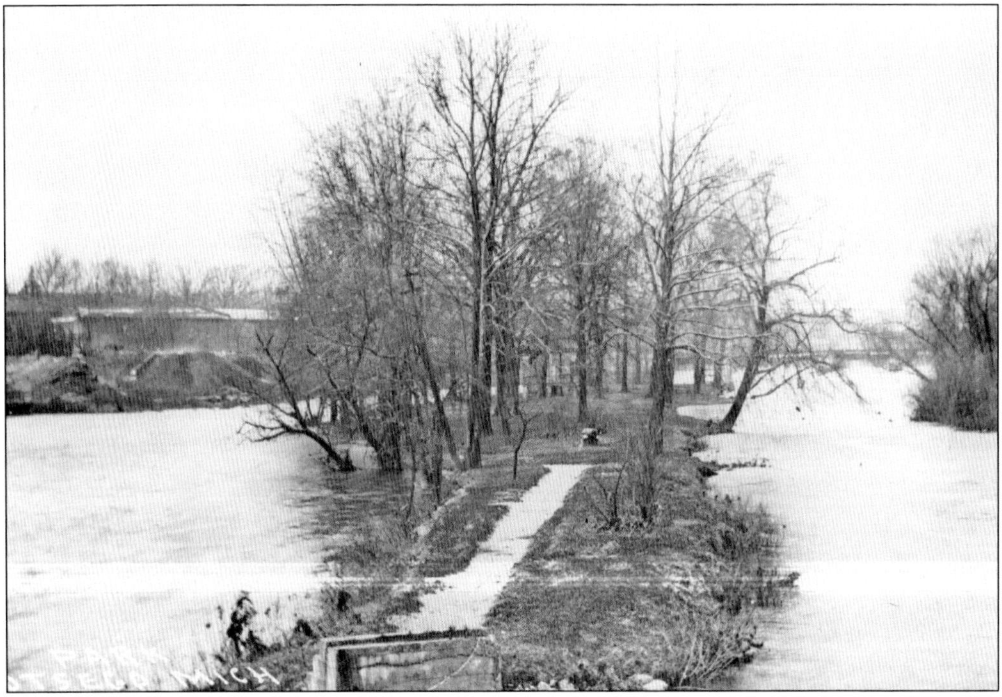

Otsego Island Park was a popular destination for families between 1870 and 1920. Building the Otsego City Dam raised the water level of the Kalamazoo River, submerging most of the island. When the dam is removed, the water level will recede once more, and the island is expected to become a popular destination once again. (DDC.)

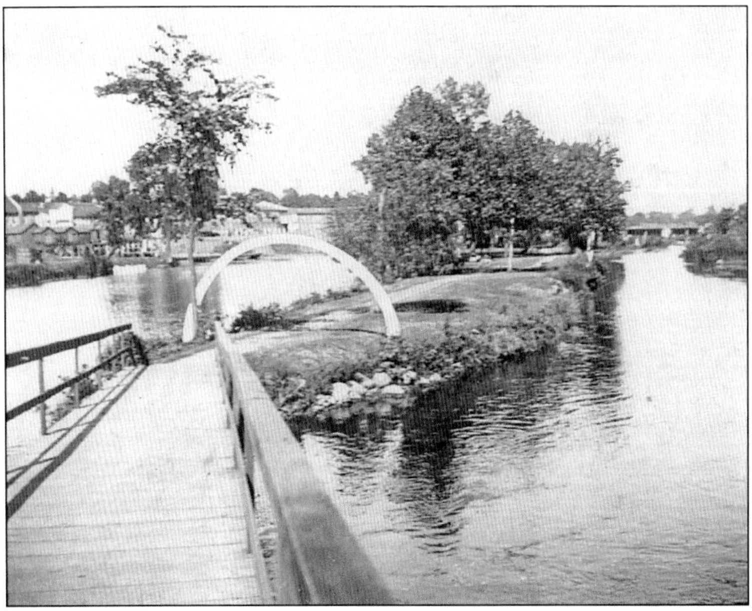

Otsego Island Park was in the Kalamazoo River just north of Farmer Street. From about 1870 to 1920, it was a popular destination for many trying to escape the summer heat. Once the Otsego City Dam had been put in place, the island became smaller and hard to reach. (OHS.)

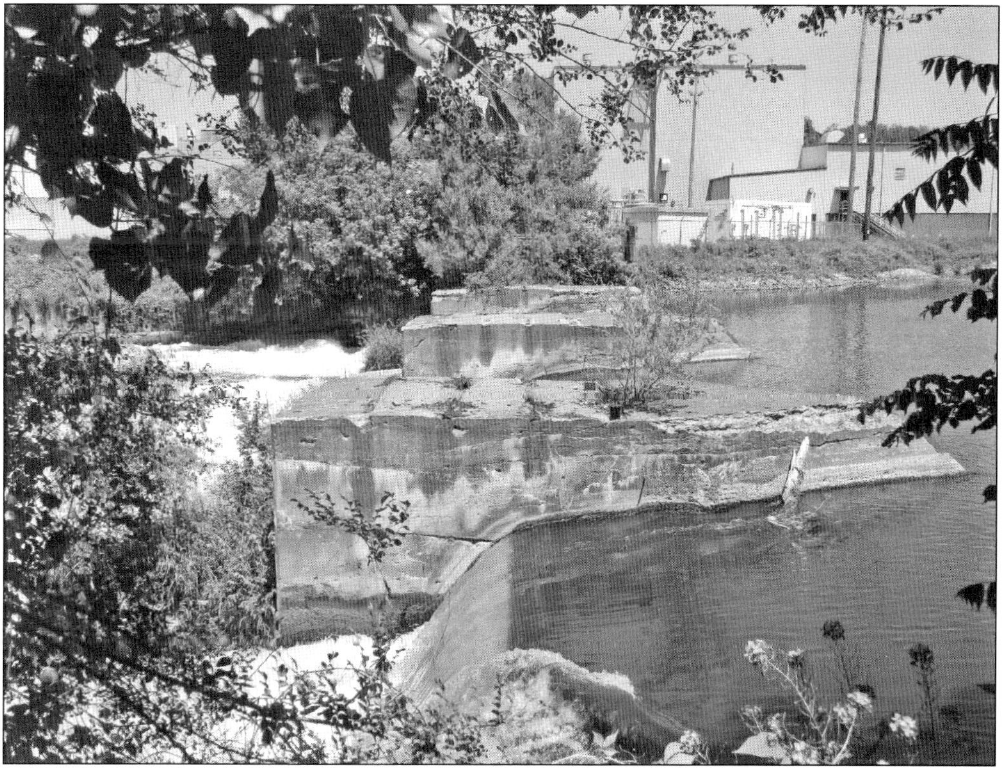

The Otsego City Dam was installed in the late 1800s. This was important for the regulation of water levels to ease shipping and to help power the paper mills along this stretch of the Kalamazoo River. However, it also changed the natural channel of the river. The dam is now in disrepair with contaminants from long forgotten industries built up behind it. City commissioners, along with the EPA, hope to remove this dam as part of a larger program along the Kalamazoo River. If the dam is removed, 1.8 miles of river would be remediated. (Both, authors' personal collections.)

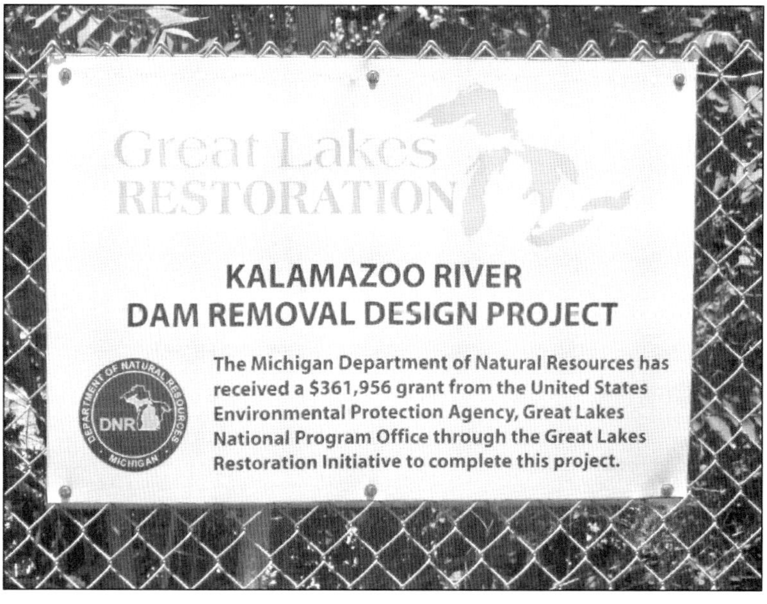

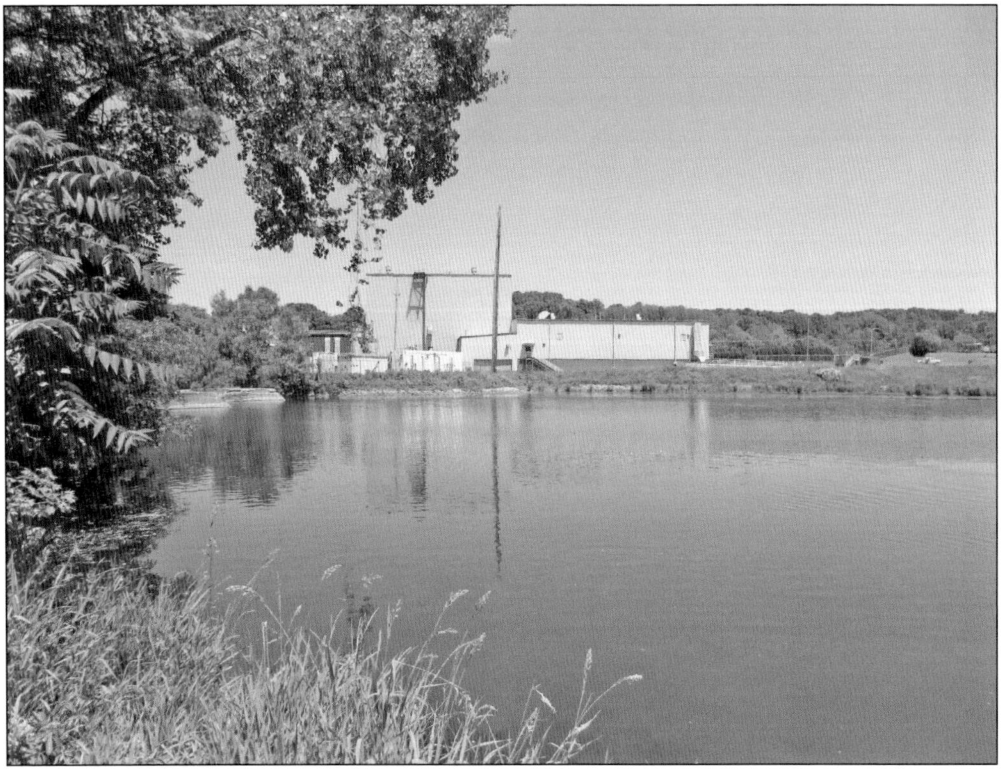

This plant lies at the corner of Farmer and East River Streets. The Otsego City Dam can be seen to the left. The business currently produces gypsum products, such as drywall. Prior to this, paper was produced and PCBs were released into the Kalamazoo River. Now that this is a gypsum plant, the river is no longer being polluted at this location. (Authors' personal collections.)

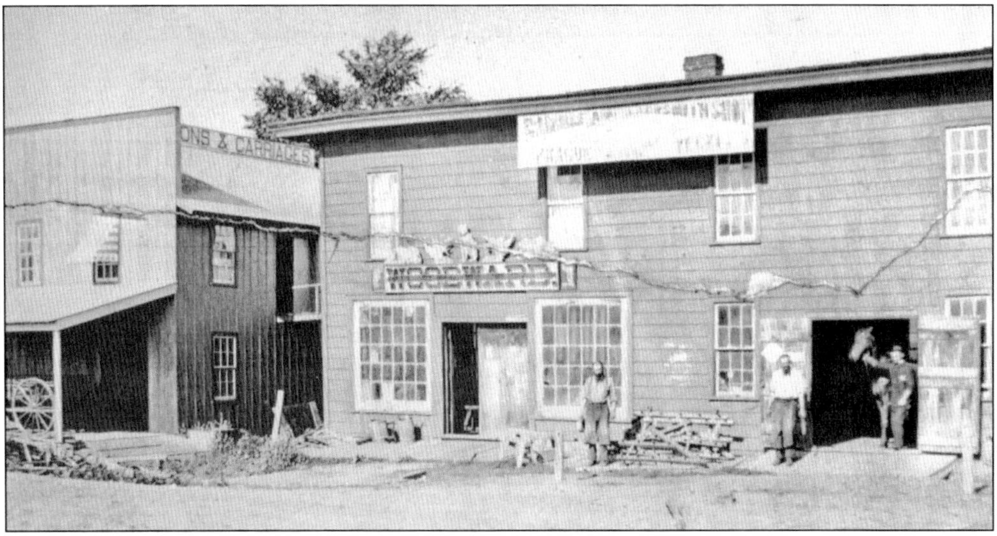

In the mid-1800s, the Sprague and Yeckley Carriage and Blacksmith Shop sat along the Kalamazoo River where the Department of Public Works building currently sits. This location is just north of the intersection of Farmer Street and M-89. This was an ideal spot for this type of business because it was convenient for travelers. (OHS.)

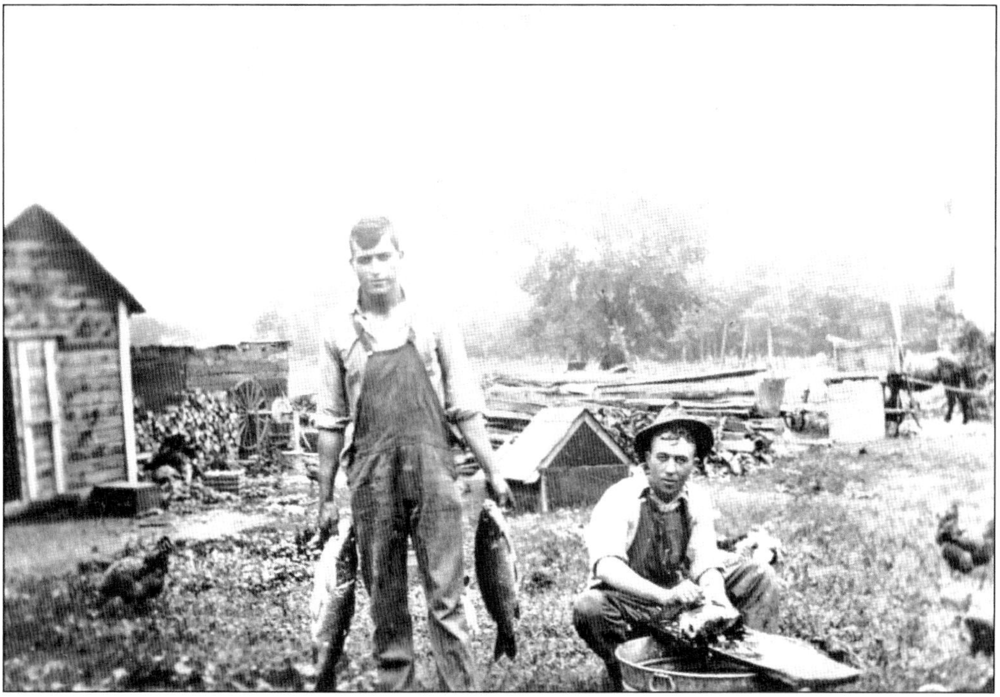

The Kalamazoo River was known for its great fishing. These men appear to have spent some of their free time fishing along the river on this day. Their catches may be enough to feed their families for dinner. The use of boats to fish had become increasingly common so the men could select their favorite fishing site, as many of these areas were no longer near the banks of the river. However, since the 1920s, the water conditions have deteriorated due to the industrial waste that has been discharged into the river, making fishing more dangerous and difficult. (Both, DDC.)

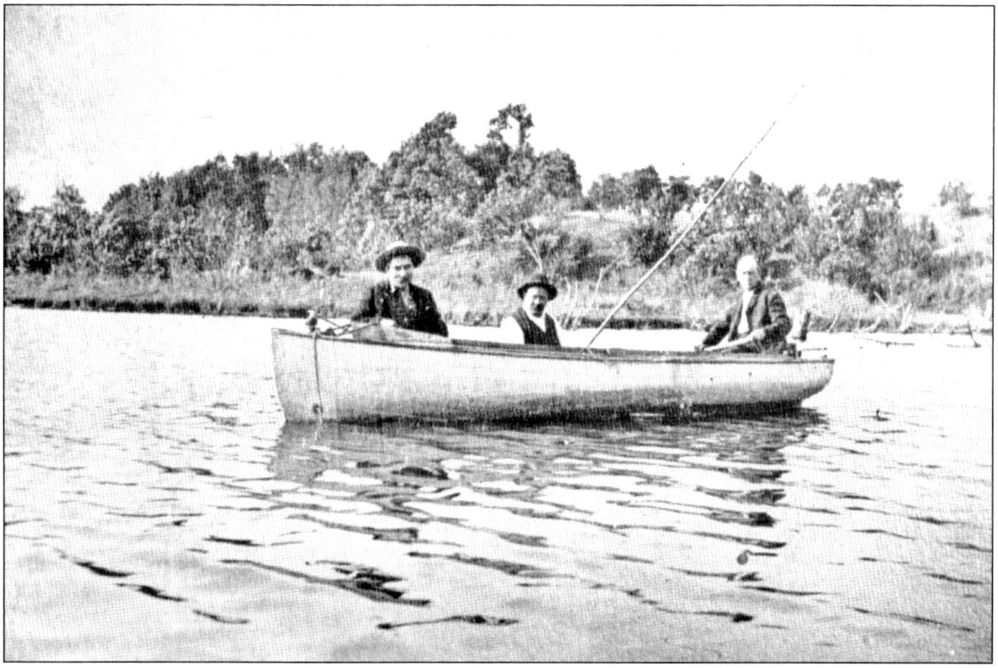

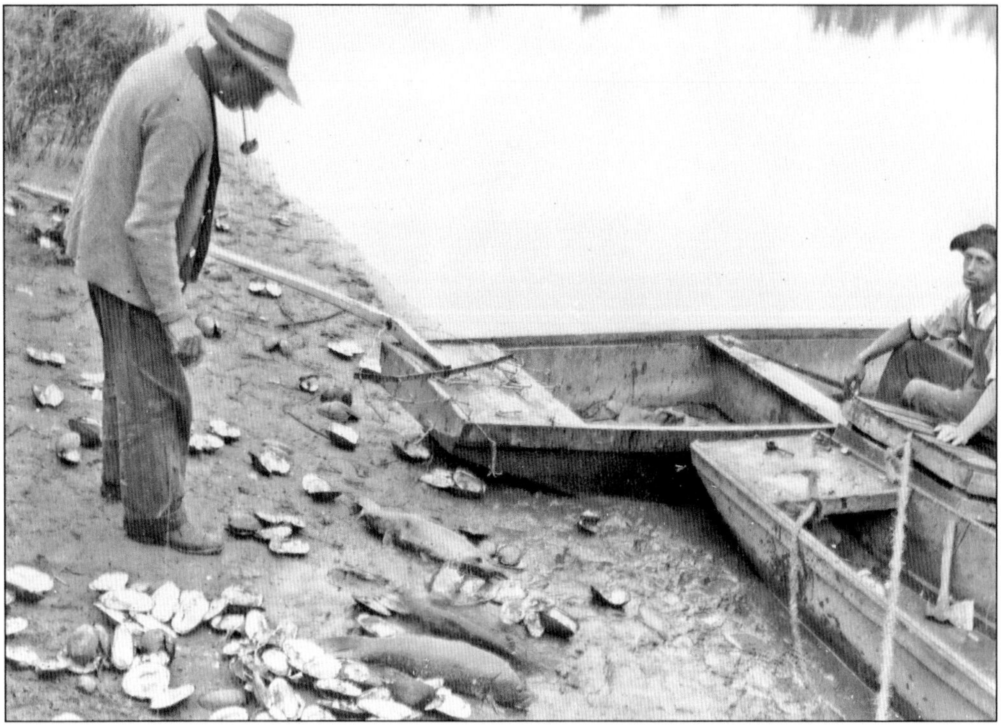

Residents along the Kalamazoo River were able to harvest large clams. This photograph shows one man admiring another's catch of the day, which also included some large fish. Clamming was curtailed because of pollution in the river devastating the clam population. More recently, clam communities are increasing due to management protection. (DDC.)

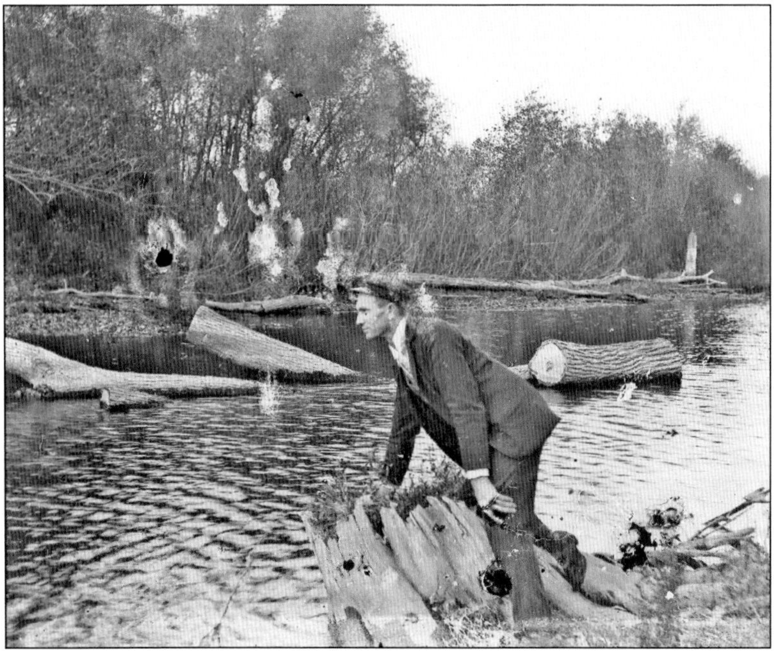

The Kalamazoo River transported many products. This was the fastest, most economical way of getting logs from the rural locations to the mills along the river. Spotters, like the man seen here, were sent out to make sure that the logs being sent down the river did not get jammed up, causing delays and potential flooding. (*Union Enterprise*, RL)

Six

West to Lake Michigan

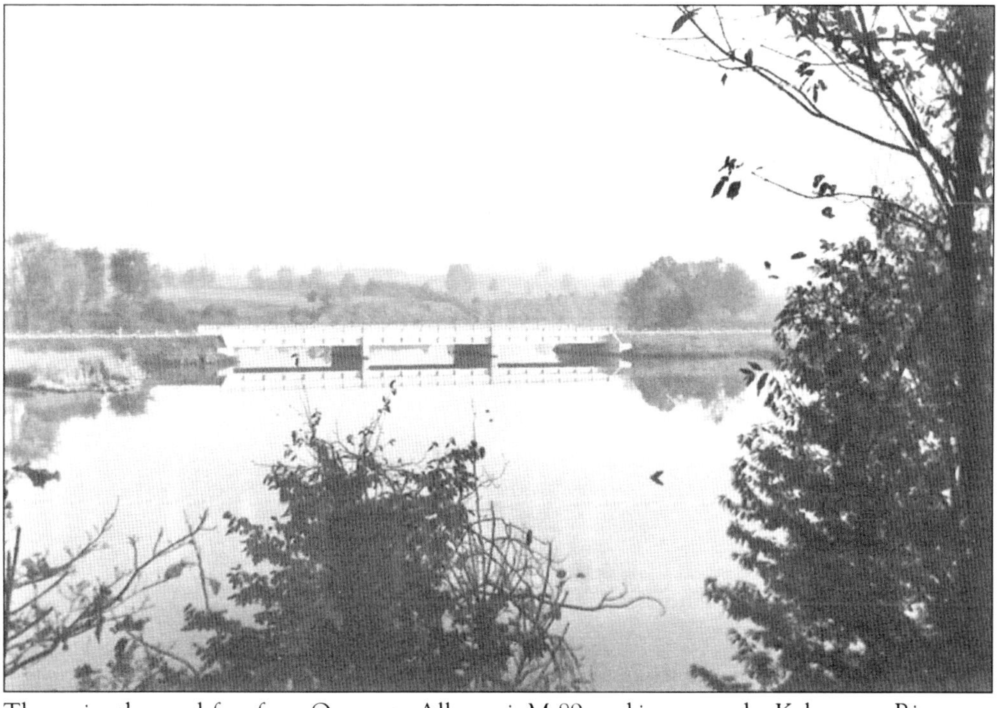

The major thoroughfare from Otsego to Allegan is M-89, and it crosses the Kalamazoo River one time in its 10-mile journey between the two cities. The M-89 Bridge is located just west of the Otsego city limits as the road begins its winding route through the peaceful countryside. (DDC.)

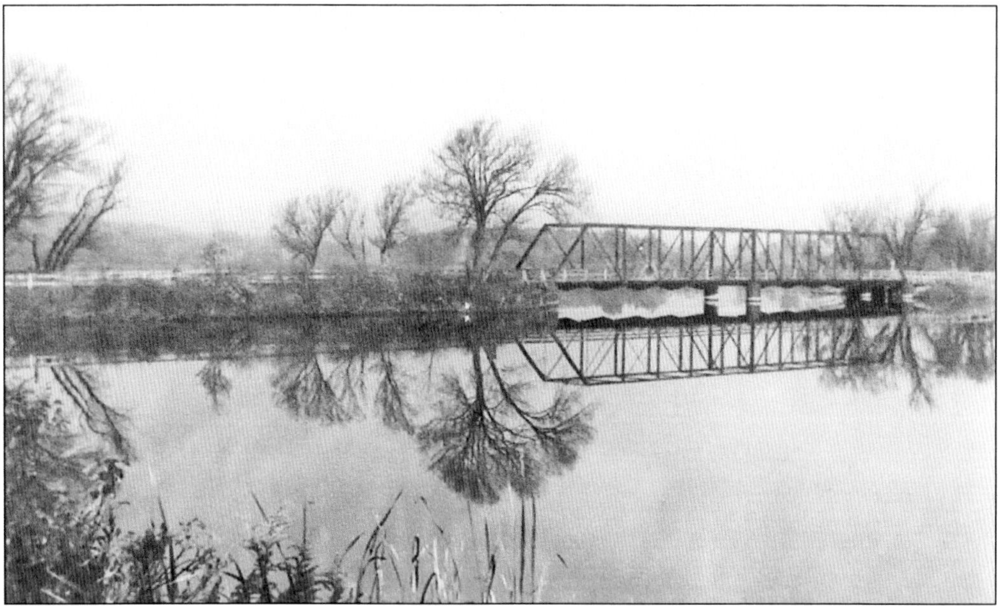

The Nineteenth Street Bridge went across the Kalamazoo River west of Otsego. However, it was torn down in 1950 and never replaced due to a large amount of swampy wetlands that Nineteenth Street traversed. It was not cost-effective or easy to maintain the bridge, and other options for crossing the Kalamazoo River were available within miles from here. (DDC.)

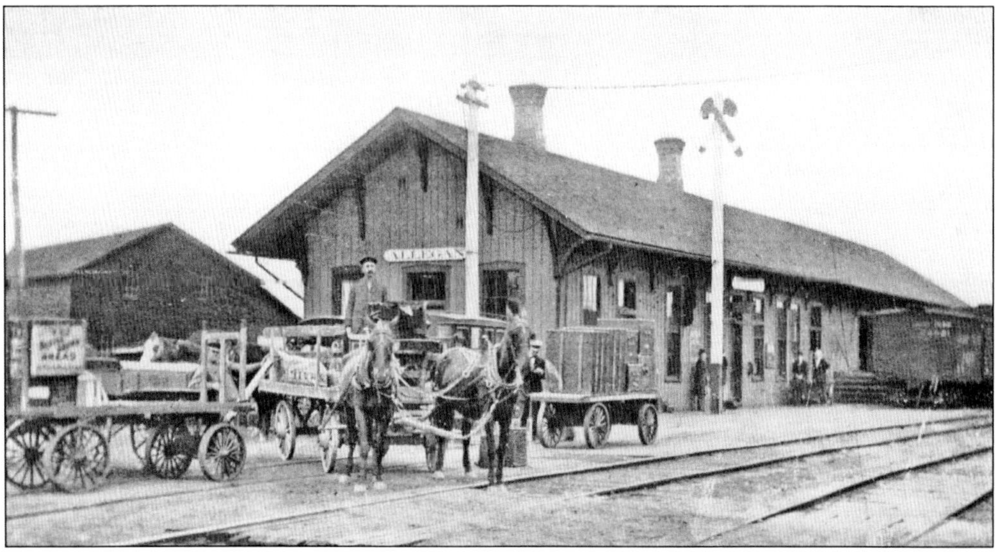

The Lake Shore & Michigan Southern Railroad had a station in Allegan. The main line connected Buffalo, New York, with Chicago, Illinois. This railroad transported passengers, coal, and iron ore between the early 1870s and late 1890s. In this photograph, some people are waiting on the train's arrival to welcome their family and friends and to pick up goods that have been transported from other cities. Others are waiting to board the train. (Craig Phillips.)

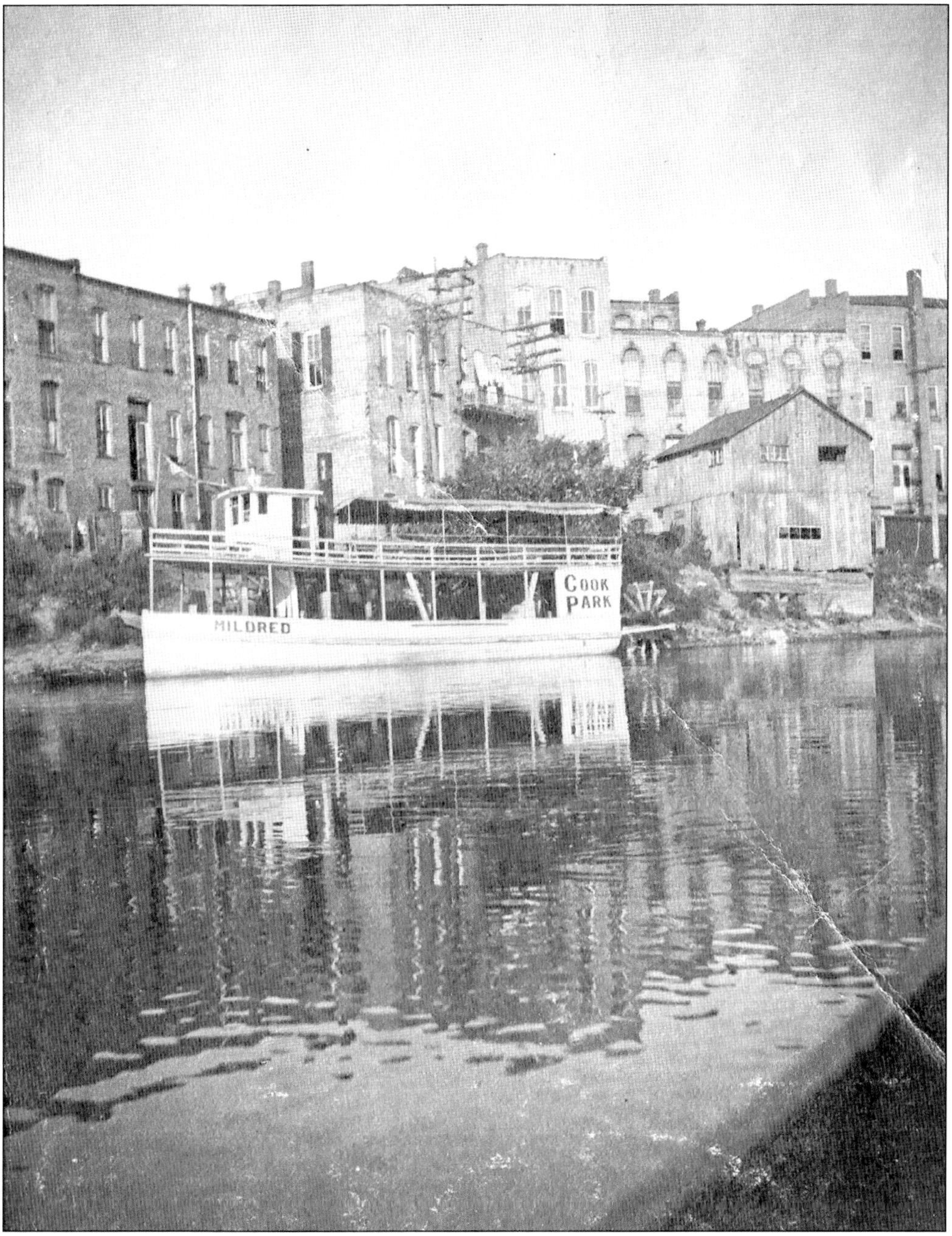

Kalamazoo River tour boat excursions have been enjoyed by residents and visitors for decades. One of the original steamers, *Mildred*, carried passengers to and from Cook Park in Allegan. Cook Park was the gathering place for families to spend time together picnicking, playing, and listening to bands that played in the gazebo. (Craig Phillips.)

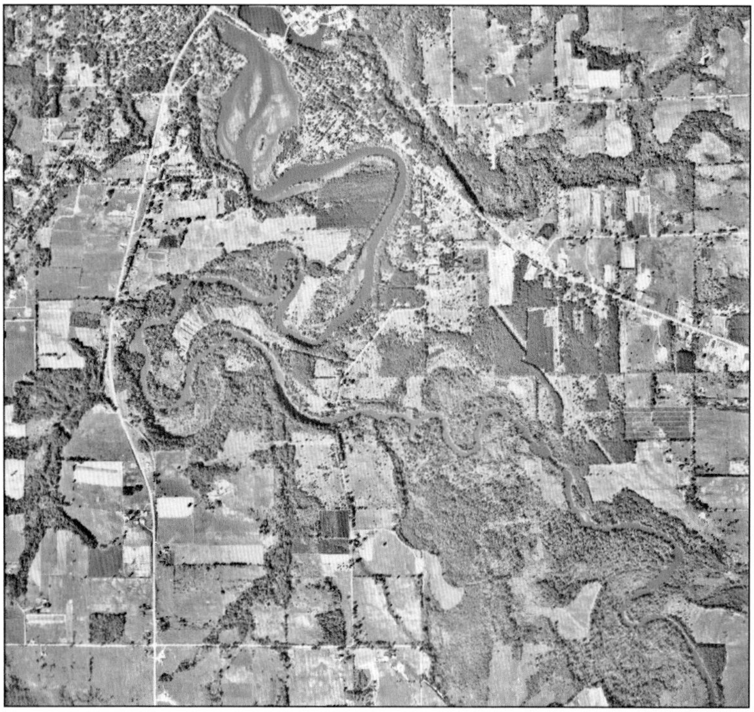

This Allegan aerial photograph is from September 1967. The white lines represent the two main roads leading into Allegan. M-40 is the north–south road on the left, and M-89 is the southeast–northwest road in the upper right. The Kalamazoo River meanders through the countryside providing freshwater to the area and a recreation location for people. (Upjohn.)

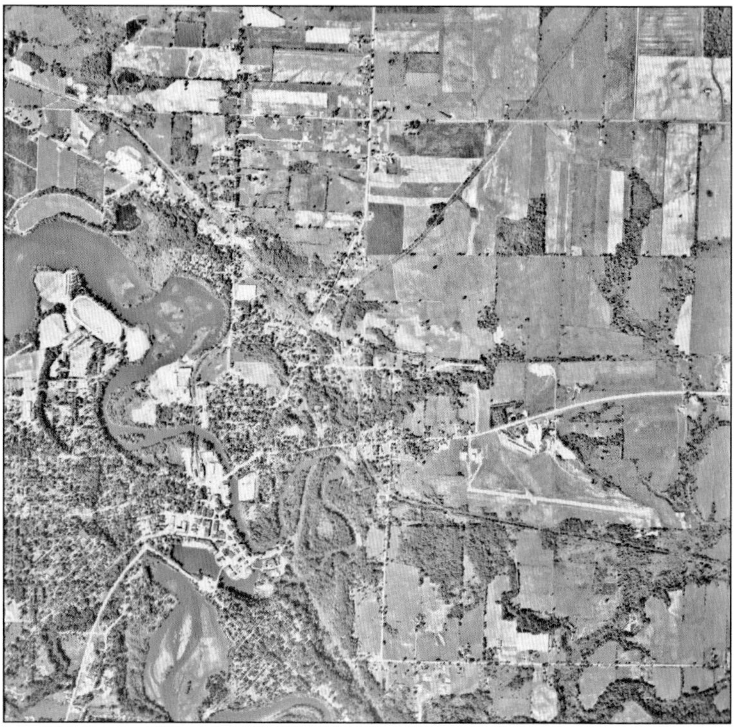

Allegan grew up along the Kalamazoo River. This 1967 aerial photograph shows that nearly every place along the river where a house or structure could be built, one was. Urban growth was greater on the southwest bank of the river because of higher elevation, so the soil was not good for farming but perfect for living above the floodplain. (Upjohn.)

This aerial view of downtown Allegan was taken prior to the 1950s when the M-89 highway was built. This is a great example of how the Kalamazoo River meanders through the landscape and cities take advantage of the waterfront. In this photograph, the river flows from right to left around the east side of Allegan. (Craig Phillips.)

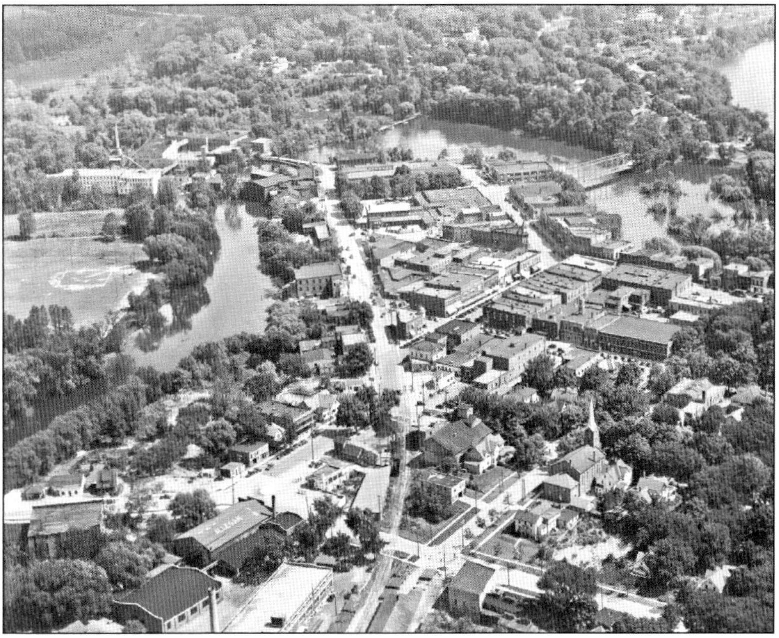

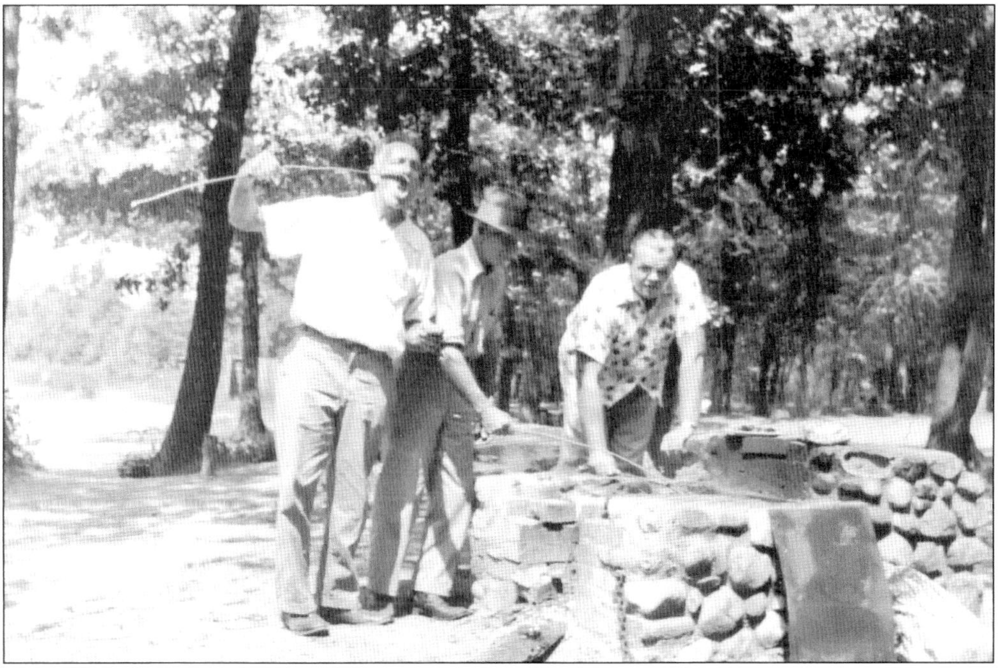

Picnicking was a frequent occurrence along the Kalamazoo River throughout Allegan. Here, men are enjoying their food at one of the many grill sites, with the river flowing behind them. Craig Phillips recalled stories about many Sunday adventures along the river with his family. (Craig Phillips.)

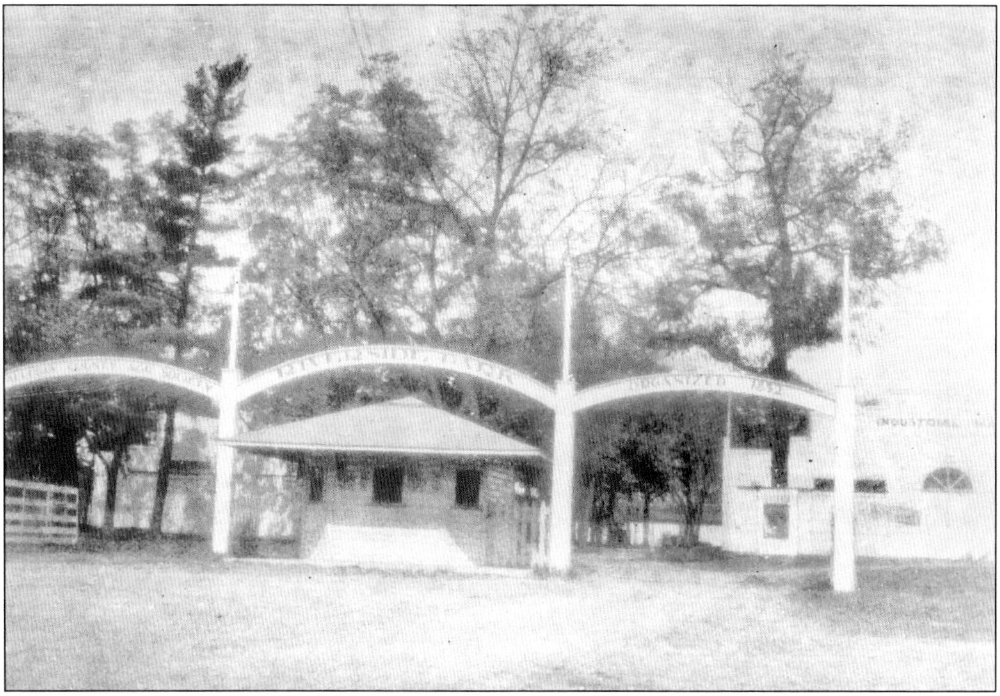

The Allegan County Agricultural Society was established in 1852. In 1854, Riverside Park, located along the Kalamazoo River, became the site of the Allegan County Fair, created by the society. It has become one of the largest in the state and the first to hold an evening fair. Among the attractions were the Great Houdini and the Wonderful Douglas. (Craig Phillips.)

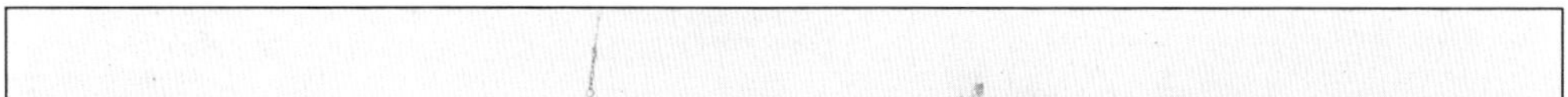

Fish from the Kalamazoo River was a staple for many families, which meant a lot of fishing needed to be done. Elaborate fishing nets were constructed in hopes of catching more than one fish at a time. This photograph from 1926 shows two such nets in the river near Allegan. The basket would be manually lowered into and raised out of the water. (Kalamazoo Valley Museum.)

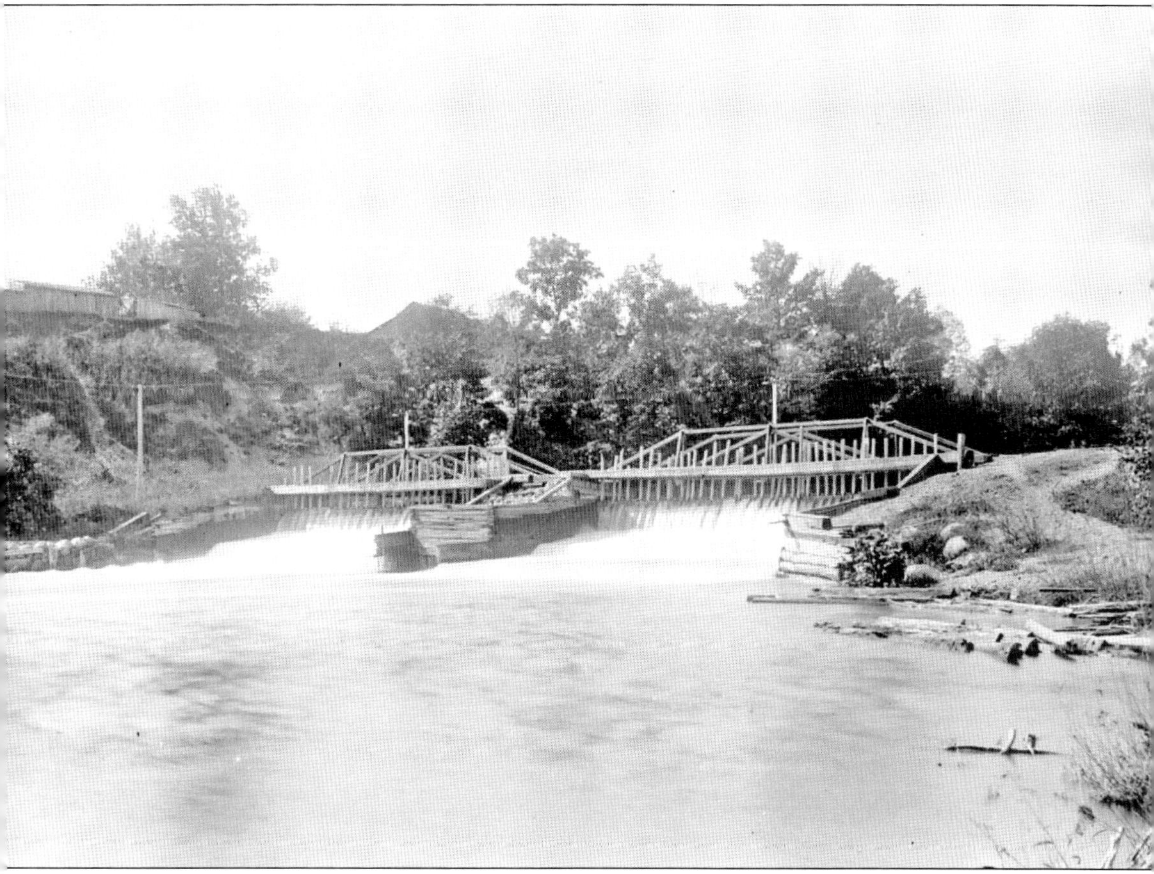

Trowbridge Dam was built to provide hydroelectric power to the residents of Allegan and all along the Kalamazoo River west to Kalamazoo. This structure was one of the more elaborate dams constructed at the time and provided large amounts of power. This view is looking back from below the dam as it was being built. (RL.)

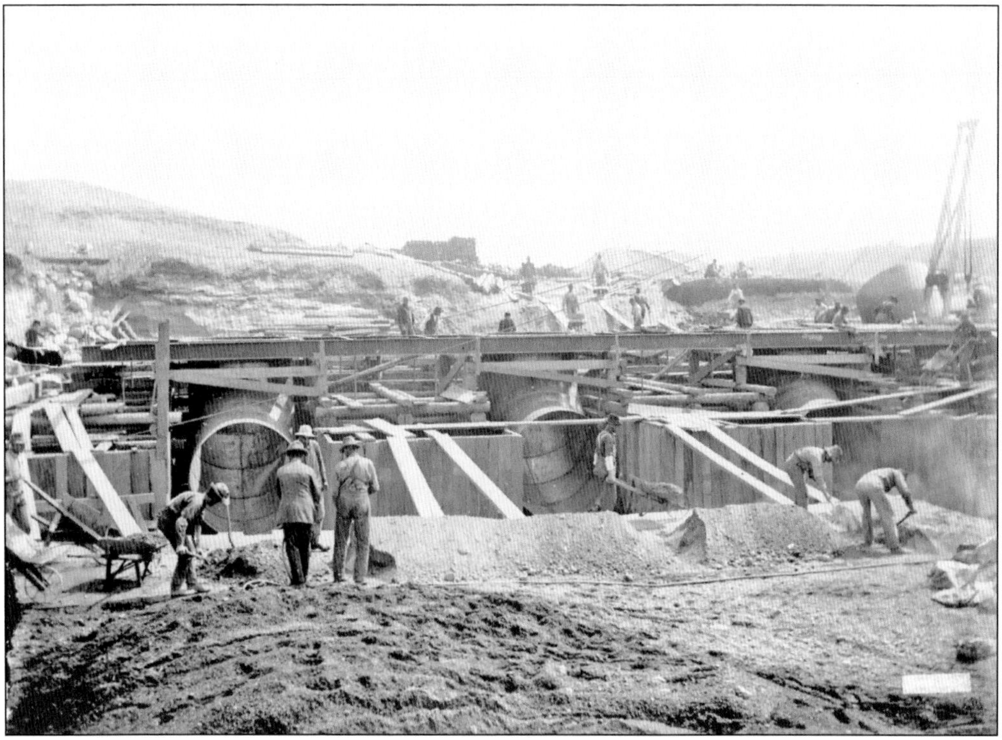

The Trowbridge Dam and Powerhouse was built in 1899 and provided hydroelectric power to the city of Kalamazoo. This project employed a large number of men from the local area with expertise in masonry as well as building construction. Although it may look like a haphazard scene, the men at right are laying boards and logs precisely where they need to be to make the dam and powerhouse as safe as possible at the time. These photographs could have been a mid-spring or mid-autumn day as some of the workers are wearing jackets over their long-sleeve shirts. (Both, *Union Enterprise*, RL.)

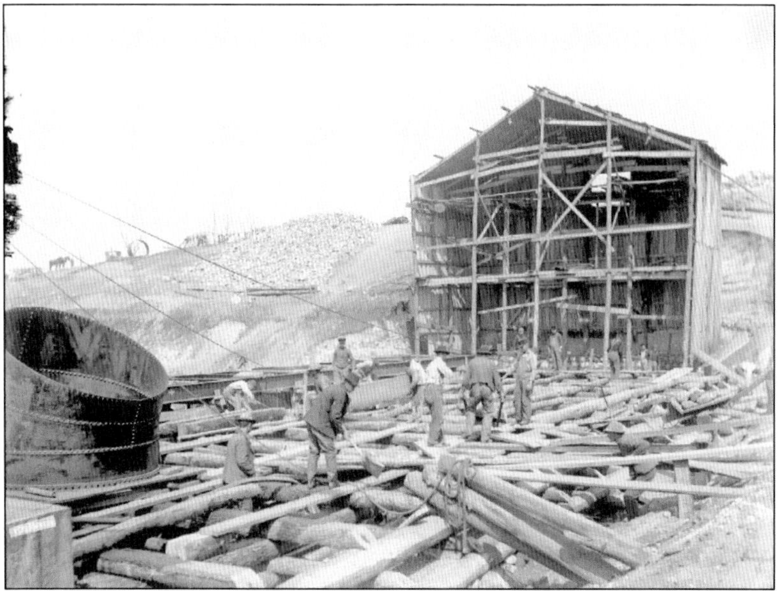

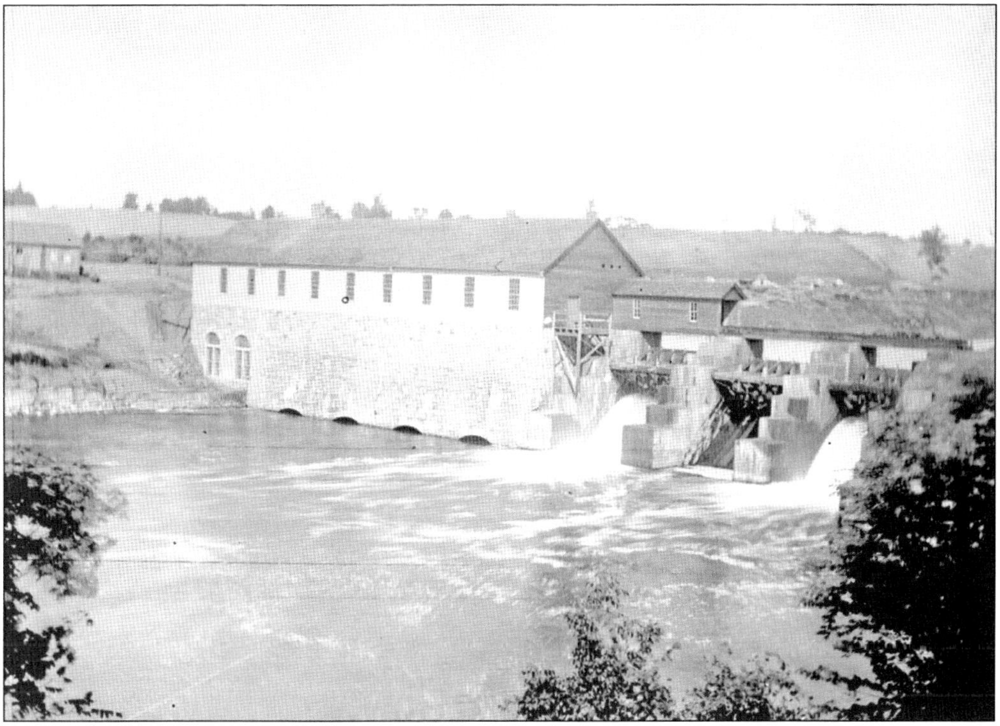

The Trowbridge Dam and Powerhouse is perhaps the most recognized dam along the Kalamazoo River. It is also one of the dams in the most disrepair. These types of dams have a 50-year lifespan, and the Trowbridge Dam is over 100 years old. There are plans to remove this dam but remediation steps need to be taken before this can happen. (*Union Enterprise*, RL.)

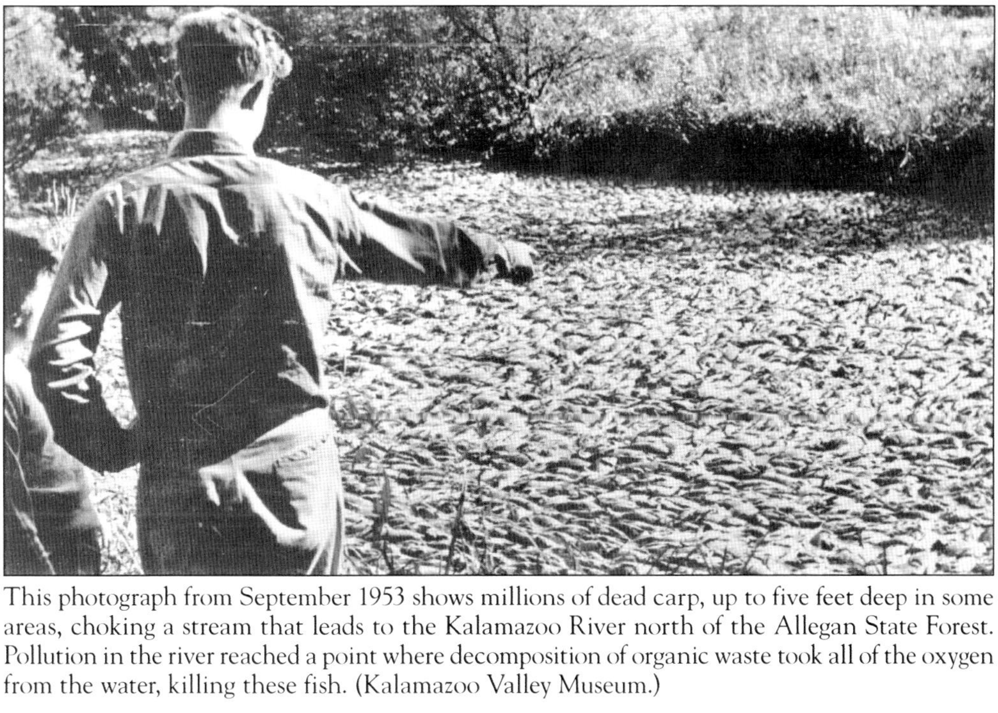

This photograph from September 1953 shows millions of dead carp, up to five feet deep in some areas, choking a stream that leads to the Kalamazoo River north of the Allegan State Forest. Pollution in the river reached a point where decomposition of organic waste took all of the oxygen from the water, killing these fish. (Kalamazoo Valley Museum.)

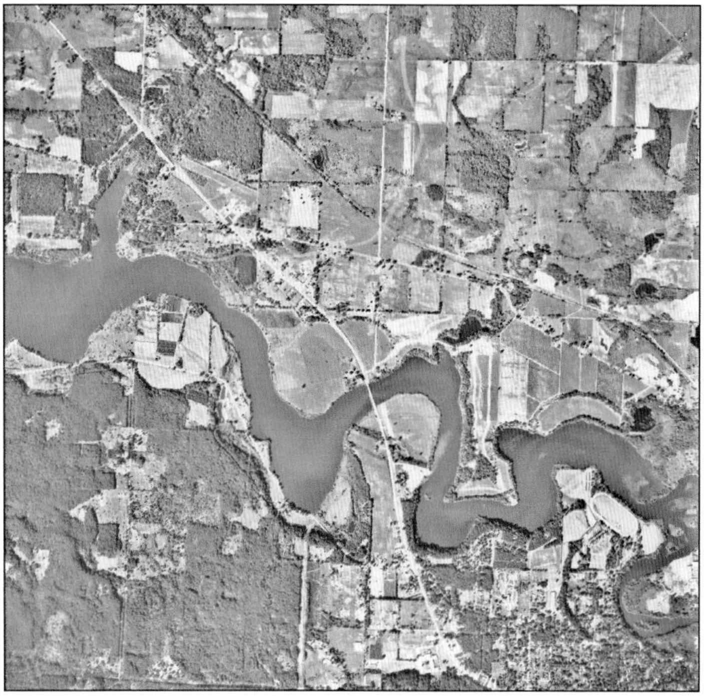

This 1967 Allegan aerial photograph show just how much the width of the Kalamazoo River varies as it winds through the landscape. The inside of the two curves of the river at center contain flat, fertile land. They are both large farming areas. (Upjohn.)

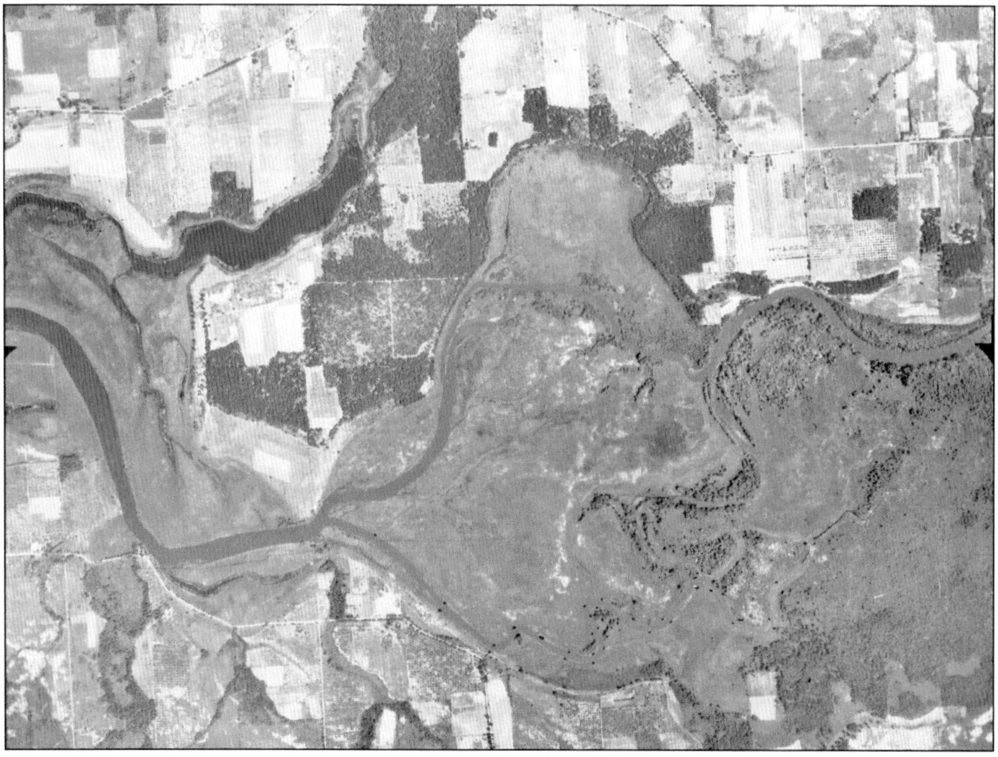

This 1938 aerial photograph shows the many decades of the Kalamazoo River modifying the landscape. As the river flows, it meanders across the easiest route and can create a wide floodplain, as seen here. The river continues to flow downstream to its destination. (Upjohn.)

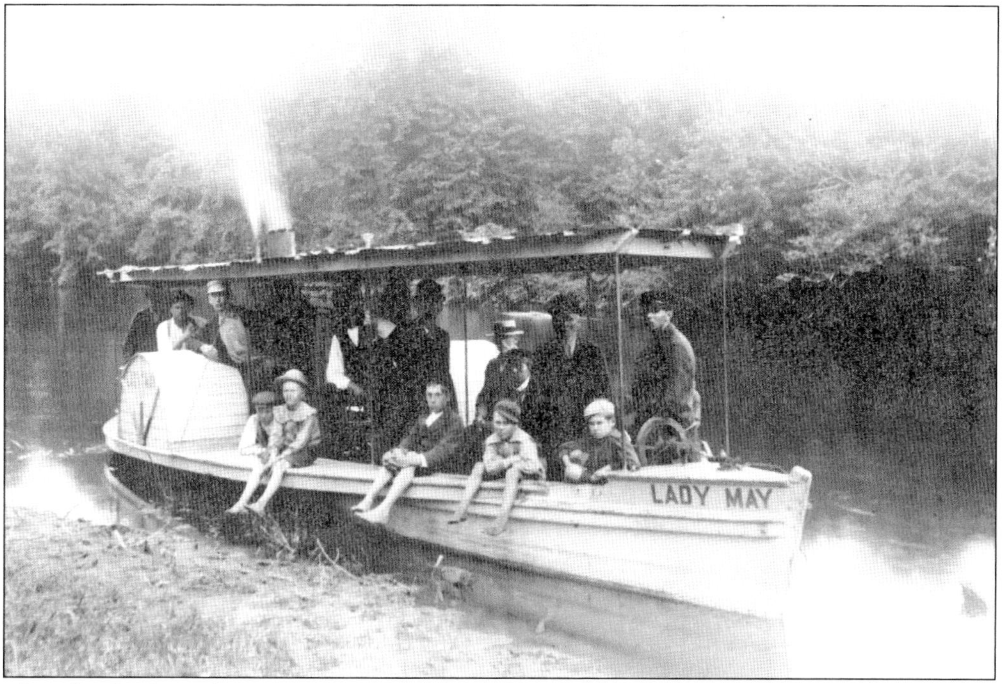

The side-wheeler *Lady May* took small groups on tours along the Kalamazoo River, mainly between Allegan and New Richmond during the 1890s. People who took the tour could see lush green woods and how the river swirled and cut the banks until tall trees fell into the water. They could also enjoy wildlife such as blue herons, eagles, turkey vultures, and white-tailed deer. (RL.)

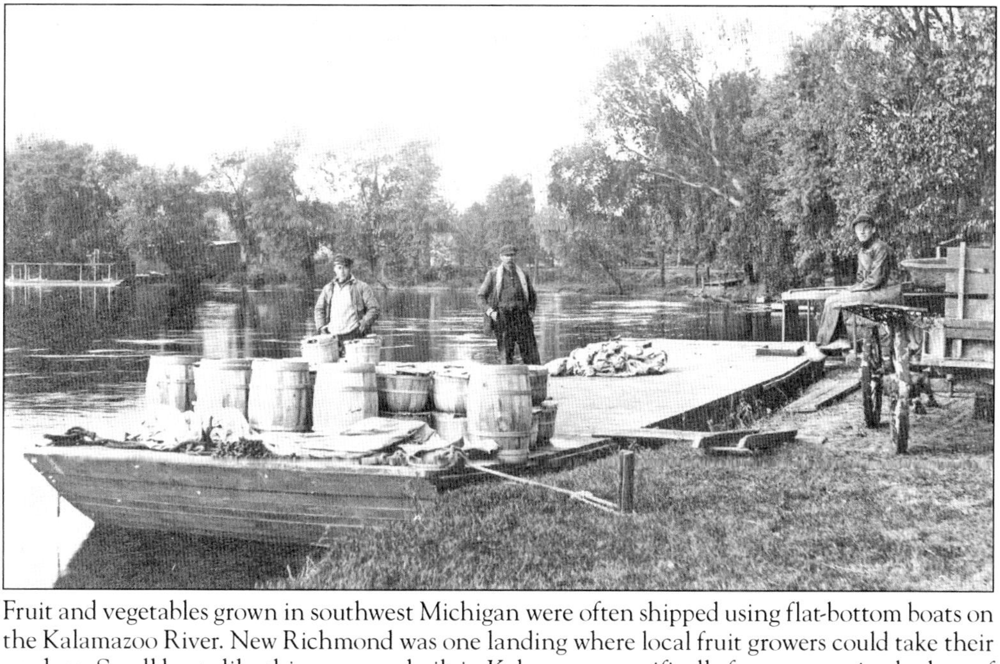

Fruit and vegetables grown in southwest Michigan were often shipped using flat-bottom boats on the Kalamazoo River. New Richmond was one landing where local fruit growers could take their produce. Small boats like this one were built in Kalamazoo specifically for transporting baskets of fruit from towns along the river to Saugatuck. The baskets were then loaded onto a lake steamer for continued transport. (SDHC.)

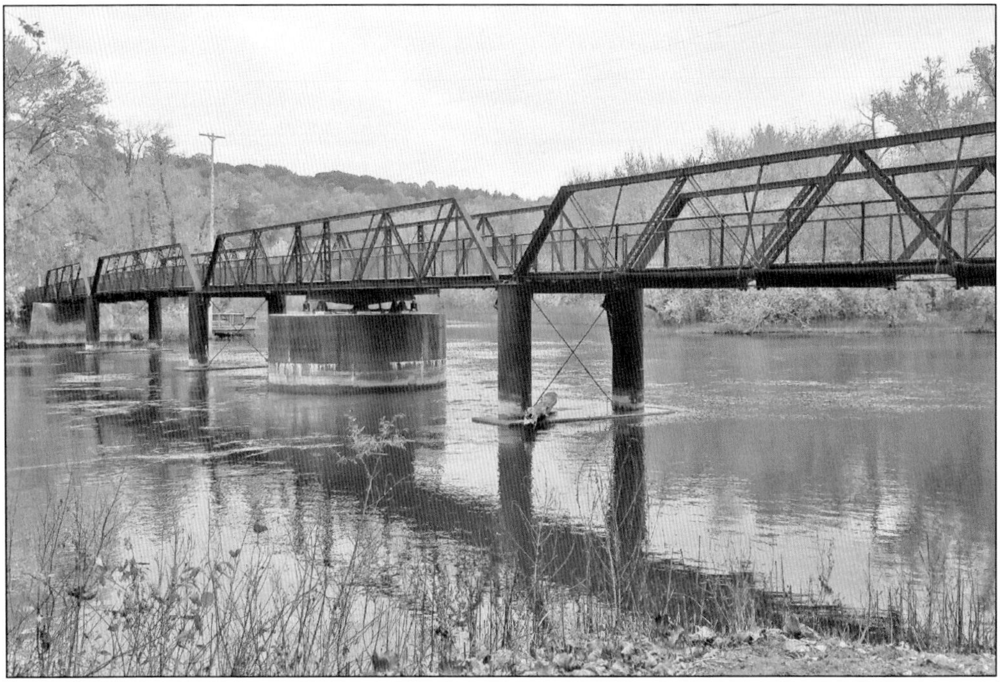

The Fifty-Seventh Street Bridge, also known as the New Richmond Bridge (above), was originally designed as a swing bridge to allow riverboat traffic to pass through here easily on the way to and from Lake Michigan. This bridge is the last surviving swing bridge in the United States and only one of four bridges that have pony truss spans in their construction. The bridge was used for auto traffic until 1980, was listed in 1998 in the National Register of Historic Places (below), and was restored for pedestrian traffic exclusively in 2005. The New Richmond Bridge is now part of the New Richmond Bridge Park, which contains five fishing piers, a half mile of boardwalk trails, a boat launch, and a railroad bridge running parallel to it. This bridge serves 30 to 40 trains a day. (Both, authors' personal collections.)

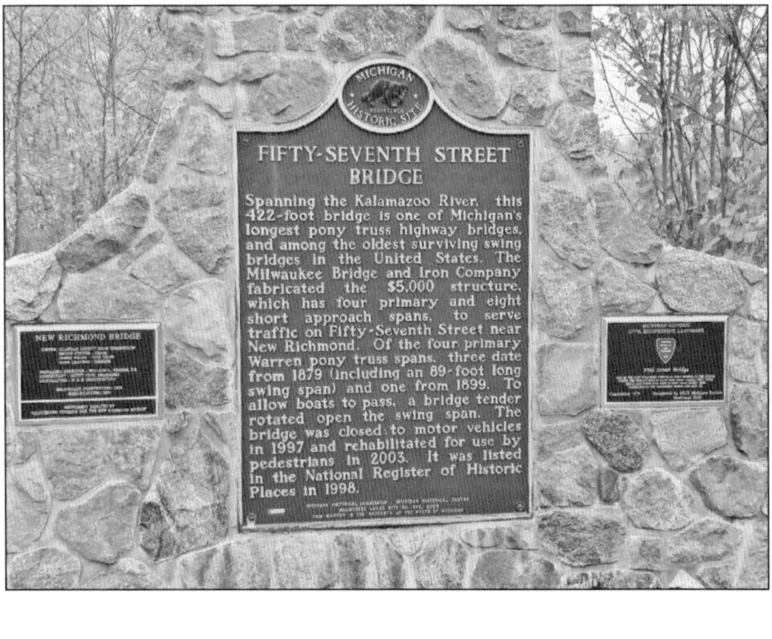

The steam-powered side-wheeler *A.R. Heath* took passengers between Saugatuck and New Richmond daily. Launched in 1901, it was publicized as the best shallow water steamer ever because it needed less than a foot of water to move. The steamer ran for 12 years before it was abandoned in Saugatuck along the riverbank. On this day, around 1900, the steamer has a full load of passengers taking advantage of the beautiful weather and river scenery. (SDHC.)

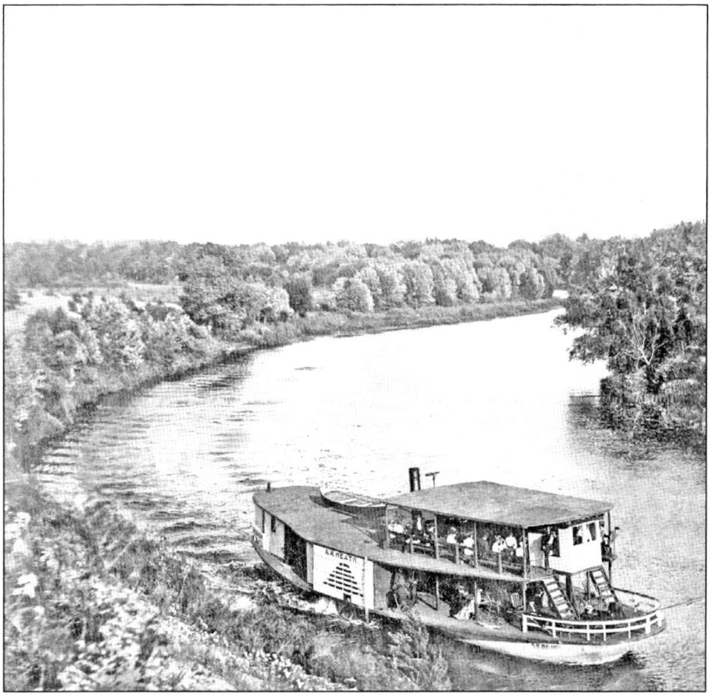

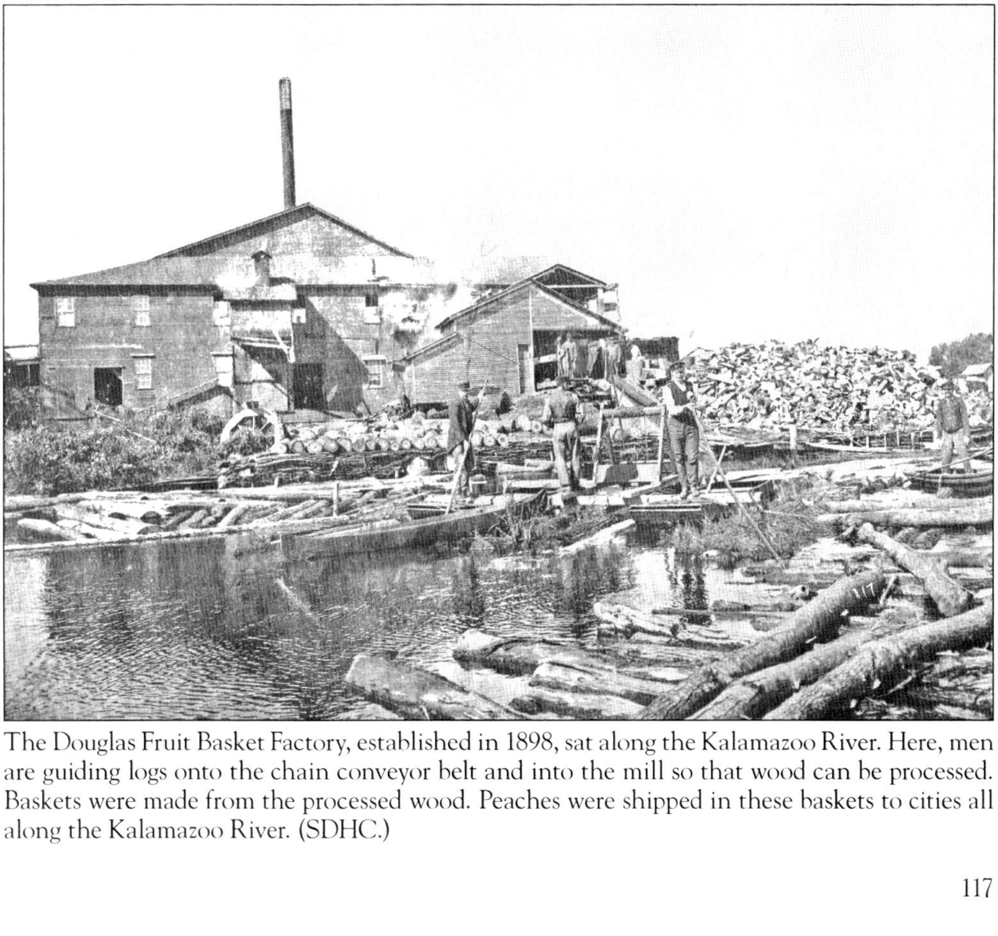

The Douglas Fruit Basket Factory, established in 1898, sat along the Kalamazoo River. Here, men are guiding logs onto the chain conveyor belt and into the mill so that wood can be processed. Baskets were made from the processed wood. Peaches were shipped in these baskets to cities all along the Kalamazoo River. (SDHC.)

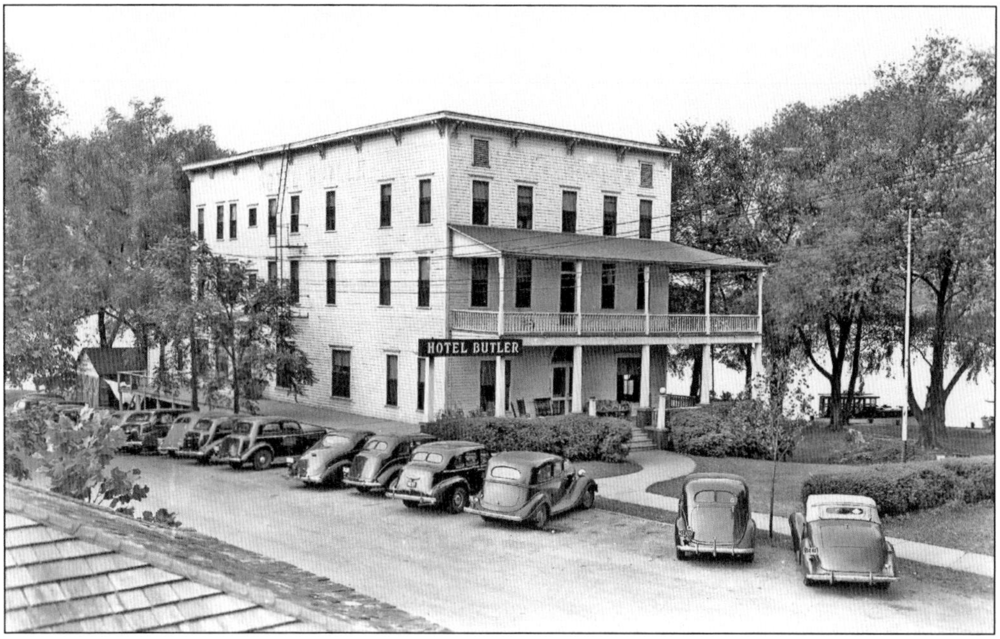

The Butler Restaurant in Saugatuck was originally a gristmill and was converted into a hotel. The Butler Hotel operated from 1901 until the 1960s when fire protection regulations were put into place. The top two floors were deemed a fire liability and were removed. Throughout the decades, it was a popular destination for visitors because it sat on the Kalamazoo River and was close to the center of town. College-age women would take jobs as waitresses and housekeepers at the Butler Hotel. They were provided with uniforms, housing, and a decent wage. As seen here, they took great pride in their appearance while working at the hotel. (Both, SDHC.)

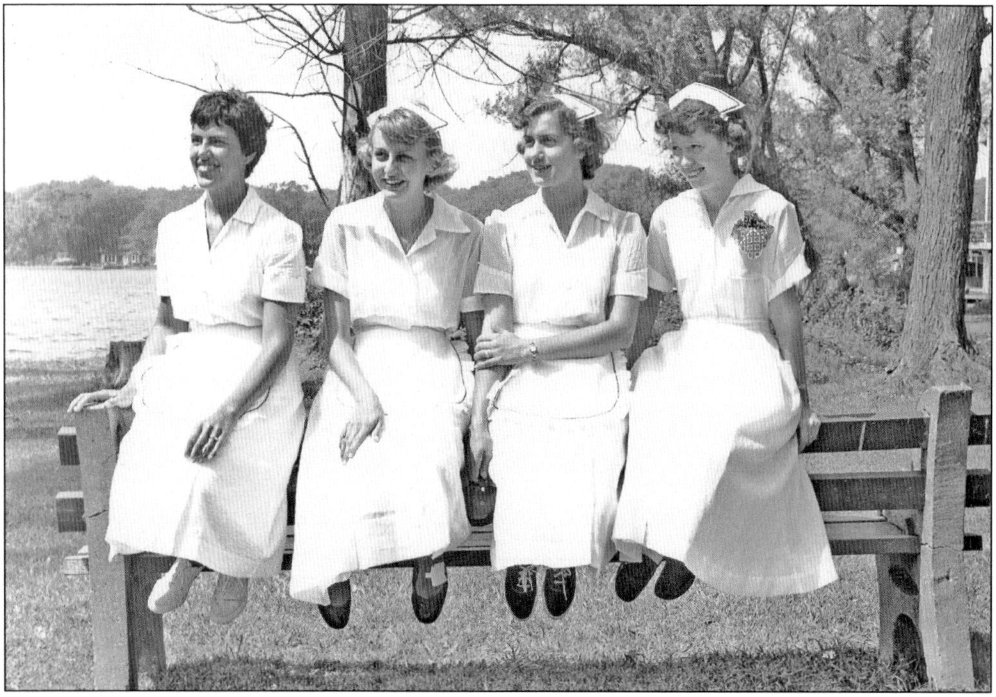

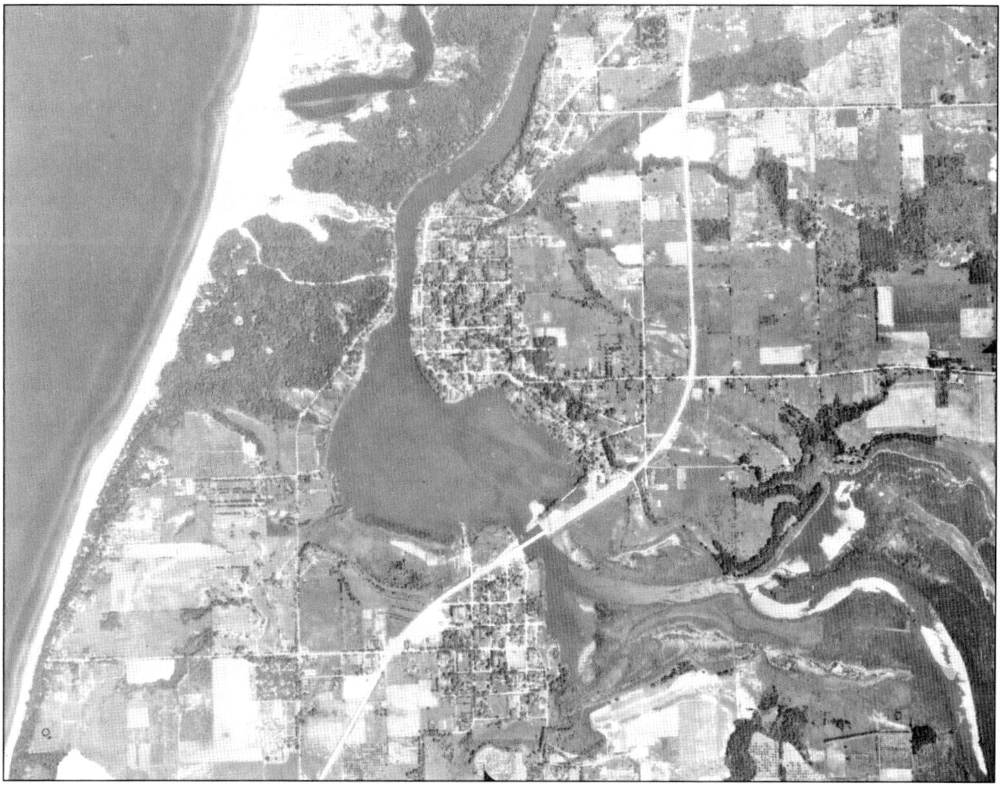

In the lower right corner of this 1938 Saugatuck aerial photograph, sediment buildup in the channel is obvious as the white areas. As the river meanders, the velocity of the flow changes. When it slows, this sediment is deposited along the bottom and sides of the channel. (Upjohn.)

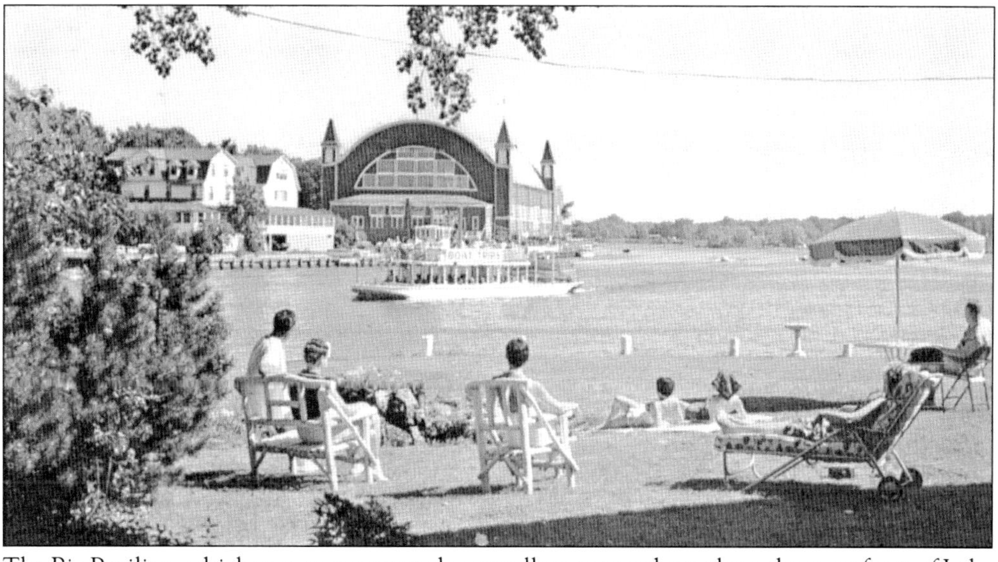

The Big Pavilion, which was enormous and unusually structured, sat along the waterfront of Lake Kalamazoo on the Kalamazoo River. The building housed restaurants, bars, a movie theater, and a large dance floor. Large lake ships, such as the steamer *Tennessee*, would bring many visitors from cities such as Chicago to enjoy the entertainment that the Big Pavilion provided. (SDHC.)

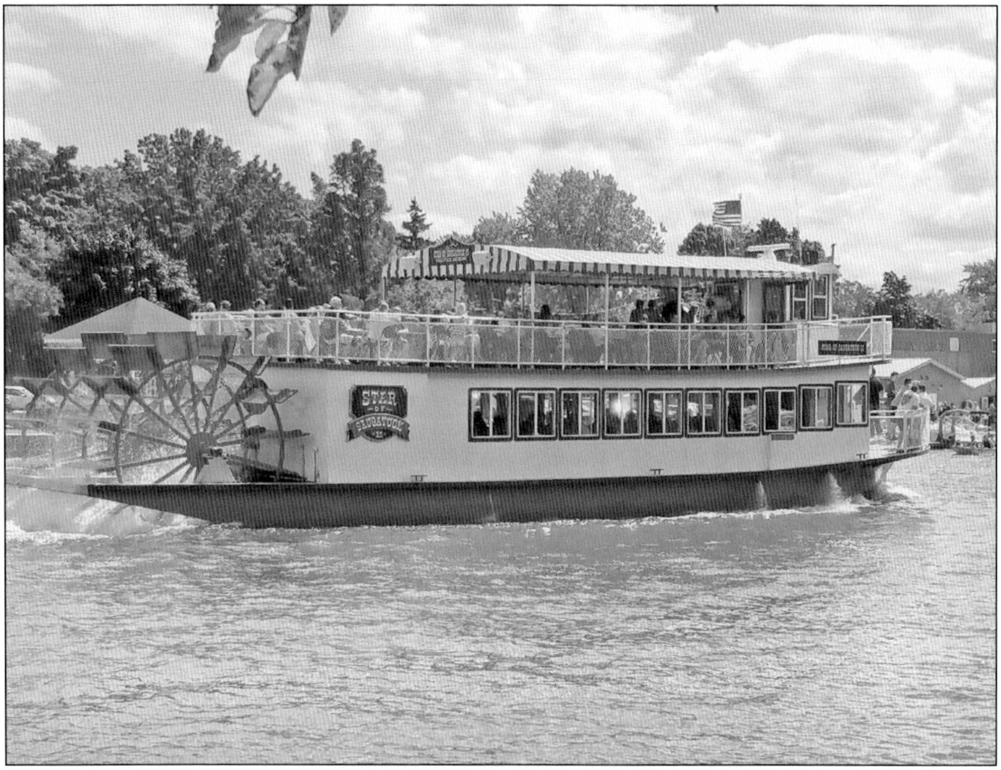

The Saugatuck/Douglas area has had boat excursions since the late 1960s because of the river's calmness and easy access to Lake Michigan. *The Queen of Saugatuck*, later renamed *Star of Saugatuck*, continued to provide tours until 2000, when the *Star of Saugatuck II* replaced it. These trips have live narration that highlights local landmarks, points of interest, and local lore. (Authors' personal collections.)

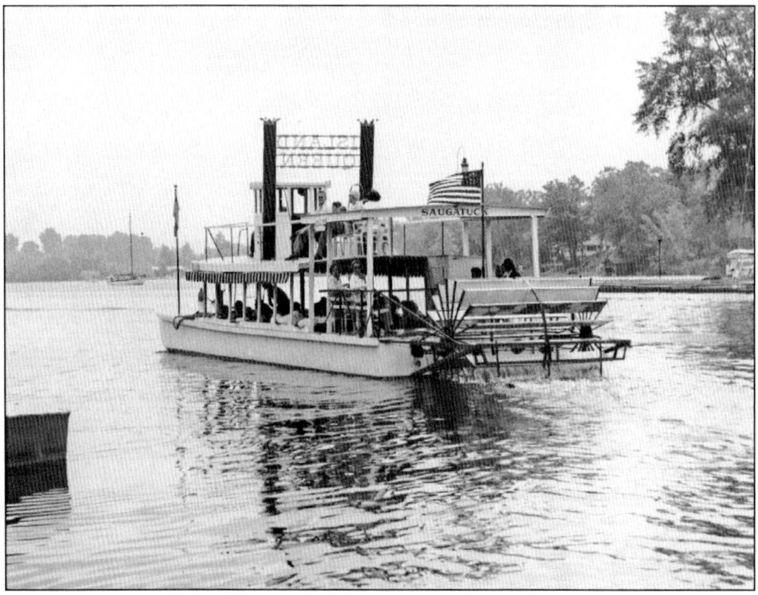

In the 1950s, the *Island Queen* paddle wheeler carried up to 40 passengers between Saugatuck and New Richmond. This boat brought a Mississippi River feel to the Kalamazoo River and was constructed with five rudders to help it navigate the strong current. (Authors' personal collections.)

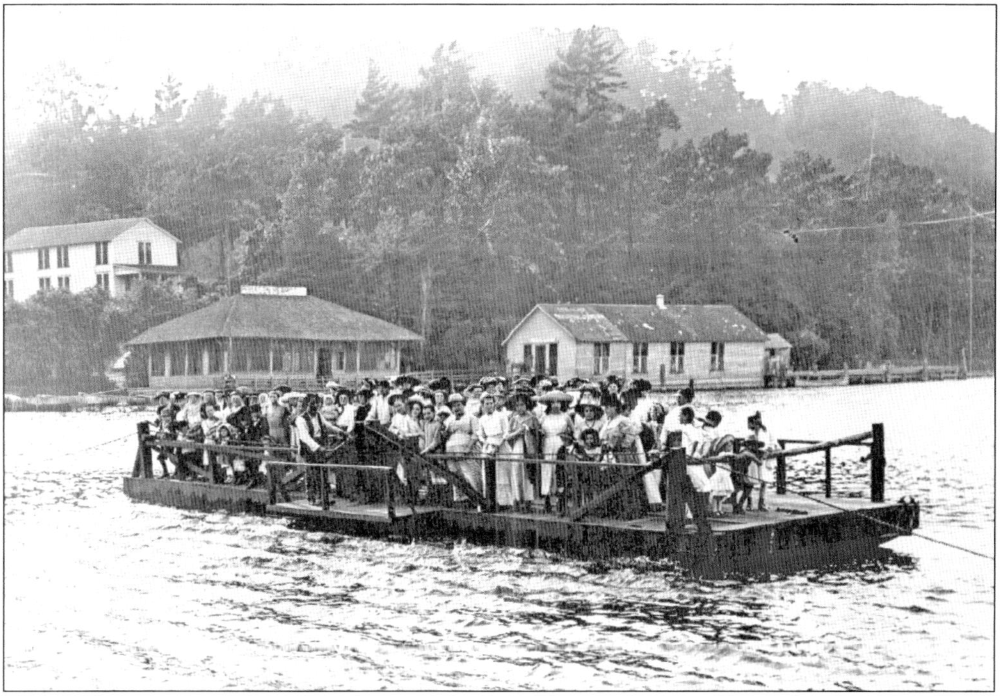

The Saugatuck Chain Ferry was built in 1838 to replace an old bridge, which was falling apart. The first ferry could carry 50 people across the Kalamazoo River and was used until 1947 (above). While the ferry was being redesigned, a rowboat was used but could only carry about nine people at a time. The new ferry, created in 1968, was a bit smaller than the original ferry and held only 45 people (below). The original ferry had a bank-to-bank setup, but now a hand-crank chain secured to both banks powers the ferry. The ride across the river takes about five minutes, or approximately 200 cranks. It serves as a tourist attraction and is the only hand-crank ferry left in the United States. (Above, WMU; below, authors' personal collections.)

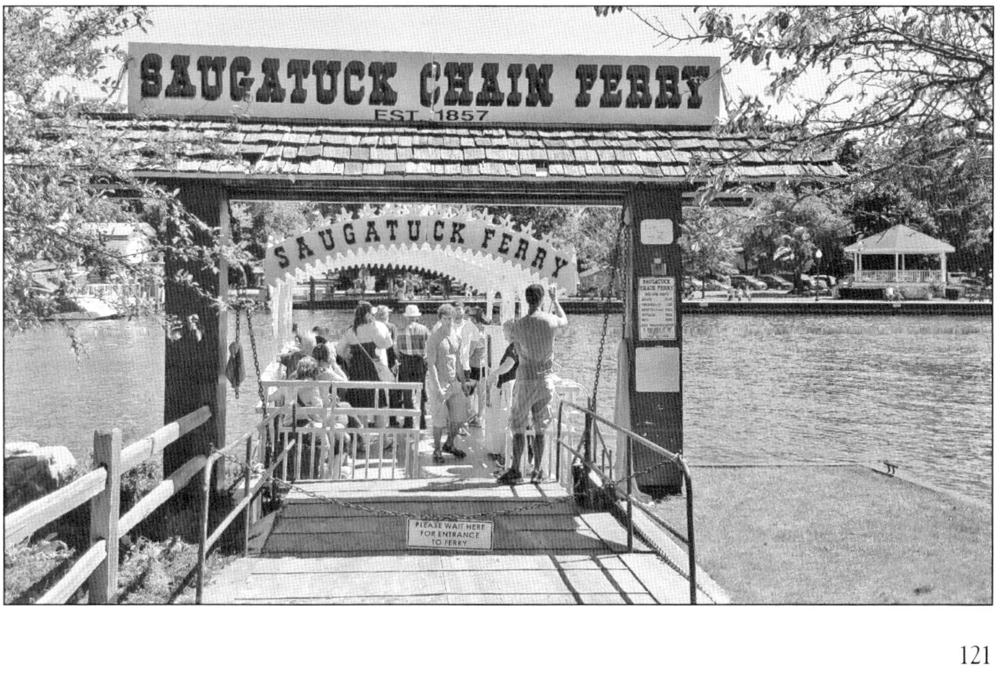

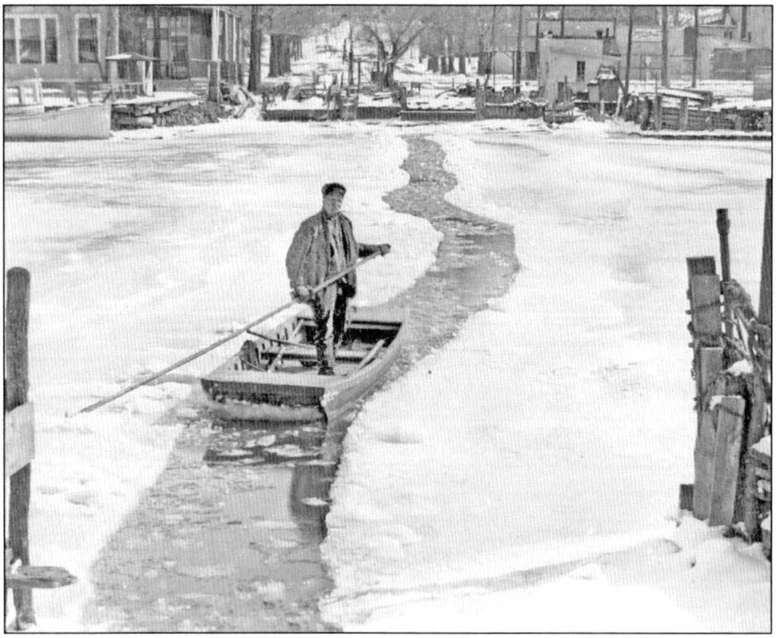

In the winter, much of the Kalamazoo River's surface would ice over. As long as the ice was not too thick, it could be broken apart and the chain ferry and other boats could still run. On this particular day, around 1925, it was this gentleman's turn to break the ice and navigate this flat-bottom boat across the channel. (SDHC.)

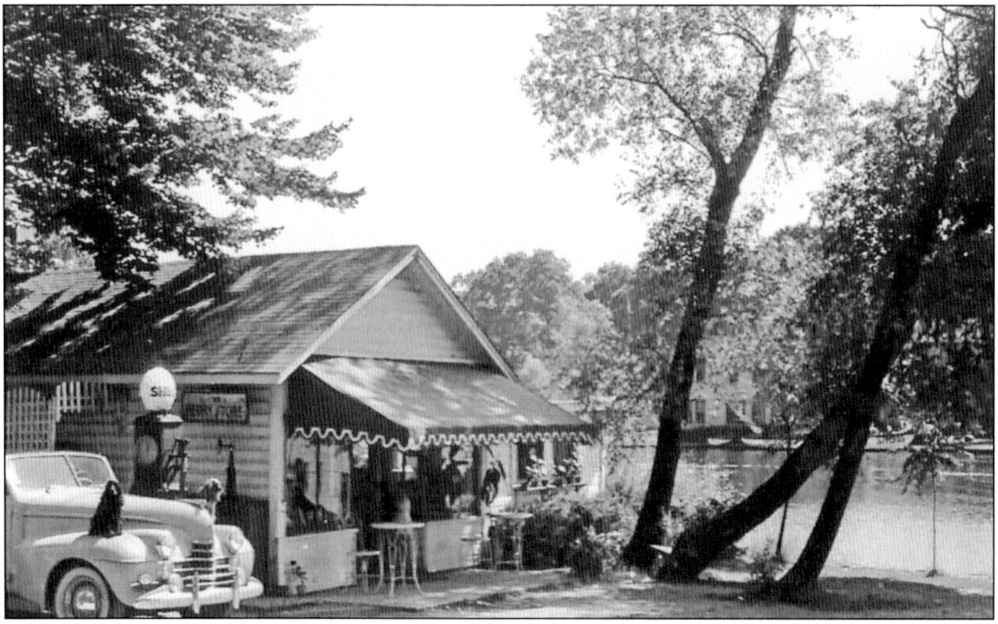

The Ferry Store was located at the west chain ferry landing along the Kalamazoo River from at least 1900 until the late 1940s. Summer residents of the wooded peninsula across from Saugatuck relied on the Ferry Store for perishables, seasonal produce, and a few staples. In the early 1940s, the owners added a large front porch that served as an ice-cream parlor. (Paul Petosky.)

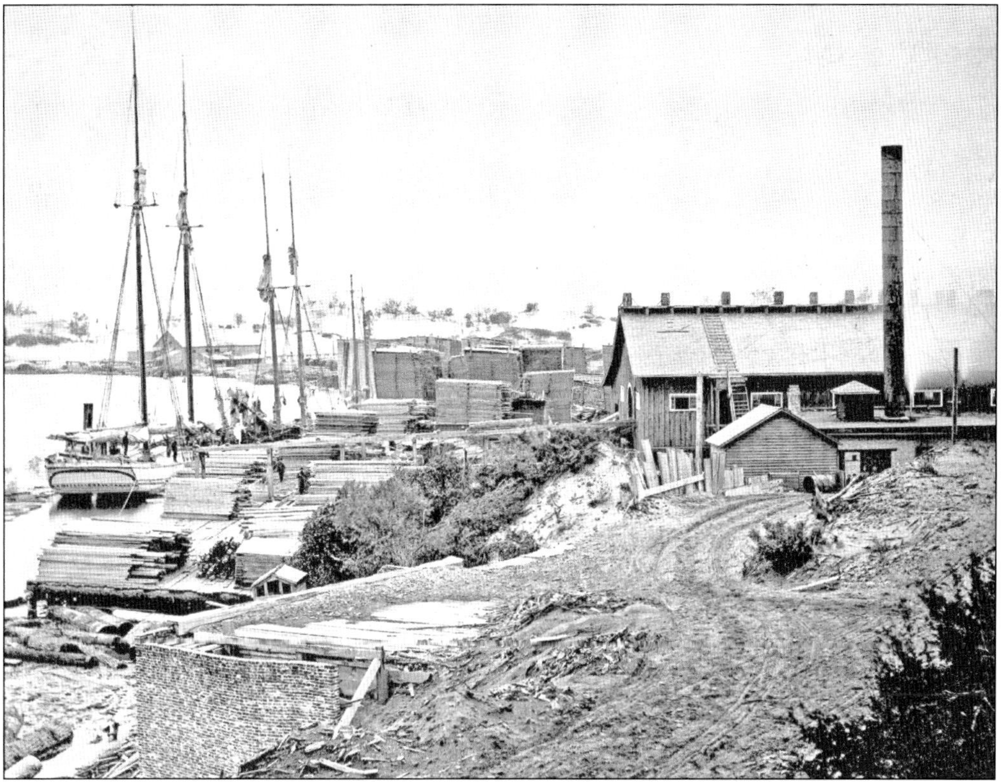

Singapore, perhaps one of Michigan's most famous ghost towns, existed from 1837 until the early 1880s. Shown here in 1869, Singapore made its mark as a lumber and shipbuilding town. Singapore supplied wood to Chicago, Holland, and Peshtigo following the fires that swept through in late 1871; this depleted the forests of Allegan County and led to the city's eventual demise. Its shipyard built two of Michigan's earliest schooners, along with the *O.R. Johnson* and one of the first steamships built in the area. The *O.R. Johnson* was known as the fastest, smartest schooner on Lake Michigan. This town was also an immigration port. Around 1850, the local boardinghouse had families from Canada, Germany, Holland, Ireland, and Norway. Today, Singapore is covered in sand but its influence on the area remains. (Above, SDHC; right, authors' personal collections.)

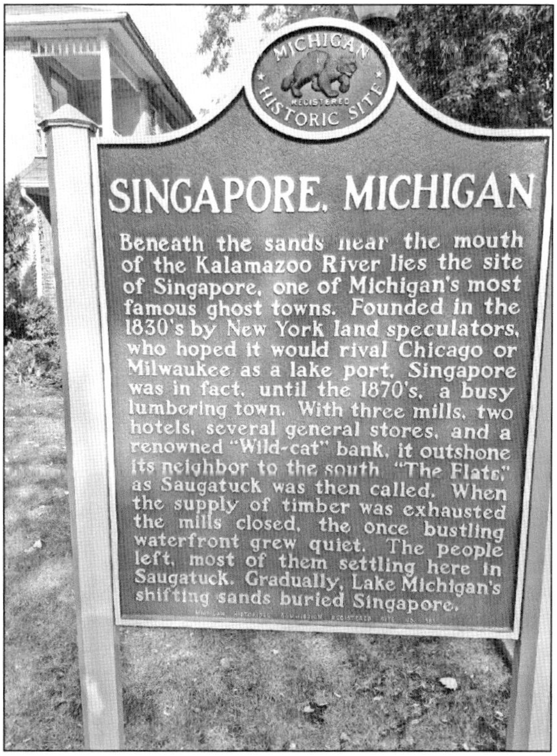

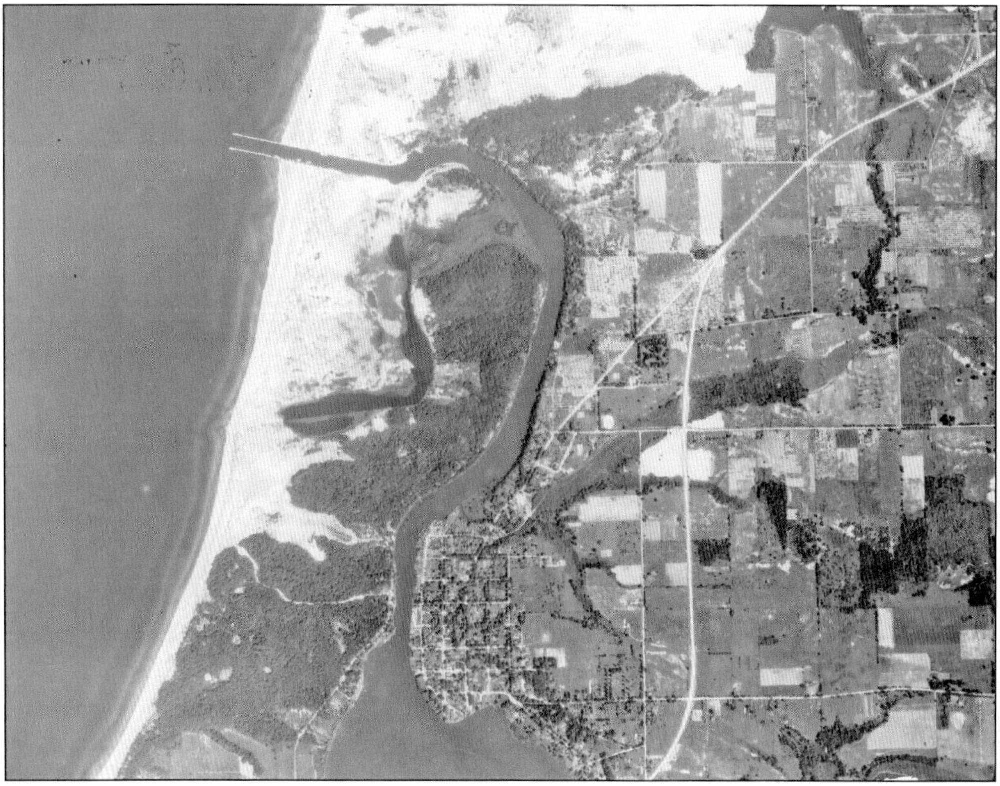

This 1938 Saugatuck aerial photograph shows loose sand (the large white areas along the coast). The outlet of the Kalamazoo River into Lake Michigan was moved in the early 1900s because sand was blown inland, choking off the channel. The old outlet area is at center, south of the current outlet. (Upjohn.)

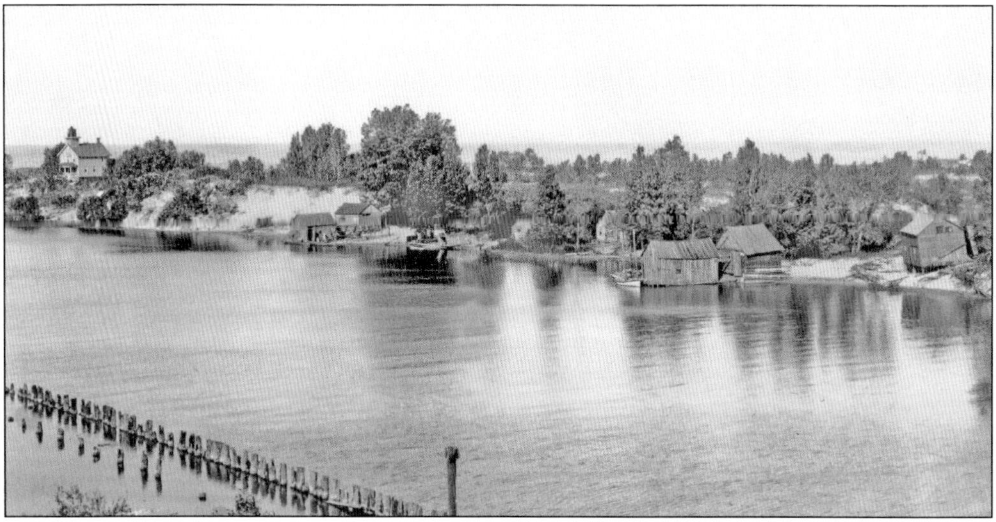

Fishtown was the last town on the Kalamazoo River before it reached Lake Michigan. This photograph, with a view looking southeast, was taken around 1910. Fishermen and their families had to move into Saugatuck because this harbor became landlocked when the new channel was established. The lighthouse that can be seen at far left was decommissioned in 1915. (SDHC.)

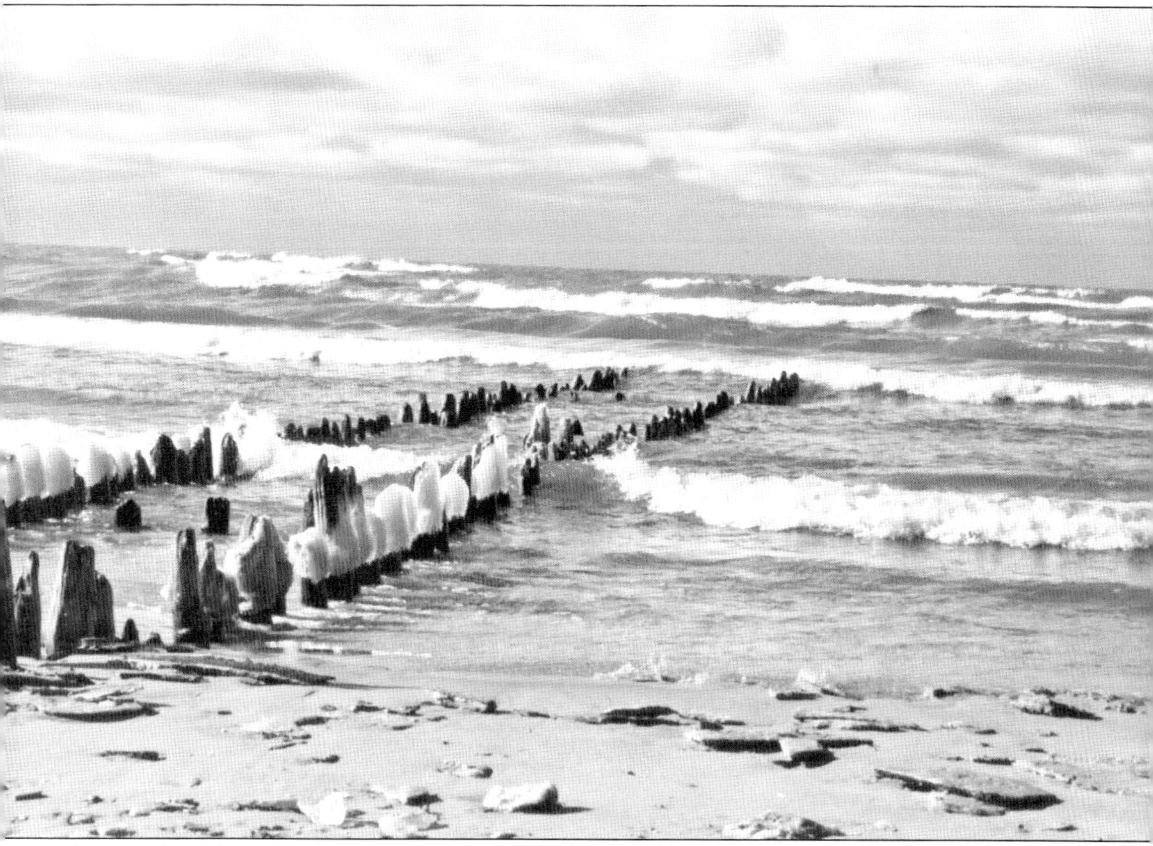

The mouth of the Kalamazoo River was moved a mile north from where it originally flowed into Lake Michigan. The old riverbed had silted along much of the sharp bends of the last mile of the river. In 1904, it was decided that moving the mouth of the river was a better course of action. This photograph shows the remnants of the original pilings. (Jeff Shook.)

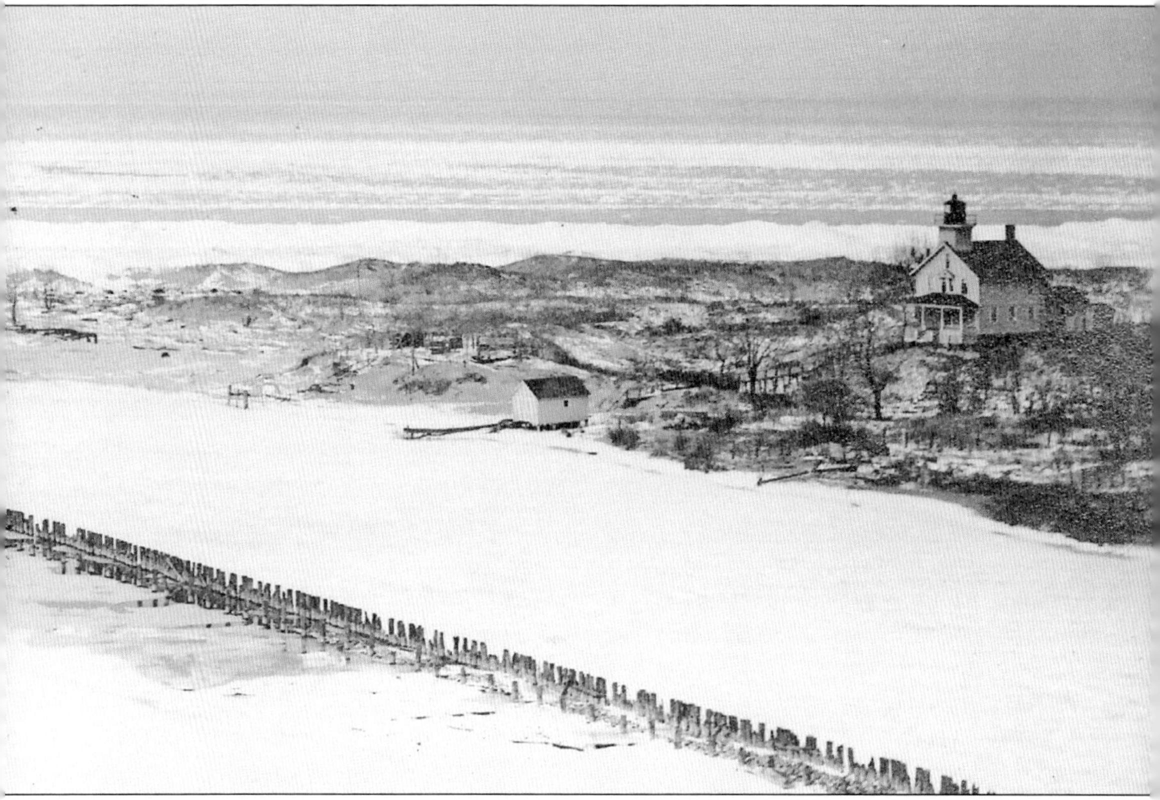

Winter along the Lake Michigan shoreline could be harsh for a lighthouse and its keeper as strong winds whipped off the water. The Kalamazoo River would often freeze over, as would the immediate shoreline of the lake, hindering ship traffic into Fishtown on the old Kalamazoo River outlet. Pictured is the lighthouse in 1909. (Jeff Shook.)

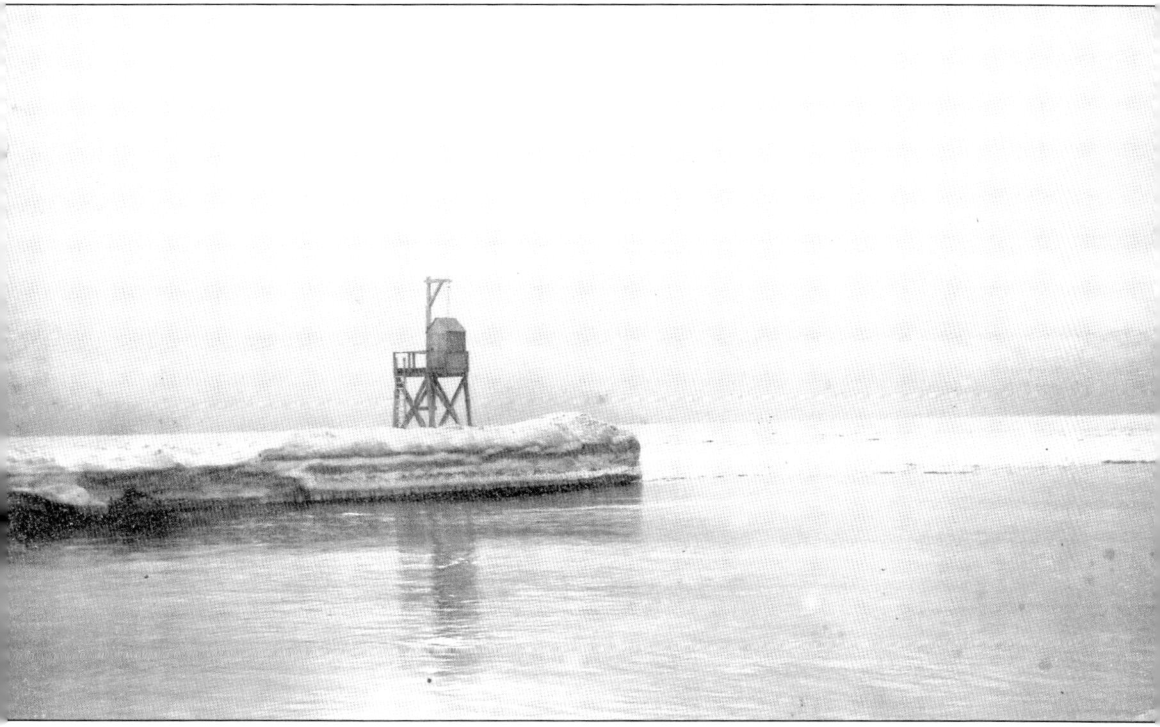

In the early 1900s, the new harbor of the Kalamazoo River was opened into Lake Michigan. It was constructed because sand continually blocked the old harbor's entrance and the last mile of the old harbor was a very sharp curve that was difficult to navigate. The marker in this 1913 photograph indicates the entrance of the new harbor. (Jeff Shook.)